RO[illegible]FERENCE

IRISH ANCESTORS

Máire Mac Conghail
and
Paul Gorry

ROBERTS
WHOLESALE BOOKS LTD

This edition published in 2000 for
Roberts Wholesale Books Ltd.
Unit 12 Benson Street Enterprise Centre
Hanover Quay, Dublin 2
by Diamond Books
77-85 Fulham Palace Road
Hammersmith, London W6 8JB

First published in 1990 by HarperCollins*Publishers*
PO Box, Glasgow G4 0NB

Reprint 10 9 8 7 6 5 4 3 2 1 0

ISBN 0 00 760465 3

Maps on pp 56–57, 95 & 105 drawn by Roy Boyd

A catalogue record for this book is available from the British Library

Printed and bound in Great Britain by
Caledonian International Book Manufacturing Ltd, Glasgow

Contents

Acknowledgements

We are indebted to many individuals and institutions for their assistance.

We record, with gratitude, the support and encouragement received from our colleagues; in particular from Steven ffeary-Smyrl, who read the work in-progress and shared his encyclopaedic knowledge with us; from Eileen O'Byrne, who clarified elements of the Penal Laws for us; and from Marie Wilson, who unravelled particular queries relating to repositories in Northern Ireland; Aideen Ireland and Gregory O'Connor, archivists, National Archives; Colette O'Flaherty, assistant keeper, Kevin Brown, library administration officer, and Jim O'Shea, senior library assistant, The National Library of Ireland; Raymond Refaussé, librarian and archivist, Representative Church Body Library; David Sheehy, archivist, Roman Catholic Archdiocese of Dublin; Siobhán O'Rafferty, librarian, Royal Irish Academy; Seamus Helferty, archivist, Archives Department, University College, Dublin; Michael Smallman, archivist, Queen's University of Belfast; Virginia Teehan, college archivist, University College Cork; Máire Kennedy, senior librarian, Dublin Corporation Gilbert Library; Revd Seán McCarthy, parish priest, Enniskean, Co. Cork; Bernard Devaney, senior library assistant, Genealogical Office; Harman Murtagh, The Military History Society of Ireland; Comdt Peter Young, Military Archives; Andrew Perry, Post Office Archives; Robert Mills, Royal College of Physicians in Ireland; Mary Casteleyn and Peter Manning, Irish Genealogical Research Society; Elisabeth McDougall, Society of Genealogists, London; Jan Gow, genealogist, New Zealand; Jennifer Harrison, genealogist and historian, Australia; Guillermo MacLoughlin, Argentina; Anne Boulter, South African Embassy, Dublin.

We acknowledge and are grateful for the help and attention

received from the directorate and staff of the following institutions: The National Library of Ireland; Genealogical Office; National Archives; General Register Office, Valuation Office; Representative Church Body Library; and Ordnance Survey of Ireland.

Máire Mac Conghail and Paul Gorry
Dublin, 1997

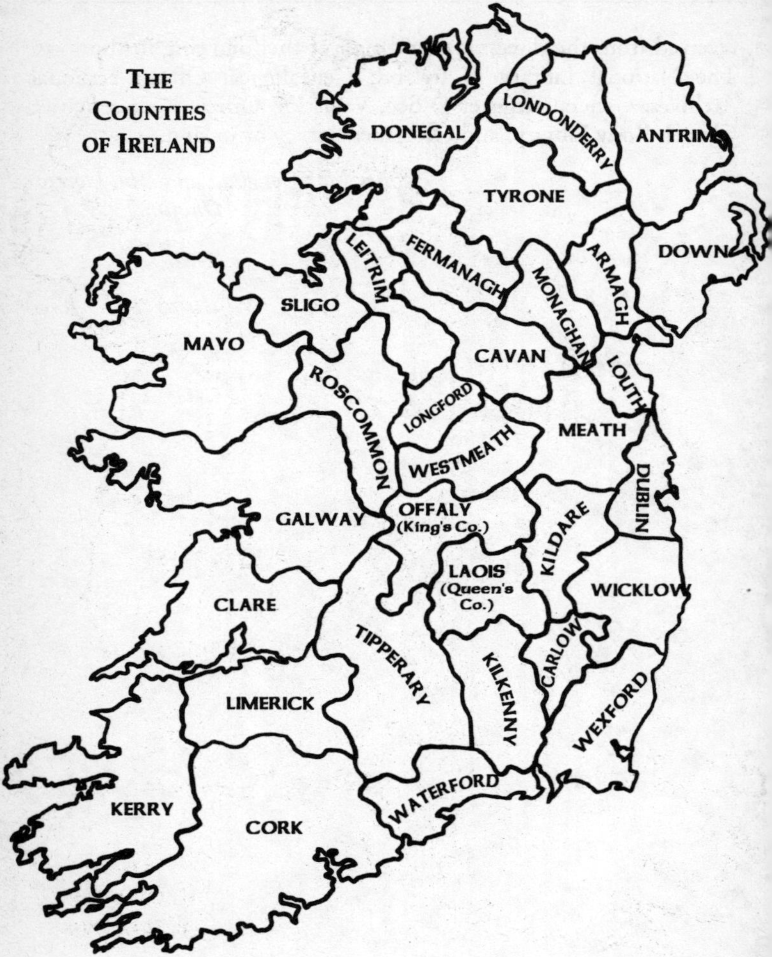
THE COUNTIES OF IRELAND
DONEGAL
LONDONDERRY
ANTRIM
TYRONE
FERMANAGH
LEITRIM
DOWN
ARMAGH
MONAGHAN
SLIGO
MAYO
CAVAN
LOUTH
ROSCOMMON
LONGFORD
MEATH
WESTMEATH
DUBLIN
GALWAY
OFFALY
(King's Co.)
KILDARE
LAOIS
(Queen's
Co.)
WICKLOW
CLARE
TIPPERARY
CARLOW
KILKENNY
LIMERICK
WEXFORD
WATERFORD
KERRY
CORK

THE PROVINCES OF IRELAND

I gcuimhne mo thuismitheoirí,
David Doran (1911–1982) agus
Nessa Ní Shéaghdha (1916–1993)
agus do mo chlann agus clann mo chlainne.

Máire Mac Conghail

To Kathleen McDermott, who brought me to the Genealogical Office when I was a boy.

Paul Gorry

1 Preparation

Researching your ancestry in Ireland is an exciting challenge. However, like any challenge, the better prepared you are the more confident you will be when it comes to carrying out the research. Genuine interest and curiosity, bucketsful of patience and a pencil and paper are the essentials.

When working on your family history you always research step by step, or generation by generation, backwards from yourself through your parents to your grandparents, great-grandparents and so on. As you progress, you will collect information on siblings of your ancestors, probably acquiring cousins many degrees removed, of whom you may have been unaware.

Remember that genealogy is a hobby that will engage your interest over months and years rather than days and weeks. So you need to allow time to prepare. Start your fact-finding long before even contemplating a research visit to Ireland.

People very often make the mistake of visiting Ireland to trace their ancestry without first doing the groundwork at home. If you only know that your ancestor left Ireland sometime towards the end of the nineteenth century, without any idea of a birth date, a place of origin or the parents' names, there is no way you can do any worthwhile research while visiting the country. There is no point, either, in commissioning an Irish genealogist or record agent without having some identifying information on the emigrant ancestor.

If your family remained in Ireland you don't have to contend with the major difficulty of making the connection from overseas. However, the initial steps are the same for everyone regardless of where you live. If you disregard them you will waste a lot of research time either getting nowhere or busily tracing the wrong family. It is important that you first tap any family sources before venturing forth to tackle the record repositories.

WHERE TO BEGIN

Family Sources

Everyone should begin with family sources; these are of two kinds: family stories and family papers.

Family Stories

Oral tradition can be an invaluable source of information, sometimes backing up documentary evidence and sometimes providing vital clues in the absence of such evidence. There is nearly always someone in the extended family who has retained the collective memories of past generations. Coaxing those memories to the surface may take a little ingenuity, but it is important not to suggest names or dates or places to the informant or you may find yourself inventing your own family lore.

Write down any information immediately or, preferably, tape the informant, as it will be difficult to remember their exact words after a few weeks of further research. It is a good idea to interview several family members separately about the same subject, as you will find all sorts of variations emerging. Don't forget to ask how they know these stories and who told them. You might find that they all emanate from the half-baked research of some earlier dabbler in your family history.

STICK TO THE FACTS

At this point you are only beginning to assemble information. It is imperative that early on you understand the importance of separating proven facts from hearsay or supposition. Your family tradition may very well be completely accurate but, until you find documentary evidence that confirms all its various points, it should remain separate in your head (and certainly on paper) from what you can safely call *facts*.

Family Papers

Every family has some type of documentation sitting around, most likely forgotten. It may be in the form of birth, marriage or death certificates, a receipt from a cemetery, events recorded in the family Bible, newspaper cuttings, photographs, deeds, letters from relatives or, in Roman Catholic families, memorial cards. Any papers that give names, dates or addresses are worth having. If you cannot get possession of the originals, be sure to get photocopies.

Once you have obtained all the information, oral or written, you can gather from family sources, it is time to look to the record repositories. Before you do so, perhaps it would be an idea to draw out a rough pedigree based on what you already have. This will help you to visualise the information and see what areas need further research. Get yourself a large sheet of blank paper; one that can be easily folded and taken along on your research expeditions.

Mapping Your Family Tree

A pedigree or family tree is simply a diagram showing either your direct ancestry or the descendants of one of your ancestors. Try drawing up one of each. On the first enter your name and those of your parents, grandparents and so on. If you don't have names for all of them just leave a blank space to be filled in later. Leave a space also for their dates and places of birth, death and marriage. This will serve as a handy reference guide while you research. It is possible to buy pre-prepared forms of this type.

Your second diagram will concern just one of your ancestral lines and an example is shown overleaf. You will get confused if you try to research all your ancestors at once, so decide on the line you first wish to pursue. It may be your paternal line or the family of the one grandparent you knew well or an ancestor with an unusual surname that interests you. It doesn't matter which line you chose. It will give you

Forbes

Draft or Work-sheet Pedigree

Others

John Forbes
Caher,
bap. 27th December 1836
m. 27th Feb. 1868
Julia Coakley
Teenah, civil parish of
Kinneigh, Co. Cork

No children

Others

John Patrick O'Shea
b. 7th July 1887 at
18 Georges St, Cork City
[m. 2ndly 1950
'Maisie' McKeefrey, widow]
d. 8th April 1971, Dublin

From 1912, known as
Seán P. Ó Séaghdha

KEY

b. : born
bap. : baptised
m. : married
= : married
d. : died

Edward Forbes
Caher, civil parish of
Kinneigh, Co. Cork

Farmer

=

Honoria 'Norry' McCarthy

Had at least 8 children

Jeremiah Kehelly
Cooleenagow, civil parish
of Fanlobbus, Co. Cork

Farmer

Widower at time of his
marriage to Anne

d. 14th June 1906
aged 76 years

=

Anne Forbes
bap. 15th March 1841
Enniskean parish
m. 20th Jan. 1867
Enniskean parish
d. 11th October 1926
Dunmanway, Co. Cork

= Catherine Kehelly
b. 10th August 1881, Cooleenagow
m. 5th October 1912
Dunmanway R.C. Church
d. 27th July 1948, Dublin

Issue/children

the experience to research the others at a later stage. For this diagram turn the sheet of paper lengthways and write the name of the ancestor you wish to begin with at the centre, along with dates of birth and death. Add his or her spouse and below, in a line across the page, add their known children and their spouses. The grandchildren's names can be added below that again. Keep the details simple and leave lots of space for additions. Hopefully your research will allow you to extend the pedigree up the page.

PINPOINTING THE EMIGRANT ANCESTOR

Family tradition may possibly say that your great-grandfather was from Cork and left Ireland at the time of the Famine. This is still not enough information on which to build a research visit and anyway, without corroborating documentation it is still only hearsay. You need to begin with the sources available in your own country and work your way back through the generations to that great-grandfather. This will involve the type of research that will give you good experience by the time you come to Irish records. If you feel you can't manage it yourself, or if you need detailed advice, you should engage the services of a genealogist in your own country. But there is no shortcut. This groundwork must be done in order to give you a chance of success.

Beware the easy options

Many people fall into the trap of consulting a book on Irish surnames to determine where their ancestor might have originated. For instance, having found that the surname Byrne is historically associated with the Wicklow area you might abandon any attempt to find the place of origin of your emigrant ancestor and waste hours searching in the wrong part of Ireland. Worse still, you might stitch this historical fact to your family tradition and engage a genealogist to conduct what would ultimately be fruitless research based on these shaky foundations.

Edward MacLysaght's *The Surnames of Ireland* and similar publications provide valuable and interesting information on the origin and background of Irish names. By all means consult them for the historical perspective, but they cannot be used as substitutes for genealogical research. The surname Byrne, for instance, had spread to many parts of Ireland by the 19th century.

Another 'easy option' is to consult the Mormon *International Genealogical Index* (*IGI*) without fully understanding its limitations. The *IGI* is a very useful research aid. It is available on microfiche (and in many cases on CD-ROM) in Mormon libraries worldwide and can even be purchased at a very reasonable price. It consists of a listing of birth/baptismal and marriage records for people in various countries all over the globe and can be of enormous assistance in pinpointing places of origin. However, in relation to Ireland it is most certainly *not* anywhere near a comprehensive listing. A very common mistake is to pick someone of the same name and approximate date of birth as your ancestor out of the *IGI* for Ireland and to try to reshape the known facts to suit his or her profile. If your information is that your Joseph Kelly was from Mayo, there is no good reason to abandon him for a Joseph Kelly of Kilkenny simply because he was the only person of the name listed in the *IGI* in the right time frame. The proper use of the *IGI* in relation to Ireland is discussed in Chapters 2 and 4; see also Glossary.

What Do You Need to Start Searching?

You can never have too much information on your emigrant ancestor, but you certainly can have too little. The very minimum you need to find out before heading for Ireland is the county of origin and an approximate date of birth. If the ancestor did not marry in Ireland you would certainly need to have the name of one of his/her parents. Of course, the very minimum is not always enough, especially if you are dealing with a relatively common surname.

KEEP AN OPEN MIND

When people start out in genealogy they very often focus too closely on their own family or even on their own ancestors within the family. You need to be less blinkered in your approach. If you decide that your grandmother's brothers and sisters are of no real interest to you and don't bother to trace their careers, you may miss out on some clues in their records that would fill the gaps in your information, or never make contact with a long-lost cousin who has all the information you have and more. If you don't bother to even glance at the names of your great-great-grandfather's neighbours, you may miss out on his brother-in-law or his first cousin. This is particularly relevant in the case of an emigrant. Even if his neighbours were not related they could very well have been from the same parish in Ireland.

Searching in the Irish Diaspora

This is, of course, a book on Irish research and we are not in a position to give detailed guidance on records in other countries. However, the following is a brief summary of the types of records in the main countries of emigration that may give identifying information on your emigrant ancestor.

Remember that a certain amount of information about most of the record offices mentioned below can be found on the Internet. If you would like to do some background reading on the patterns of Irish migration, Donald Harman Akenson's *The Irish Diaspora: A Primer* (Canada, Belfast, 1993) is a good introduction.

Argentina

- Civil records of births, marriages and deaths are not centralised, but held locally in each province. Registration began for Buenos

Aires city in 1888, for Buenos Aires province in 1890 and for other areas about the same time. Birth records include the parents' ages and nationality and earlier ones sometimes include the grandparents' names. Marriages give the bride and groom's parents' names and nationality. Irish people are more often listed as British or even English. Surnames are sometimes hispanicised or given complete translations into Spanish.

- Church records are, of course, of use in the period prior to the introduction of civil registration. The very early registers of parishes in the Buenos Aires area were destroyed by fire in 1955 but those from the 19th century are held in their respective churches. Those for other areas have survived and are in local custody.
- Census returns for the entire country are available for 1855, 1869 and 1895 at the Archivo General de la Nación in Buenos Aires and at provincial archives. As well as occupation and age, the returns state each individual's nationality. As with births and marriages, Irish people are usually recorded as British or English. Surnames are even more prone to corruption in the case of census returns. Earlier census material is available at the Archivo General. Some of it concerns the entire country while the rest covers only the province of Buenos Aires, where most of the early population was concentrated.
- Gravestone inscriptions are one of the best sources for finding an immigrant's place of origin in Ireland. Unfortunately, few have been transcribed so it is necessary to visit the relevant cemeteries.
- Newspaper obituaries are another good source for place of origin. *The Southern Cross*, the Irish-Argentine newspaper founded in 1875, contains such material. *The Standard*, another publication for the English-speaking community, *La Nación* and local newspapers are also worth trying.

- Passenger lists are held at the National Immigration Office. They may give nationality, age, occupation and marital status. Those concerning Irish people for a period in the 19th century have been published by Eduardo Coghlan along with information taken from the 1869 Census in Buenos Aires province and the 1895 Census throughout the entire country. Naturalisation papers are not generally of use as they do not usually state the place of birth.

Australia

- Civil registration of births, marriages and deaths was controlled separately by each colony state. The dates of commencement and conditions of access vary by area. By comparison with other countries Australian civil records are very detailed. Marriages are particularly useful since they give the place of birth and parents' names for the bride and groom and the information was supplied by the couple themselves. They also indicate how long the individuals were resident in Australia, if immigrants. Deaths also give valuable details but, of course, they were supplied by third parties, thus, are less reliable for parents' names.

- Church records are of use for baptisms and marriages and some burials in the period prior to civil registration but are much less detailed than the civil records.

- Immigration records may give a clue as to immigrants' origins but, most importantly, they may indicate which ship he/she travelled on and the passenger list may show that he/she made the journey with relatives.

- Convict records concern the earliest European settlers, who were transported to the Australian colonies as convicts from 1788. The last convicts arrived in 1868; though transportation ceased to New South Wales in 1840 and Tasmania in 1852, it continued to

Western Australia between 1850 and 1868. The majority of records originating in Australia are held in the Archives Office of New South Wales in Sydney along with the Archives Offices of Tasmania in Hobart and of Western Australia in Perth. These include Convict Indents (lists of convicts on each ship) which give the date of trial, sentence and in later years the native place, and indication of Conditional or Absolute Pardons. They are published on microfilm, are widely available in Australian repositories and are indexed. They are complemented to an extent by the Transportation Records from Ireland's National Archives (see Chapter 9) which are also available in the National Library in Canberra and in each State Library. There are further records originating in England. Most of these are held at the Public Record Office in Kew, but are also largely available on microfilm in Australian repositories.

Canada

- Civil records, as in Australia, are kept by each province, with varying commencement dates.
- Censuses were conducted every ten years from 1851 in what are now Ontario and Quebec, and in other provinces as they joined the Dominion. The census returns up to 1901 are available for consultation. They state each individual's place of birth (country or Canadian province) and religious denomination. There is an index for the 1871 returns for Ontario. There are earlier returns for various provinces but these (with the exception of New Brunswick for 1851, which is indexed) only list heads of household. Some 20th-century records for Newfoundland are also available.
- Church records are, of course, useful for pre-civil registration years but in the case of Roman Catholic marriages they can also supplement the information in the civil records. Catholic marriage regis-

ters tend to give both parents' names and often their addresses. Most of them have been microfilmed by the Church of Jesus Christ of Latter-day Saints (Mormons). Records of Protestant denominations are generally held in local custody.

- Gravestone inscriptions can provide invaluable information and large numbers of transcripts are available in the various provincial archives.
- Newspaper death and marriage notices are another potential source and many have been transcribed and published.
- Passenger lists are not a major source because they are generally not available before the mid-19th century and do not usually give the place of origin. However, they may record your ancestor arriving with relatives. You would need to know the port of entry and the year of arrival before pursuing such records.
- Land grant petitions and petitions for Crown land purchases can provide valuable information on early settlers. Free land grants were given prior to 1826 and thereafter Crown lands could be bought. Petitions concerning these are held in some cases at the National Archives of Canada, based in Ottawa, and in others at the various provincial archives and are indexed.
- The National Archives of Canada will provide their free booklet, *Tracing Your Ancestors in Canada*, on request.

England and Wales

- Civil registration of births, marriages and deaths in England and Wales commenced on 1 July 1837. Yearly indexes may be viewed free of charge at the Family Records Centre, 1 Myddelton St, London EC1R 1UW, and on microfiche at many major libraries. The certificates give similar details to Irish ones (see Chapter 2).

- Censuses were conducted every ten years. The earliest existing returns are for 1841 and those up to 1891 may also be consulted at the Family Record Centre. A comprehensive names index to the 1881 Census, arranged by county, is now available. There are indexes to other years for certain areas but generally it is necessary to have an exact location for the family. For Irish people the returns may give place of birth simply as 'Ireland', but the county is often given.

- Church records are located in various repositories. Many are held in some form in county record offices while others are retained in local custody or held centrally by church authorities. In the case of Roman Catholic marriages, it is worthwhile to try the church record as well as the civil one as the church record may give the place of origin in Ireland or the mothers' names.

New Zealand

- Civil records date from 1848 for European settlers and are available at the Central Registry in Lower Hutt. Indexes to them are available free of charge in various libraries and branches of the New Zealand Society of Genealogists throughout the country. From 1876, birth records give the parents' age, place of birth and date and place of marriage. From the same date, death records give the deceased's date and place of marriage. They also state his/her parents' names and father's occupation but, as with all death records, the details are not as reliable as those supplied by the individuals themselves. Prior to 1880 marriages do not include the parents' names but from that date forward they do, adding the father's occupation. This information, being supplied by the couple, is more trustworthy.

- Church records are generally centralised in one of the archives of the relevant denomination. The Presbyterians have only one repository, which is in Dunedin. Those for the other main denominations are in Auckland, Christchurch and Wellington.

- Gravestone inscriptions from most burial grounds in the country have been transcribed and are available on microfiche in various libraries and branches of the New Zealand Society of Genealogists.
- Newspaper notices of birth, marriage and death have been indexed in many cases and are available in local libraries.
- Shipping records are not held in one location, but usually in the area of the port of arrival. They can be a disappointing source as passenger lists are not always available and the information on them is generally sparse. However, they can identify an ancestor as arriving with relatives.

Scotland

- Civil registration began in Scotland in 1855. Yearly indexes may be viewed for a fee at the General Register Office, New Register House, Edinburgh. The certificates are more detailed than Irish ones. Birth records (other than those in 1856–1860) give the date and place of the parents' marriage. Marriage records give the names of both parents for the bride and groom. Death records give the parents' names and father's occupation but this information is less reliable, since it was provided by a third party.
- Censuses were conducted every ten years. The earliest existing returns are for 1841 and those up to 1891 may be consulted at New Register House for a fee. A comprehensive names index to the 1881 Census, arranged by county, is now also available there.
- Church records are in a number of locations. Pre-1855 parish registers of the Church of Scotland may be examined for a fee at New Register House. Many registers of non-conformist Protestant

denominations are available, free of charge, at the Scottish Record Office, Edinburgh (ref: CH.3 & 10–16), while the remainder are in local custody or in other repositories. Likewise, Roman Catholic registers are at the Scottish Record Office (ref: RH.21), in local custody or in other repositories.

- New Register House will provide on request their free leaflet on family history research.

South Africa

- Death notices are the most useful source of genealogical information in South Africa. They are not civil death records or newspaper obituaries, but part of the files gathered by the Master of the Supreme Court on the estates of deceased individuals. There are no death notices for those with very small estates, but the majority of deceased adults would be worth checking. The information given in most cases includes occupation, parents' names, age or date of birth, place of birth, date of last marriage, name of surviving (or any previous) spouse, names of surviving children, and date and place of death. All these details are not always given and, of course, their accuracy depends on the informant's knowledge. An estate file may also include the deceased's will. Death notices were introduced in the Cape Colony in 1834. They were in use in all four provinces as well as Rhodesia (now Zimbabwe) by the late 19th century and in South West Africa (Namibia) by 1920. The most recent estate files are held in the Master's Office in each provincial capital (in Cape Province there are also regional offices in Grahamstown and Kimberley). The earlier files, for example pre-1950 for Cape Province and pre-1974 for the Transvaal, are at the Archives Depots in each provincial capital. Those for Namibia are held in Windhoek. Those for Zimbabwe are held in Harare, but Rhodesian death notices for 1890–1976 are on microfilm at the Human Sciences Research Council in Pretoria.

- Church records are in a number of locations. The archives of the Nederduitse Gereformeerde Kerk (the main Dutch Reformed denomination) in Cape Town holds copies of the registers of all its congregations in Cape Province from 1843 as well as original registers down to that date. It also holds records relating to other provinces and to Namibia and Zimbabwe. The NG Kerk archives in Bloemfontein, Pietermaritzburg and Pretoria hold records for other congregations but some registers are still in local custody. Most early registers of the Nederduitsch Hervormde Kerk and the Gereformeerde Kerk are held in their respective archives in Pretoria and Potchefstroom. By and large, the registers of all other denominations are still in local custody.
- Civil registration, as in Australia and Canada, began at different times in the various provinces. Unfortunately, they are not open to the public and certificates will only be supplied if the date and place of the event and the parties' names can be stated on application. Records prior to 1923 do not contain all details reflected in current certificates. The custodian is the Director General for Home Affairs in Pretoria.

The United States

- Federal censuses were conducted every ten years from 1790 but the early ones only give the name of the head of household and the number of family members. Those from 1850 give details for all occupants, including their state or country of birth. With the exception of the 1890 returns, which were almost entirely destroyed by fire, the returns up to 1920 are available for consultation at the National Archives in Washington, DC, and at regional offices of the Archives. The 1880, 1900 and 1920 returns have a soundex system (see Glossary) of identifying families, arranged by state. That for 1880 only covers households containing children aged 10 or under. The returns rarely give a more precise place of birth for an immigrant than 'Ireland' but they can give an indication of when the family arrived in the US by the birth places of the children. If any of the children were born in Ireland you have a better chance of tracing their birth records in Ireland than those of the parents.

- Registration of births, marriages and deaths was the responsibility of each state and the certificate format, commencement dates, locations and conditions of access vary. Death records generally give the names of the deceased's parents but, as they were supplied by third parties, they are not always reliable. In many cases similar records pre-dating the state-wide registration are available at county level.
- Church records are, of course, useful in the years prior to state registration. However, they can also supplement the state records, particularly in the case of Roman Catholic marriages.
- Cemetery records and gravestones, where available, can turn up unknown relatives who, when investigated, may provide the link to a location in Ireland. The gravestone inscriptions of immigrants quite frequently give their county of origin in Ireland.
- Newspaper obituaries are worth checking, especially if the ancestor lived in a small community. They may give the birth place within Ireland or other vital clues to their background.
- Naturalisation papers are unlikely to give a location within Ireland, but they will indicate how long an individual was living in the country. They are held in various locations depending on the state.
- Passenger lists may be worth looking for, in that they may show your ancestor arriving with a group of relatives and may (in extreme cases) give a place of origin. However, you would need to know the port of entry and at least the year of arrival. They are generally unindexed and thousands of Irish people passed through

large ports such as Boston and New York each year. However, *The Famine Immigrants – Lists of Irish Immigrants Arriving at the Port of New York, 1846–1851*, edited by Ira A. Glazier and Michael Tepper, covers an important period. It is arranged chronologically in seven volumes, each with an index.

PASSENGER LISTS

There are virtually no passenger lists available from the Irish end.

Name Variations

Surname Spellings

One of the first things you need to rid yourself of when dealing with family history, particularly in Ireland, is the idea that the spelling of your surname has any significance. This idea is very much a product of the 20th century. Today we make a point of distinguishing between Carney and Kearney, Donahue and Donoghoe, or McDermot and MacDermott. Up to the latter half of the 19th century people seem to have paid little attention as to how their surname was spelt. This was not just because of high levels of illiteracy, though that was a factor.

In any case, you must remember that most of the records you will be using to trace your ancestry were compiled by third parties. When the priest or clerk was recording a baptism he would not have enquired as to the precise spelling of the name, no more than would the surveyor who was compiling the *Primary Valuation*. Anyway, the spelling of a surname is ultimately of no importance. Donaghoe, Donaghue, Donahoe, Donahue, Donoghoe, Donoghue, with or without the prefix O', are all simply anglicised variants of the original Gaelic surname Ó Donnchadha.

SURNAME VARIATIONS

Check all possible variations of the surname when working on an index.

Prefixes O and Mac/Mc

In their original state, the majority of Gaelic surnames had either the prefix O, as in Ó Donnchadha, or Mac as in Mac Diarmada. By the 18th century they had been by and large anglicised and among the ordinary people most O surnames had lost their prefix, as had some of the Macs. The family of Daniel O'Connell, who was of the landed gentry, was a notable exception to the rule. People in Gaelic-speaking areas would have retained the prefix, but the written record was, as we already said, usually compiled by a third party. It was with the Gaelic Revival in the final years of the 19th century that ordinary people began to re-adopt the prefix O.

Mc is simply an abbreviation of Mac. Contrary to the widely held belief in North America that one is Irish and the other Scottish, the prefix is found in surnames of both origins.

Interchangeable Forenames

In Ireland many of the variations occurring in regard to forenames were brought about by phonetic translations of Gaelic names into Latin or English. For instance, Brigid was latinised as Bedelia (possibly because of the pet form Biddy) and subsequently Delia. Brigid and Delia were regarded as the same name and used interchangeably even into the 20th century. Other examples of this type of quasi-translation are Owen (originally Eoghan) to Eugene; Brian to Bernard and Gubby (Gobnait) to Abby (Abigail) or Deborah.

English forenames of separate origins were also confused in records because of common pet forms. Judith and Julia were usually interchanged, as both were shortened to Judy. In the southern province of Munster, Johanna was also confused with Judith and Julia. In the same area Johanna and Honoria might easily be confused in records because of the shared pet form of Hannah. Many Roman Catholic parish registers are in Latin. While most names are recognisable in their Latin form there are some which may not seem familiar. Some of these are mentioned in Chapter 4.

Naming Patterns

It was traditional in Catholic families, but not an absolute rule, that the eldest son was called after the father's father, the second son after the mother's father and the third after the father himself. The daughters were similarly named, though the first and second might have either grandmother's name. This did not happen in all families, but it is worth keeping in the back of your mind as it may allow you an educated guess at some stage.

Another point worth remembering concerns middle names used by emigrants to North America. Until the late 19th century the majority of Irish Catholics had only one forename. However, in crossing the Atlantic many men appear to have acquired a second one; John Sullivan in Kerry became John Patrick Sullivan in Philadelphia. Again it is not an absolute rule, but it is generally found that the middle name was actually his father's. In such cases this stems from colloquial naming traditions.

As surnames were usually heavily concentrated in specific areas, there were often several people of the same name, even within a townland. To distinguish between two John Sullivans, they might have been referred to locally as Black John and Red John. Alternatively, if one was the son of Patrick and the other the son of Michael, they might have been called John Pat and John Mike.

Generally these secondary names did not find their way into written records. However, you may come across them in *Griffith's Valuation* or related land records (see Chapter 5).

A FEW IMPORTANT POINTS

The next eight chapters deal with the sources for Irish genealogy which may help to trace your ancestors. They are followed by a further chapter giving detailed information on the various record repositories mentioned in the text. At the back of the book is the Glossary, which contains explanations of administrative divisions and some of the terms frequently used in the text. If you are unfamiliar with the geography of Ireland it would be worthwhile to glance at that section before reading on. Certainly you should consult the Glossary as you proceed through the book.

In relation to the record repositories, you should note that *copies of most genealogical sources are centrally available in Dublin or Belfast.* These may be originals, transcripts, photocopies or microfilm copies. While a visit to your ancestor's county of origin can be profitable for research as well as having sentimental value, you would be wasting time visiting graveyards and making enquiries locally before making use of the centralised records. So start in Dublin. If your ancestors were from one of the nine counties of Ulster there will undoubtedly be records for you to look at in Belfast as well.

Record repositories can be daunting at first. You may feel out of place, especially as everyone else seems to know exactly what to do. If you follow the advice in Chapter 10 and read the house rules where applicable you should feel very much at home within a short time. However, we have one golden rule that you should remember no matter where you research: *handle all original material with extreme care.*

WRITING TO IRELAND

As we have already indicated, the general theme of the following chapters consists of a 'hands on' guide to tracing your ancestors while in Ireland. However, you may not be able to come to Ireland, or, if you do visit, the length of time you spend in the country may not be sufficient to pursue your family research. So, what can you do from your home base? Having followed through some of the suggestions already made, you will have assembled as much documentary evidence and oral family lore as possible and using this material, it is possible to advance significantly your researches by writing to sources in Ireland.

The National Library of Ireland

In conjunction with the Association of Professional Genealogists in Ireland (APGI), the National Library of Ireland provides a genealogy service free-of-charge. The service is designed to facilitate your researches in Ireland by providing you with:

- an overview of the records most commonly used by geaealogical researchers in Ireland
- advice on the most appropriate next step in your researches
- access to reference material and finding aids including:
  - genealogical publications
  - relevant National Library of Ireland finding aids
  - the computerised index to Griffith's *Primary Valuation*
  - the database version of Grenham's *Irish Recordfinder*

LDS family History Library

If you avail of the postal service, you then may wish to inquire of the LDS Family History Library in Salt Lake City or the LDS centre within your catchment area (see Chapter 10) whether they have copies of any of the sources referred to in your postal consultation; for instance, civil registration indexes and records (see Chapter 2), census returns (see Chapter 3), parish church records (see Chapter 4). If Salt Lake City has the appropriate material, the LDS Family History Centre in your area will requisition it for you, if requested.

The LDS has Family History Centres worldwide and on request, these centres will requisition from Salt Lake City material relevant to your research. If there is a centre within your catchment area you may be able to carry out some ancestral research, within reach of your home base (see Chapter 10).

Magazines

Two genealogical magazines worth noting, with regard to informative articles and to the space and attention given to readers queries are *Irish Roots*, a quarterly magazine, edited by Tony McCarthy and published in Cork, and *The Irish at Home and Abroad*, also a quarterly magazine, edited by Kyle J. Betit and Dwight A. Radford and published in Salt Lake City. If you are faced with problems or come up against the proverbial brick wall, a letter to the editor(s) may result in loosening up some of those bricks!

PROFESSIONAL RESEARCHERS

If you have difficulty making progress with your research from your home base, or, on the other hand, when you have examined the genealogical material easily available to you, you might wish to commission a professional genealogist, researcher or record agent to carry out, or, continue, your family research.

The Association of Professional Genealogists in Ireland (APGI) is an all-Ireland professional body, whose individuals, in addition to acting as consultants for the National Library of Ireland's Genealogy Service (see p. 32), undertake commissioned genealogical research. Members are full-time genealogists and are not employed in any other full-time occupation; they adhere to a strict code of practice, which incorporates maintaining high standards among its members and in protecting clients' interests. If reported, a complaints panel will investigate any dissatisfaction or grievances a client may have experienced.Their address is APGI, c/o The Genealogical Office, Kildare Street, Dublin 2. Telephone + 353 1 603 0200; fax + 353-1-662 1062.

The Association of Ulster Genealogists and Record Agents (AUGRA) is confined to members living in Ulster; members need not be full-time nor professional genealogists and membership is also open to Record agents.

Virtually all repositories and libraries include a list of researchers with their information sheets and if you have access to the Internet you will note that many of the individual web sites also include a list of researchers.

WRITING TO REPOSITORIES

If you wish to write to a specific archive, repository or library in Ireland, how can they assist you? Virtually all repositories, libraries and such institutions can be contacted by telephone, by fax and in writing (see Chapter 10). Some of the principal repositories, such as the National Archives, Public Record Office of Northern Ireland (PRONI) and the National Library maintain web-sites on the Internet, the information on which can be both informative and of assistance. The repositories and libraries usually respond to queries and requests for straightforward information within a reasonable time span.

Generally speaking, genealogical or historical research is not undertaken by repositories or libraries. If you request research of a particular repository or library, they will send you a list of independent genealogists, researchers and record agents, who undertake such research. A rider is usually included indicating that the repository does not recommend any particular individual nor can it accept any responsibility for the research carried out, nor for the payment arrangements entered into between the client and the genealogist or record searcher. That said, what services are available?

Services on Offer

The General Register Office

The General Register Office (see Chapter 2) will carry out limited birth, marriage and death searches. For a birth, marriage or death which took place during the 1800s, the GRO will carry out a two-year search. (General civil registration commenced in 1864 and registration of non-Roman Catholic marriages commenced in 1845 – see Chapter 2.) If the event took place during the 1900s a three-year search will be carried out. For instance, if you can supply the Office with the full name(s), place and year of the particular event the index will be examined for the year mentioned and for the following year, if the event took place during the 1800s and for the 1900s a further year will be added. You will be informed in writing of the outcome of the search. It may happen that the information you have is somewhat uncertain or vague about some specifics, such as, if requesting a birth record, you may not be certain about the mother's name before marriage or, with regard to a death record, you may not know where the particular death took place. In cases similar to these it could happen that the GRO search staff might note more than one entry, but would not have sufficient information to be able to pinpoint a specific record as the relevant one. In these circumstance details from those records noted will be sent to you.

For example, John Barry was born in 1870 in Cork City and his father's name was probably John: a search for his birth record would be made for the year 1870 and 1871. However, allowing for the probability that the surname Barry would be relatively numerous in Cork City, more than one birth record of a John, son of John Barry, could be noted within the two-year search. Details of the records would be sent to you.

You may have undertaken a birth marriage or death search yourself through microfilm copies of the indexes (see Chapters 2 and 10) and thus have the appropriate references; if you want a certified copy of the particular record you can send the references to the GRO.

Remember, a marriage search involves the examination of marriage indexes under two distinct names, that of bride and groom, and both names have to list the same references, thus, the relevant marriage entry usually can be identified from the index.

At present the two- or three-year search costs *IR£1.50. *IR£4 (including postage) is payable for a full certificate, *IR£5.50 for a search and certificate. Sterling and US dollar cheques and International Money Orders are acceptable. Fees are payable in advance.

*It is anticipated that there will be a significant increase in GRO fees before the end of 1998.

If an expansive or general search is required the GRO will send you a list of researchers.

BIRTH REGISTRATION SHORT-CUT

Virtually all births registered in the years 1864, 1865 and 1866 and a substantial number of those registered in the later 1860s are included in the 1992 edition of the *International Genealogical Index (IGI)* (see Glossary).

THE GRO'S HOLDINGS

Remember: The GRO (Dublin) holds annual indexes and copies of all births, marriages and deaths registered within the whole of Ireland up to December 1921 and from January 1922 for the Republic.

The General Register Office of Northern Ireland

The General Register Office of Northern Ireland will undertake specific five-year searches, provided sufficient information is given: for a birth certificate; the full name of the person whose birth certificate is required, together with the approximate year and place of birth and the parents' names, including the mother's name before marriage.

With regard to marriage and death searches prior to 1922, the Office cannot carry out a search unless the district where the marriage or death was registered is known.

Photocopies of civil records are not available at the GRO Northern Ireland. £2 sterling covers a five-year search, or part of five years and a certified copy of birth, marriage or death entry, including the search, costs £6 sterling.

The National Archives

The National Archives has a web site on the Internet (for address, see Chapter 10). Their main holdings of genealogical interest are listed, as are the names and addresses of independent researchers. The National Archives does not carry out research on behalf of the public. However, if you wish to have a photocopy of a testamentary record, which you have already established exists (see Chapter 7), you can order a copy by post, supplying the name and address of the deceased, the date of death and most importantly, the date of the grant of probate or administration. The fee, which is payable in advance, amounts to approximately IR£1.50 (US$2) per copy; cost of postage is extra.

The National Library of Ireland

The National Library of Ireland will photocopy printed material if you can supply the title, author, pages and call-up number. Manuscript material can be photocopied if on microfilm otherwise, it can be photographed. There is a photocopy fee: IR£0.60 (approx. US$1) per page.

The Genealogical Office

Queries relating to the Genealogical Office's holdings can be addressed to the in-house researcher. For a reasonable fee, a search of the manuscript collection can be made for specific queries and when relevant material is found it can be copied by hand, if not available on microfilm. Some of the more important manuscripts have been microfilmed, copies of which are held at The National Library.

Registry of Deeds

You can obtain a photocopy of a registered memorial from the Registry of Deeds, once you can furnish the Registry with the memorial number (see Chapter 6). The fee is approximately IR£4 (approx. US$6) per memorial.

The Public Record Office of Northern Ireland

The Public Record Office of Northern Ireland has an expansive and informative web site on the Internet (see Chapter 10 for address). PRONI is unable to carry out genealogical or historical research and includes a web page with a list of professional researchers.

Genealogical Indexing Centres (Heritage Centres)

Financially supported by state agencies, there are approximately 36 indexing or heritage centres throughout the whole of Ireland, engaged in indexing and computerising genealogical records relevant to their particular area, county or counties. The records from church registers of all denominations, up to at least 1900, are the basis of the databases. Many centres are also indexing the civil records, census returns, land and house holders' records and gravestone inscriptions. Computerisation is ongoing, and several centres are at an advanced stage of completing the computerisation of, at least, the Roman Catholic parish registers of their particular county or area. These databases can be of assistance if (i) you know the county, but not the particular parish or area within the county, in which your ancestor was born or married; (ii) if she or he was born or married prior to the commencement of civil registration; (iii) if your ancestor's surname was a relatively common or numerically strong one, thus making the examination of civil registration indexes difficult (see Chapters 2 and 4). The visitor or public does not have access to the databases. Many of the centres can provide a service to the customer, based on the contents of their particular database and indexes. A varying range of fees are payable.

For information relating to the individual county centres you can write to The Chief Executive, Irish Genealogy Limited, ESB Complex, Parnell Avenue, Harold's Cross, Dublin 12. Telephone: + 353-1-6042134; Fax: + 353-1-4544042; or email: pbrinkley@igl.ie. A fee of US$5 is requested to defray postal costs. Irish Genealogy Ltd is the umbrella organisation for genealogy throughout the island of Ireland (that is, the Republic of Ireland and Northern Ireland).

Information on the heritage centres, their databases and fees also can be found on the Internet: website http://www.mayo-ireland.ie/roots.htm.

THE INTERNET

Many are familiar with computers and with the variety of software and user services available. The Internet, which can be described as computers from different corners of the world interconnected through telecommunication lines, sharing information, became accessible to the ordinary person from the late 1980s. Electronic mail (email), which allows you to send messages and letters within seconds to anywhere in the world, and the WorldWideWeb (www), which can incorporate sound, graphics, and videos with the written word, are the most common and regular uses of the Internet.

Web pages relating to genealogy are to be found on the Internet and their number is constantly increasing. Both the National Archives and the Public Record Office Northern Ireland (PRONI) have helpful and interesting web sites. Web pages are provided by some professional genealogists and by individual providers, groups, magazines, associations and societies. Several of the web pages offer some general information and usually include a list of related web sites, which you can easily call up.

MATERIAL FROM THE INTERNET

It is worth noting that you can print out material you may wish to retain for future reference from web sites or down load them on to your hard or floppy disks; such as, information sheets from the web site of the National Archives; from those of PRONI or the PRO (London). Generally, copyright material can be reproduced without prior permission once it is for personal or in-house use. It is important, however, to always check information you receive from a web page for possible inaccuracies.

2 Civil Registration of Births, Marriages and Deaths

To start off your family research with information obtained from a birth, marriage or (to a lesser extent) a death record is invaluable. The vital particulars gleaned from, for instance, a birth or marriage record, can lead you to the census return for your ancestor's family (see Chapter 3) and to the parish church register (see Chapter 4) in which baptismal or marriage entries of an earlier generation or two may be found.

From the commencement of civil registration and onwards to the present day certified copies of all records were sent from the individual Superintendent Registrar's Districts (see Glossary) to the Registrar General of Births, Deaths and Marriages in Dublin, where annual indexes were created and are available to the public at the General Register Office (GRO). Thus, if there is the possibility that your ancestor or his/her family's births, marriages and deaths were registered by the state, the General Register Office probably will be your first 'port of call'. To make the best use of the records and facilities of the GRO, it is essential to know how to use the Indexes to Births, Marriages and Deaths, which will be central to your research.

In Ireland the start of compulsory civil registration of births, marriages and deaths came in two stages: the registration of *non* Roman Catholic marriages commenced 1st April 1845; and the registration of births, deaths and *all* marriages commenced 1st January 1864.

If your ancestor was born, married or died in Ireland after 1st January 1864 and, in the case of a non Roman Catholic marriage, if he/she was married after 1st April 1845, the particular event should be registered. However, many births, marriages and deaths were never registered, particularly during the earlier years.

RESEARCHING AT THE GENERAL REGISTER OFFICE, DUBLIN

The General Register Office, which is located in Dublin, holds copies of all civil records for the whole of Ireland, from the commencement of registration, up to and including the year 1921; from 1922 onwards, the GRO holds copies of the records for the Republic of Ireland. The GRO's separate annual indexes to births, marriages and deaths are available for consultation in the research room of the GRO, on the payment of a fee.

NORTHERN IRELAND RECORDS

The civil records, from 1st January 1922 onwards, for Northern Ireland (the counties of Antrim, Armagh, Down, Fermanagh, Londonderry and Tyrone), are *not* available at the GRO.

Prior to arriving, you will have your search plan already prepared and laid out; thus, having some idea as to the indexes and approximate period of years you will need, to start off your family search. Find yourself a table and chair, complete the search form with the required information regarding the type of index and the period of years you wish to consult and hand it over to a member of staff, together with the fee; the index volumes will be then made available to you. Using the suggestions and guidelines appropriate to your particular family search, work methodically through the indexes, making a note of each index consulted. When it comes to noting references, be systematic and methodical so that you will not have to spend your precious time returning to indexes already consulted.

At present a fee of £IR1.50 (approx. US$2) allows you to examine specific indexes over a period not exceeding five consecutive years. This process can be repeated any number of times. However, it is

PREPARATION

Before you start your research at the GRO:

- have as much preparation as possible done beforehand;
- have your search plan laid out on paper;
- note the opening hours of the GRO and try to be there as soon as it opens, as the research room can get very crowded;
- note that the research room closes from 1230 to 1415 hours;
- give yourself plenty of time to get accustomed to working through the indexes;
- as search and photocopy fees are payable, remember to bring Irish currency.

anticipated that there will be a significant increase in GRO fees before the end of 1998.

Even if you have a specific year for the civil birth, marriage or death record of your ancestor, it is wise to allow for some margin of doubt, so include, perhaps, two years before and two years after the year of the event in question. For example, Mary Doran, daughter of John Doran born Dublin, 1871: the *Indexes to Births* from 1869 to 1873, which incorporates five consecutive years – two years before and two years after 1871 – would be examined. If there was no reference to the birth of a Mary Doran registered in the Superintendent Registrar's District of Dublin, North or South, a further five-year search would be undertaken, probably from 1868 back to 1864, for which a further fee would be paid. Maybe two or more Mary Doran birth references would be noted, within that period. Thus, it might be necessary to request a photocopy of each birth record to find out which one, if any, might be the relevant one. At present each photocopy costs £IR1.50. A general fee of IR£12 (approximately US$20) allows you self-service access to the indexes in whatever order you wish.

INDEXES AND RECORDS

You have access to the Indexes only, not to the actual records. However, one of the great advantages of the research facilities of the GRO is that you can get photocopies of records almost immediately. Then, having gleaned the information from the birth, marriage or death record you might be able to take your family research a step further at the GRO. For instance, if you retrieved your ancestor's birth record, from which you learnt, for the first time, the mother's surname; now with both parents' names and taking into account the commencement years of marriage registration, a search for the marriage record could be feasible.

WORKING WITH THE GRO INDEXES

The research room displays on open shelves the volumes of the *Annual Indexes to Births* (red binding); *Marriages* (green binding) and *Deaths* (dark blue); the *Indexes to Non-Roman Catholic Marriages 1845–1863* (dark green binding) are kept separately in an enclosed press.

Births, Marriages and Deaths

The individual Indexes to Births are arranged in alphabetical order, according to surname and Christian/forename and include the following information, running in a single line, across a column:

- Surname;
- Christian name (forename); ('female' or 'male' in the case of the birth having been registered prior to name-giving);
- Name of the Superintendent Registrar's District in which the birth, marriage or death took place.

- Volume and page number of the register in which the entry is recorded.

From the year 1878, the annual indexes are divided into four quarters: births registered during the quarter ending 31st March, 30th June, 30th September and 31st December.

The Indexes to Marriages include the names of both spouses, under the appropriate letter of the alphabet. The year, the name of the Superintendent Registrar's District, the volume and page numbers entered against each spouse's name have to correlate in every respect before you should anticipate having found the relevant marriage record reference. From the year 1878 onwards, the annual indexes are divided into four quarters: marriages registered during the quarter ending 31st March, 30th June, 30th September and 31st December.

The Indexes to Deaths include the age of the deceased at last birthday (as the age is reported by a third party, it may not be accurate). From the year 1878, the annual indexes are divided into four quarters: deaths registered during the quarter ending 31st March, 30th June, 30th September and 31st December.

Late Registrations

At the back of each yearly birth and death index, the births and deaths which occurred in the year in question but were not registered within the obligatory time period are listed. In the early years 'late marriage registrations' are usually inserted in ink in the appropriate place within the marriage index proper.

How the Indexes are Arranged

As already indicated, from 1878 each yearly index volume to births, marriages and deaths is divided into four quarters: births, marriages and deaths registered in the quarter year, ending 31st March, 30th

June, 30th September and 31st December. Thus, when consulting any of the Indexes from 1878, remember to examine the four separate sections of each volume and the late registration section at the back of the particular volume.

From 1903 to 1927 inclusive, the layout of the Indexes to Births alters: annual volumes are not sectioned into quarters, but encompass the calendar year, and importantly, the child's date of birth and the mother's maiden name (before marriage) are included with each entry in the index. Each annual Index to Births for the years 1903–1927 consists of four books, arranged alphabetically: A–D; E–L; M–O; P–Z. Late registrations are at the back of the last book (P–Z), after Z.

From 1928 the Indexes to Births revert to the pre-1903 layout, i.e. annual volumes sectioned into quarters. However, they include the mother's maiden name, but not the child's date of birth

AVAILABLE INDEXES

The following are the Indexes available to the public at the General Register Office:

- Indexes to non-Roman Catholic marriages 1845–1863 for the island of Ireland.
- Indexes to Births 1864–1921 for the island of Ireland.
- Indexes to Births 1922 onwards for the Republic of Ireland.
- Indexes to Marriages 1864–1921 for the island of Ireland.
- Indexes to Marriages 1922 onwards for the Republic of Ireland.
- Indexes to Deaths 1864–1921 for the island of Ireland.
- Indexes to Deaths 1922 onwards for the Republic of Ireland.

NAME VARIANTS

When searching under a surname that can be preceded by O or Mac, such as (O')Sullivan; Mac/Mc Carthy/Carty; (O')Donnell etc., or a surname, which can commence with a different letter of the alphabet, such as Carney – Kearney; Kane – Cane/Cain; etc., you will need to consult more than one book for the year in question: for example, the books A–D and M–O would be consulted in relation to the surname (Mac/Mc) Carthy and (O') Donnell; the books M–O and P–Z for (O') Sullivan; the books A–D and E–L for Carney and Kearney.

Special Registers and Indexes

Some 'specialist' registers and indexes at the GRO include:

- Army: The Births, Deaths and Marriages (Army) Act 1879 required registration of the births, marriages and deaths of those Irish born who were serving abroad in the British Army. From 1883 these births, marriages and deaths are indexed and are included at the back of the appropriate annual indexes.
- Marine Registers: From 1864 separate *Marine Register Books of Births and Deaths* of Irish subjects were kept and from 1886 indexes to these births and deaths are included at the back of the appropriate annual indexes.
- Schulze Register and General Index consists of several thousand marriages and a small number of baptisms performed in Dublin between 1806 and 1837 by the unlicensed clergyman Rev. J.G.F. Schulze.
- South African War 1898–1902 ('The Boer War'): There is an index to deaths of Irish subjects killed during the 'Boer War'.

- Foreign Birth Register: From 1864 births abroad of Irish subjects, if notified, were obliged to be registered.
- Index to deaths of Irish serving in the British Army during the First World War (1914–1918): What is available is the appropriate reference with which to apply to the Family Records Centre, 1 Myddelton St, London EC1R 1UW, for a certificate.

BIRTH REGISTRATION SHORT-CUT

Virtually all births registered in the years 1864, 1865 and 1866 and a substantial number of those registered in the later 1860s are included in the 1992 edition of the *International Genealogical Index (IGI)* (see Glossary).

Searching for a Birth Record

A birth record usually includes:

- date and place of birth
- child's name (or 'female' or 'male')
- sex
- father's name, place of residence and occupation
- mother's name and maiden name (name before marriage)
- name, address and qualification of the informant of the birth

UNREGISTERED BIRTHS

Remember that many births, marriages and deaths were never registered.

- date of registration, name of the registrar
- Superintendent Registrar's District and County of registration.

If you already know the year and place of your ancestor's birth, together with the names of the parents, the quest for the birth record should not be troublesome, nor should it be if your ancestor had an unusual or rare surname, even though you might have very little specific information, with regard to when and where in Ireland he/she was born. On the other hand, searching for the birth record of, let us say, Mary Sullivan, daughter of John Sullivan, born *c.* 1867 in Co. Kerry, presents difficulties, even before you open an index. You will note from the map that, for the purposes of civil registration, six Superintendent Registrar's Districts cover Co. Kerry (Dingle, Tralee, Listowel, Killarney, Kenmare and Caherciveen). The name (O') Sullivan is very numerous throughout Co. Kerry and the forename Mary is also numerous. With an approximate year of birth, it is advisable to commence with examining at least five years of indexes – two years before and two after the approximate year. Then, from each *Index to Births* you note all the references for Mary O'Sullivan and Mary Sullivan whose births are registered in any of the six

REMEMBER SPELLING VARIANTS

Before you undertake any research, write out and keep in front of you all the possible variant spellings of both the surname and forename of the subject of your search. Take all variations into consideration when examining records and indexes, for example: Catherine, Katharine, Kate; Brian, Bryan; Honoria, Hanah, Hannah, Hanora, Nora; (O')Neill, Neil; Dillon, Dillan, Dillane; (O)Callaghan, Callahan; (Mac) Carthy, Carty; (O) Rahilly, Reilly, Riley; (O')Donoghue, Donohue; Cain, Cane, Kane; Phelan, Whelan; etc.

Superintendent Registrar's Districts covering Co. Kerry; you will probably end up with many references just for the one year. You could order up a photocopy of each entry, a costly exercise, only to find that there are several Mary (O')Sullivans, whose fathers were named John; without knowing your particular Mary's mother's maiden name, you have no way of finding out whether your ancestor's birth record is among the pile.

Another troublesome quest would be searching for the birth record of, for example, James Ryan, son of James Ryan and Margaret Kennedy, born *c.* 1870 in Thurles Town, Co. Tipperary. Ryan and Kennedy are very numerous surnames throughout Co. Tipperary, and the Superintendent Registrar's District of Thurles not only incorporates the town of Thurles, but also other towns, villages and townlands within a large catchment area. Very many references to James Ryan, Registrar's District of Thurles, could be extracted from five years of birth indexes.

If it proves difficult for you to make progress at the GRO because of one or more of the troublesome situations illustrated above, there are alternative possibilities open to you:

- If you know the names of both parents, search for the marriage record; remember that if you identify both names in the same index, it is essential that the references to year, Superintendent Registrar's District, volume, page and quarter (if applicable), are similar.
- Identify the relevant parish church registers (see Chapter 4). Search through the baptismal register for the years you want; you may find the baptismal record of your ancestor (and maybe a sibling or two). The date of baptism can then help to pinpoint the relevant year for the Index to Births at the GRO. A civil record usually is more informative than a church record. (Generally, children, particularly children of Catholics, were baptised within a few days of birth).

- If your search involves an entire county, inquire whether the Indexing Centre of the particular county has the church registers indexed (see chapters 3 and 11).
- Virtually all the births registered in the years 1864, 1865 and 1866 and a substantial number of those registered in the later 1860s are included in the 1992 edition of the *International Genealogical Index* (*IGI*) (see Glossary).

The civil birth record, together with the church baptismal/birth record, sometimes can pose interesting questions. If you retrieve both the civil birth record and the church birth/baptismal record and you find that the date of birth given on the civil record is several months later than that which is entered in the baptismal register, which one is considered accurate? The responsibility to register a birth with the District Registrar lay with the parents or a person present at the birth and a fine was payable if the birth was not registered within three months. However, in many areas, it took several years to inform the public about the process of registration. In addition, for many, the District Registrar's dispensary was a distance from home, so when it came to registering, three months or more might have elapsed – to avoid having to pay the fine some months might have been taken off the child's age. However, the child, particularly of Catholic parents, would have been baptised within a few days of birth.

Searching for a Marriage Record

A marriage record includes:

- date and place of marriage (specifying the religious denomination of the church or the name of the Registrar's Office)
- surname and forename of both spouses

- ages (usually noted as 'of full age', that is, over 21 years, or 'minor', under 21; sometimes the actual age is stated)
- condition, that is, spinster, bachelor, widow or widower
- occupation
- place of residence of each spouse at the time of marriage
- father's name and occupation of each spouse (it may state that the father is 'alive' or 'deceased/dead'); but *not* the fathers' addresses
- names of two witnesses to the marriage
- name of the clergyman/registrar who performed the ceremony
- Superintendent Registrar's District and the county in which the ceremony took place.

A marriage search can be most rewarding: to carry out a marriage search you need to know the surname and forename of both spouses. Check the indexes under both names remembering that, before you request a photocopy of what you hope will be your ancestor's marriage record, the references – year, Superintendent Registrar's

HELP IS AT HAND

When you receive a requested photocopy of a birth, marriage or death record, read it immediately – the handwriting can be hard to decipher; and some essential particulars, such as the name of the townland or street where your ancestors lived could be incomprehensible. Ask for assistance, a member of the staff may enlarge the particular detail; also, the *Townlands Index* (see Glossary) is available if you wish to check the townland.

UNREGISTERED MARRIAGES

Remember that many births, marriages and deaths were never registered.

District, volume, page and quarter (if applicable) for both spouses should be similar. The bride's and groom's fathers' names are given on the marriage record, which enables you to add another generation to your family tree. Unfortunately, the mother's names were not included in marriage records until the 1950s.

Sometimes, a marriage record can be traced with the name of only one of the parties. If that surname is unusual or rare, it could 'stand out' on the marriage index page. If you have succeeded already in tracing your family in the 1901 or 1911 census returns (see Chapter 3), the information given on the census returns, such as ages of children, forename of wife, county of birth and the number of years married (all included in the 1911 census returns), can help to assemble enough facts to warrant a return visit to the GRO to search for the marriage certificate (see the Forbes marriage search at the end of Chapter 3).

There could be many a John Murphy and Mary Doyle of the civil registration district of Wexford or many a James Reilly and Mary Sheridan of Cavan listed in the same *Index to Marriages*. It is essential, when carrying out a marriage search, to have the names written out in front to you, with all the possible variant spellings of each surname and forename. If you find the names of both the bride and groom in the same index, it is essential to cross-check the entries to ascertain that both names have the common references for civil registration district, volume and page numbers. Remember, also, that from 1878 the annual indexes are sectioned into quarters; thus, if you find what may look like the relevant couple, recheck to ascertain that both spouses' names are listed in the same quarter of the same year.

Then fill in the white form with the names and relevant references, and for the required fee, you will receive a photocopy of the marriage record. Ask for assistance if you have difficulty in deciphering the script.

Searching for a Death Record

A death record includes:

- date and place of death
- name of the deceased
- sex
- whether the deceased was married or a widow(er), spinster or bachelor
- age of the deceased at last birthday
- occupation
- cause of death
- name, address and qualification of the informant
- date of registration and name of the Registrar
- Superintendent Registrar's District and County of registration

Death certificates are often the least satisfactory of records from the family researcher's point of view. Unlike some countries, such as Scotland and Australia, Irish death certificates do not include date of birth or parents or spouse's names, thus, genealogical information is minimal. As the age of the deceased stated on the certificate has been given by a third party, it is probably inaccurate. It can be difficult to identify the death record of an ancestor, even if you have specific information, such as date, age and place of death. The fact that certain surnames are associated, in numerical strength, with particular counties or parishes and thus with civil registration districts, can make examining the Indexes to Deaths (and the Indexes to Births) very frustrating. The options suggested, in relation to a troublesome or difficult civil birth search, do not always hold for a death search (see Chapter 4's section on dealing with Catholic parish registers). However, let us not be too negative about death records, as they can include information to add on to our family tree. In connection with the Forbes family, an informative death record was retrieved: Julia Forbes, died on 23 June 1897 in the townland of Milane, Superintendent District of Dunmanway, Co. Cork; she is recorded as 88 years of age; the widow of Richard Forbes, a dairyman; John Forbes of Milane, son of the deceased was present at her death.

The Superintendent Registrar's Districts

The Superintendent Registrar's Districts, of which there are approximately 163, retain their respective original registers; and each register is indexed. In more recent times, some rationalisation has taken place

CHECK THE AGE

The inclusion of the age of the deceased in the Indexes to Deaths can help to eliminate or set aside references that are not of immediate relevancy; for example:
Index to Deaths 1874: Forbes, Mary, 0, Skibbereen;
Index to Deaths 1876: Forbes, Mary, 60, Skibbereen.
Remember, the deceased's age as entered on the death record may not be accurate, after all the deceased did not have a direct input into his or her own death record!

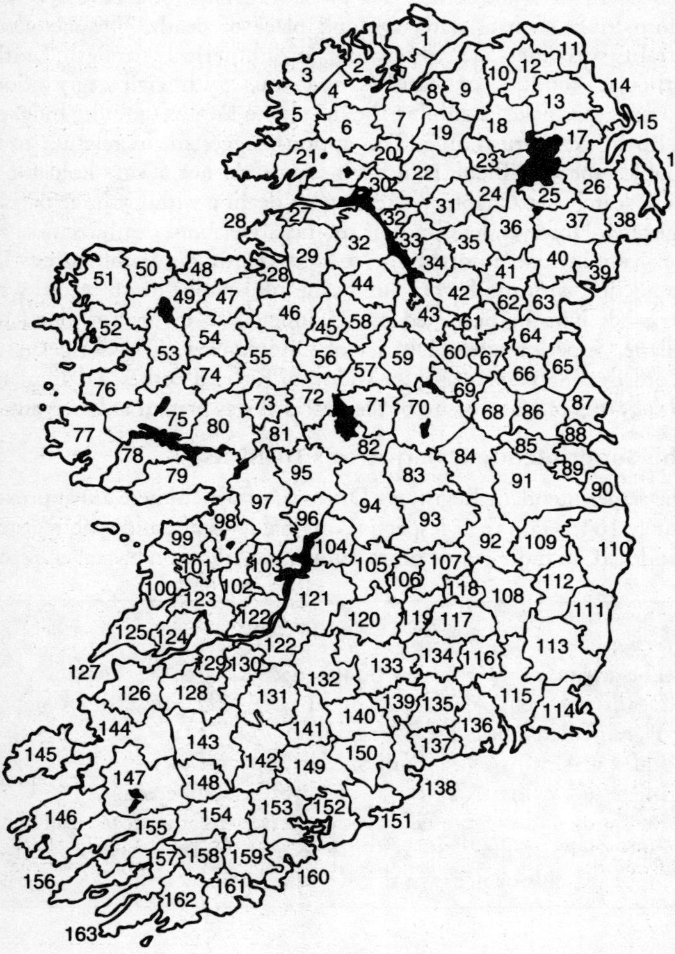
1
11
2
10
12
3
14
8
9
4
13
5
7
15
6
18
19
17
16
21
20
23
22
26
30
24
25
31
28
27
32
37
38
36
33
29
32
35
51
50
48
40
34
39
28
41
44
49
47
42
62
63
46
58
43
61
52
45
64
54
53
60
67
55
56
59
57
65
74
66
76
69
73
72
71
87
70
68
86
75
80
81
77
88
82
85
84
78
89
79
95
83
91
90
97
94
93
96
98
99
92
109
110
104
105
107
101
103
106
112
100
102
118
108
121
123
111
122
120
119
117
125
124
113
122
134
116
129
130
133
127
132
126
128
131
115
139
135
114
140
136
144
141
143
137
150
145
142
149
147
148
138
153
152
146
154
151
155
157
158
159
156
160
161
162
163

CIVIL REGISTRATION DISTRICTS: Key to map

1 Inishowen
2 Millford
3 Dunfanaghy
4 Letterkenny
5 Glenties
6 Stranorlar
7 Strabane
8 Londonderry
9 Newton-Limavady
10 Coleraine
11 Ballycastle
12 Ballymoney
13 Ballymena
14 Larne
15 Belfast
16Newtownards
17 Antrim
18 Magherafelt
19 Gortin
20 Castlederg
21 Donegal
22 Omagh
23 Cookstown
24 Dungannon
25 Lurgan
26 Lisburn
27 Ballyshannon
28 Sligo
29 Manor-hamilton
30 Irvinestown (Lowtherstown)
31 Clogher
32 Enniskillen
33 Lisnaskea
34 Clones
35 Monaghan
36 Armagh
37 Banbridge
38 Downpatrick
39 Kilkeel
40 Newry
41 Castleblayney
42 Cootehill
43 Cavan
44 Bawnboy
45 Carrick-on-Shannon
46 Boyle
47 Tubercurry
48 Dromore West
49 Ballina
50 Killala
51 Belmullet
52 Newport
53 Castlebar
54 Swineford
55 Castlerea
56 Strokestown
57 Longford
58 Mohill
59 Granard
60 Oldcastle
61 Baileborough
62 Carrick-macross
63 Dundalk
64 Ardee
65 Drogheda
66 Navan
67 Kells
68 Trim
69 Delvin
70 Mullingar
71 Ballymahon
72 Roscommon
73 Glenamaddy
74 Claremorris
75 Ballinarobe
76 Westport
77 Clifden
78 Oughterard
79 Galway
80 Tuam
81 Mt Bellew
82 Athlone
83 Tullamore
84 Edenderry
85 Celbridge
86 Dunshaughlin
87 Balrothery
88 Dublin North
89 Dublin South
90 Rathdown
91 Naas
92 Athy
93 Mt Mellick
94 Parsontown (Birr)
95 Ballinasloe
96 Portumma
97 Loughrea
98 Gort
99 Ballyvaughan
100 Ennistymon
101 Corofin
102 Tulla
103 Scarriff
104 Borrisokane
105 Roscrea
106 Donaghmore
107 Abbeyleix
108 Carlow
109 Baltinglass
110 Rathdrum
111 Gorey
112 Shillelagh
113 Enniscorthy
114 Wexford
115 New Ross
116Thomastown
117 Kilkenny
118 Castlecomer
119 Urlingford
120 Thurles
121 Nenagh
122 Limerick
123 Ennis
124 Killadysert
125 Kilrush
126 Listowel
127 Glin
128 Newcastle
129 Rathkeale
130 Croom
131 Kilmallock
132 Tipperary
133 Cashel
134 Callan
135 Carrick-on-Suir
136 Waterford
137 Kilmacthomas
138 Dungarvan
139 Clonmel
140 Clogheen
141 Mitchelstown
142 Mallow
143 Kanturk
144 Tralee
145 Dingle
146 Cahersiveen
147 Killarney
148 Millstreet
149 Fermoy
150 Lismore
151 Youghal
152 Midleton
153 Cork
154 Macroom
155 Kenmare
156 Castletown
157 Bantry
158 Dunmanway
159 Bandon
160 Kinsale
161 Clonakilty
162 Skibbereen
163 Skull

REMEMBER SPELLING VARIANTS

Before you undertake any research, write out and keep in front of you all the possible variant spellings of both the surname and forename of the subject of your search. Take all variations into consideration when examining records and indexes, for example: Catherine, Katharine, Kate; Brian, Bryan; Honoria, Hanah, Hannah, Hanora, Nora; (O')Neill, Neil; Dillon, Dillan, Dillane; (O)Callaghan, Callahan; (Mac) Carthy, Carty; (O) Rahilly, Reilly, Riley; (O')Donoghue, Donohue; Cain, Cane, Kane; Phelan, Whelan; etc.

with the Superintendent Registrar's Districts' registers now being kept in one or more centres within the particular county; for instance, the registers of each of the six Superintendent Registrar's Districts covering Co. Kerry are held in Killarney.

If you know the place of origin of your ancestors, the facility of examining these registers could be rewarding as you could easily assemble information on several members and maybe, generations of the family, gleaned directly from the registers.

In principal, for a fee, the public can examine these registers; however, due to lack of space and/or shortage of staff, some centres cannot facilitate the public at all, but the staff may carry out requested research. Before you consider approaching your family research from within the county make sure that the office of your particular Superintendent Registrar's District has a research facility.

THE GENERAL REGISTER OFFICE NORTHERN IRELAND

The General Register Office Northern Ireland (GRONI), located in Belfast, holds the civil records for Northern Ireland only. The GRONI holds the original registers of births from 1st January 1864, the original registers of deaths from 1st January 1864 and the original registers of marriages from 1st January 1922. Pre-1922 marriage records are held at local government level throughout Northern Ireland. The Indexes available are Indexes to Births 1864 onwards, Indexes to Deaths 1922 onwards and Indexes to Marriages 1922 onwards.

Other registers held at the GRONI, include the Marine registers of births and deaths from 1922; the British Consular returns of births and deaths from 1922 and marriages from 1923; registers of births, marriages and deaths from 1927, covered by the Army Act, 1879; and the Adopted Children Register, from 1931.

Working at the GRONI

By appointment, usually on one day's notice, the Indexes to Births, Deaths and Marriages (see above) are available for consultation; a fee of £2 sterling is payable for a five-year search. If you wish to establish that a particular entry in the index is the record you want, a member of the staff will give you limited verification. Then you can order a certified copy of the entry for the fee of £4.00 sterling. The GRONI does not provide photocopies of records.

The research facilities at the GRONI are very limited. To carry out a general search of the birth, marriage and death indexes for any period of years and for any number of entries, during a particular day not exceeding six hours duration, you need to book at least six months in advance. The fee payable is £5.50 sterling. A member of staff is in attendance to handle the registers and to read out the details to you. You then may wish to order certificates.

PRE- OR POST-1922?

The GRONI does not hold marriage records prior to 1922; these are held at local government level. The GRO, Dublin, holds copies of the births, marriages and deaths registered in the whole island (including present-day Northern Ireland) up to December 1921, and from January 1922 for the Republic of Ireland.

PRACTISING RESEARCH TECHNIQUES

The following illustrates how some of the suggestions in this chapter were put into practice. We started off with Catherine Kehelly's birth certificate, which records that she was born 10th August 1881 in the townland of Cooleenagow, Superintendent Registrar's District of Dunmanway, Co. Cork, the daughter of Jeremiah Kehelly and Anne Forbes; we also knew that they were small tenant farmers; and that Catherine had six or seven older siblings. We took note of the variant spellings of Kehelly – Kehely; Kehilly, Kehily and Keahily, and of Forbes – Forbus, Forboes and Firbush.

A Marriage Search

The Indexes to Marriages were examined for the marriage record of Jeremiah Kehelly and Anne Forbes; allowing that Catherine had at least six older siblings, the Indexes to Marriages were examined from 1875 back in years until both surnames were found in the same index and with the same references: Indexes to Marriages, 1867; Kehely, Jeremiah; Forbes, Anne; Superintendent Registrar's District of Bandon; volume 5; page 21 (pre-1878 marriages were registered within the calendar year and not within a specific quarter). These particulars were transcribed on to the required form, the fee paid and the photocopy was promptly received.

A Death Search

The 1901 Census Return for the Kehilly household of the townland of Cooleenagow records Anne Kehilly, aged 60 years; she is not recorded in the 1911 Census Return for the same household. She may have died between 1901 and 1911. (For information on census returns, see Chapter 3.)

The Indexes to Deaths were examined from 1901 up to and including the year 1911 for the reference to Anne Kehilly/Kehelly's death record, bearing in mind that the 1901 Census recorded her as aged 60 years and that her death probably would be registered in the Superintendent Registrar's District of Dunmanway (the townland of Cooleenagow being situated within that district).

No reference to Anne Kehily/Kehelly was found within that period. Perhaps her death was not registered; however, the search was continued and a reference which fitted the requirements was noted in the Index to Deaths for the year 1926 – Kehelly, Anne, 76 years, Superintendent Registrar's District of Dunmanway volume 5, page 155, December quarter. She had died at the home of her married daughter in the town of Dunmanway. It became apparent, as progress was made with this family research, that, sometime after the death of her husband, in 1906, Anne Kehelly made the farm over to her son Cornelius Kehelly and went to live with her married daughter.

A Birth Search

The marriage record confirms that Catherine Kehilly married John Patrick O'Shea at Dunmanway Catholic Church on 5th October, 1912. According to the marriage record, John P. O'Shea's father was James O'Shea, a compositor, but was dead at the time of their marriage. Although John P. O'Shea had a Dublin address at the time of his marriage, family tradition was that he was born either in the western part of Co. Cork (possibly Skibbereen) or in Cork City. It was accepted that he was a few years younger than his wife (who was born 1881).

The Indexes to Births were examined from 1882 and note was taken of all references to John Patrick (O') Shea and to John (O') Shea, whose births were registered in the Superintendent Districts of Cork City, and of Macroom, Bantry, Skull, Skibbereen, Clonakilty, Bandon, Dunmanway and Castletown, all of which cover west Co. Cork. Fifteen references in all were noted between 1882 and 1887, and only one referred to a John Patrick O'Shea. The Index to Births for the year 1887 includes the reference: O'Shea, John Patrick, Cork

[City], volume 5, page 127, September quarter. A photocopy of the entry was ordered and it proved to be the right one: John Patrick was born at 18 Georges Street, Cork City on 7 July 1887, the son of James O'Shea, printer and Minnie O'Shea, formerly, O'Brien.

These searches were part of extensive research, carried out over several months. Prior to each visit to the GRO, the work plan was prepared and laid out on paper, as described in Chapter 1. To avail of suitable workspace and of the initial uncrowded atmosphere, a special effort was made to arrive at the GRO at the time of opening, 0930.

Civil registration of a non-Roman Catholic marriage

Registration of non-Roman Catholic marriages commenced, as already indicated, on 1st April 1845, 18 years and 9 months prior to general civil registration.

Oscar Wilde, the brilliant Irish writer, was born in Dublin in 1854, the second son of the renowned surgeon and antiquarian Sir William Wilde and his wife Jane Elgee, who wrote poetry under the name 'Speranza'. The family were Church of Ireland, that is, Protestant. The birth of Oscar Wilde took place ten years prior to the commencement of compulsory civil registration. However, as the civil registration of non-Roman Catholic marriages commenced in 1845, the marriage of his parents should be registered by the civil authorities.

The Index to non-Roman Catholic Marriages for the year 1851 includes the names of William Robert Wilde and Jane Francesca Elgee – under the appropriate letters of the alphabet and with similar references – volume 5, page 354. They were married by Licence, on 12 November 1851 in the Parish Church of St. Peter, Dublin City.

The Index to Dublin Will and Grant Books 1800–1858 (see Chapter 7), in which the Index to Marriage Licence Bonds for the Diocese of Dublin is incorporated, lists William Robert Wilde and Jane Francesca Elgee, under the appropriate letters of the alphabet, the year 1851; type of grant: Marriage Licence.

3 Census Returns

The earliest complete census surviving for the entire country is that of 1901, and the only other currently open to the public is that of 1911. The first full census of Ireland was conducted in 1821 and thereafter there was one every ten years. However, after statistics were extracted from the 1861, 1871, 1881 and 1891 censuses, the returns themselves were routinely destroyed by government order. The bulk of the 1821, 1831, 1841 and 1851 returns were subsequently destroyed when the Public Record Office was burned during the Civil War in 1922. What survive of them are fragmentary. These are discussed below, as are Census Search Forms (which relate mainly to 1841 and 1851 returns) and 18th-century census-type records.

THE 1901 CENSUS

The original returns from the 1901 Census are held at the National Archives but they are also available on microfilm in various other repositories. For instance, most county libraries now have the returns for their area. Full name indexes to the returns for Counties Fermanagh and Tyrone have been published on microfiche by Largy Books and these are available in various repositories, including the National Archives. David Leahy's *County Longford and its People* is an index to heads of household and household members of other surnames in the 1901 Longford returns.

In order to use the census, you need to know exactly where your family was living on 31 March 1901 – the townland or small town in rural areas; the street in large towns or cities.

Townlands and small towns

The 1901 edition of the *Townlands Index* (see Glossary) will give you the name and number of the District Electoral Division (DED) your townland or town is in. You then need the file number of your townland or town within the DED. You find this in the 1901 Census

Catalogue on the open shelves in the Reading Room. The Catalogue is divided into several volumes (with purple bindings), arranged by county. Within each county volume, the DEDs are arranged numerically. Within each DED the townlands are arranged numerically and some small towns are subdivided into streets, each with a separate file number. Disregard the numbers to the right of the townland or street name, as they merely indicate how many households were returned. Once you have found your townland or street file number you can complete an Order Docket. For example, if you were looking for the Forbes family from Caher townland (file no. 6) in Kinneigh DED (no. 115), Co. Cork, you would fill in the following details:

1901 Census
Cork
DED 115/6

Large towns

The 1901 edition of the *Townlands Index* will give you the names and numbers of the DEDs over which your town extends. To find your street file number you need to check the 1901 Census Catalogue for each of these DEDs. With this information you can then complete the Order Docket in the same manner as the above example, remembering that it is always the name of the county and not that of the town that you state.

Cities

On the open shelves, beside the volumes of the 1901 Census Catalogue, are indexes to streets in the 1901 Census for Belfast, Cork, Dublin, Kingstown (now Dun Laoghaire) and Limerick. These give the DED number and (with the exception of Limerick) the street file number, allowing you to complete an Order Docket without referring to the Catalogue itself. However, it is always best to double-check.

FINDING YOUR FAMILY'S STREET

If you don't know what street the family was in at the time of the census, you could try the following. If they were shopkeepers or relatively prosperous residents you could try a trade directory (see Chapter 9). *Slater's* 1894 and *Kelly's* 1905 would be the publications nearest the date for large towns. The various city directories would have 1901 editions. If they were of a working-class background, they are unlikely to be recorded in trade directories, and they are likely to have moved home quite frequently, especially in the cities. Your best bet is to locate the birth of a child of the family at the General Register Office close to the date of the 1901 or indeed the 1911. With a large town it is practicable, though time consuming, to trawl right through each street in search of the family. With a city this would be a daunting task.

The street index for Belfast has the DED/street reference prefaced by the letter 'A' or 'D', indicating whether the county concerned is Antrim or Down. The Cork and Dublin volumes give both 1901 and 1911 references. Frequent use has shown that the Dublin index omits quite a number of addresses, so you might have to seek assistance from an archivist.

How to Use the 1901 Census Returns

You will be given a series of census returns bound into a volume. The volume will cover part, or possibly all, of a DED. Within the volume, the files are bound in numerical order, separated by coloured cardboard sheets. Once you have found your correct townland or street file, the first pages you will see are summary sheets for the townland or street. Those headed 'Form B.1' list the heads of household for the entire file. The number of the individual household return will be given in the extreme left-hand column. You may then turn to the sheets headed 'Form A', which are in numerical order, and find the very return your ancestor completed in 1901. Remember, you are dealing with original documents so *please handle with care.*

How to Order Census Returns on Microfilm

The microfilm copy is also arranged by DED and it is accompanied at each repository by a copy of the Census Catalogue, so you would use it in the same way as the original. However, many DEDs are filmed out of sequence and in cities, the streets are arranged in rough alphabetical order rather than numerically. You can view either the original or the microfilm copy (MFGI 1–32) at the National Archives. The one advantage of using microfilm is that you can print out a copy on the spot.

CHECK THEIR AGES

It is generally expected that 'official' documents such as census returns and marriage and death certificates should be accurate in regard to ages given. In reality this is rarely the case. It is quite common to find a person ageing, by as little as five, or, as many as twenty years between the 1901 and 1911 returns. You cannot always explain this as, on one hand, vanity or, on the other, a wish to show qualification for the state pension, which was introduced in 1908. Regardless of their social standing, people appear to have had little knowledge of or concern about their exact age. For this reason, it is important that you obtain an ancestor's age from a variety of sources so as to counteract their inaccuracy.

What the Returns tell You

The information given for each individual in the household is as follows: name, relationship to head of household, religious denomination, ability to read and write, age, occupation, marital status, county of birth, ability to speak Irish and serious infirmities.

What's Your Next Step?

You might as well try the 1911 returns as well, if you are in the National Archives. You could return to the General Register Office to search the birth records for one of the children now that you have a fair estimate of when they were born. Pick one with an unusual forename. The birth record would give the mother's maiden name, allowing for a search for the parents' marriage.

THE 1911 CENSUS

The original returns from the 1911 Census are also held at the National Archives and are in the process of being microfilmed. As with the 1901, you need to know exactly where your family was living on 2 April 1911.

Townlands, Small and Large Towns, and Cities

There is no 1911 edition of the *Townlands Index* so you again use the 1901 edition to get the DED name (which will be unchanged) and number (which may be slightly different). To confirm the DED number and find the townland, town or street file number, you use the 1911 Census Catalogue. Again, this is on the open shelves and divided into several volumes (light brown bindings this time), arranged by county. As in the case of 1901, within the county the DEDs are arranged numerically, with the DED name and number given on the top of each page. If the DED number is not the same as in the 1901 Catalogue, it is simply a matter of checking the names of a few DEDs before and after that number to identify the correct one. Again, within the DED the townlands or streets are arranged numerically and once you find the correct file number you can complete an Order Docket in the same format as in the 1901 example above. (The 1911 Census Catalogue for Co. Cork shows that Kinneigh DED has moved up a digit from 115 in 1901 to 116 for 1911, whereas Caher townland is still number 6).

When researching city returns to the 1911 Census, there are indexes to streets in the 1911 Census for Belfast, Cork and Dublin only. Those for Cork and Dublin are combined 1901 and 1911 street indexes. They give the DED and street file numbers.

How to Use the 1911 Census Returns

You will be given a folder or possibly a large cardboard box containing a number of folders. Each folder contains the file for a particular townland, town or street and the DED/file reference is written on it. The box will cover part, or possibly all, of the relevant DED, but it may cover others also. Within the box the folders should (but very likely will not) be in numerical order. Again, once you have found the relevant folder, the first pages you will see are summary sheets for the townland or street. Find those headed 'Form B.1' which give the heads of household for the entire file. The number of the individual household return will be given in the extreme left-hand column. This will lead you to the relevant 'Form A'. Don't forget; you are dealing with the original document, so handle with care.

What the Census Returns Tell You

The information given for each individual in the household is the same as in 1901. However, in the case of a married woman additional information was required. The householder was obliged to state how many years any married woman residing there was married, how many children she had born alive and how many were still living. This can be the most important information in this census.

Very often these details were completed for a widow and crossed through or erased by the enumerator because they were only asked of women in existing marriages. Usually it is possible to make out the figures despite the enumerator's best efforts.

Your Next Step

With a fair estimate of a marriage date you can now go back to the General Register Office to search for the marriage record.

SURVIVING 19TH-CENTURY CENSUS RECORDS

As already stated, there are no surviving census returns for 1861, 1871, 1881 and 1891. What survive from the 1821, 1831, 1841 and 1851 census returns are fragments of the originals and miscellaneous extracts, most of which are housed at the National Archives. These censuses were arranged by county, barony, parish and townland, so their structure is more straightforward than that of 1901 and 1911.

The 1821 Census

The first full census was commenced on 28 May 1821. The enumerators were issued with notebooks in which they entered details concerning each household. The process took several weeks. When they had all the information gathered they transferred it to the census forms which they submitted. The information given for each individual in these original returns consisted of name, relationship to head of household, age and occupation. The returns also stated the number of storeys in each house and the number of acres held by each family. The originals survive for Derryvullen parish and part of Aghalurcher in Co. Fermanagh, the complete baronies of Arran and Athenry in Co. Galway, the complete baronies of Navan Lower and Navan Upper in Co. Meath, and the complete barony of Ballybritt in Co. Offaly. In addition, full copies for 15 parishes and part of another in Co. Cavan are available. You will find call numbers for all of these in the 'Pre-1901 Census Material' Catalogue in the National Archives. They are also on microfilm (MFGI–34).

One original enumerator's notebook is known to exist. It is held in Armagh Public Library, with a copy in PRONI (T.450), and covers eight townlands in Kilmore parish, Co. Armagh. The details for one of these townlands, Derryhale, were published in *Ulster Folklife* in 1961. There are extracts of returns scattered through various collections. The most significant and accessible are those made by Edmund Walsh Kelly. His extracts from Waterford City were published in the *Irish Genealogist* in 1968–69. His full transcripts from Aglish and Portnascully parishes in Iverk barony in Co. Kilkenny were published in both the *Irish Ancestor* (1976) and the *Irish Genealogist* (1976). Finally, his extracts from other parishes in Iverk barony appear in the *Irish Genealogist* of 1977–78. The other substantial extracts are from Killarney town and Kilcummin parish in Co. Kerry – also from the 1841 and 1851 Censuses but mainly for Sweeney/McSweeney households (Royal Irish Academy, McSwiney Papers, Parcel F, No. 3), Carrigallen parish in Co. Leitrim – erroneously labelled 'circa 1833' (National Library Pos. 4646), and Clonmel town in Co. Tipperary – full names and occupations of heads of household only (National Archives M.242/2).

The 1831 Census

This census was conducted at varying times over a considerable period. The information given in the original returns was much less than in 1821. Only the head of household was named. The other information consisted of the number of individual families in each house, the number of males and females in each family, the number of male and female servants and the numbers engaged in various forms of occupation. However, no original returns survive. Walsh Kelly's extracts from Iverk barony in Co. Kilkenny and Dungarvan parish in

Co. Waterford are at the Genealogical Office (Ms 684). They are complete for Aglish and Portnascully parishes.

In 1834 the Commissioners of Public Instruction, Ireland, enquired into the religious affiliation of the population. To this end they had copies made of the 1831 returns, excluding the occupational information, and added a blank column in which to insert the religious denomination. These copies were returned to the original enumerators and the extra statistic was added.

The resulting hybrid census is confusingly referred to as that of 1831/4, though the information relates entirely to the situation in 1831. The 1831/4 Census for all of Co. Londonderry (Derry) is available at the National Archives. Again, you will find the call numbers in the 'Pre-1901 Census Material' catalogue. An index to these Londonderry returns, compiled by the Derry Inner City Trust, is also available on microfiche at the National Archives.

The Commissioners also requested the clergy of all denominations to conduct original censuses in their areas in 1834 in order to supplement the 1831 returns. Many responded to this call but few of their documents are now available. The 1834 census of Granard parish in Co. Longford, listing heads of household with numbers of male and female Catholics, Protestants and Presbyterians, contained in the Roman Catholic parish register (National Library Pos. 4237), would appear to be one.

Some Catholic leaders suspected that the Protestant population would be exaggerated. The politician Daniel O'Connell called on Catholic priests to co-operate with the Commission, but to make a second copy of their census. A small number did so in 1834 or 1835 and the resulting records ended up in a number of locations, including the Catholic Association papers in the Dublin Diocesan Archives. Those for seven civil parishes in Co. Kerry were published in *The Journal of the Kerry Archaeological and Historical Society* in 1974–5 and those for Templebredin in counties Limerick and Tipperary in the *North Munster Antiquarian Journal*, Vol. 17 (1975). The censuses for Tallanstown, Co. Louth, published in the *Journal of the Co. Louth Archaeological Society*, Vol. 14 (1957), and Kilcumreragh in counties Offaly and Westmeath, on microfilm at the National Library (Pos. 1994), would also appear to be part of this Catholic survey.

The Commissioners stated that many Church of Ireland parishes in Dublin had conducted censuses in 1832. A religious census of St Bridget's parish, bearing the date January 1831, is very probably part of this process. It is on microfilm at the National Library (Pos. 1994).

The 1841 Census

The 1841 census was taken on 6th June 1841. The information given for each individual in the original returns consisted of name, age, relationship to head of household, marital status (with year of marriage, or years if more than one), occupation, ability to read and write, and native county. There were two additional tables. The first concerned living family members who were absent from home. The information given for each consisted of name, age, relationship to head of household, occupation, and the country, county or city then residing in. Needless to say, this was a potential source of great importance in relation to emigrants. The second additional table concerned household members (including servants or visitors) who had 'died while residing with this Family' since 6 June 1831. The information given for each consisted of name, age, relationship to head of household, occupation, cause of death and year of death.

The originals survive for all of Killashandra parish in Co. Cavan and for 46 households elsewhere; 26 in Co. Cork, 13 in Currin parish in Co. Fermanagh, 4 in Lismore parish in Co. Waterford and 3 unidentified. You will find call numbers for these in the 'Pre-1901

Census Material' catalogue. The Killashandra returns are also available on microfilm (MFGI–36). The only significant collection of extracts are Walsh Kelly's for Aglish (all but Curraghmartin and Mountneill townlands) and Rathkieran civil parishes (three full townlands) in Co. Kilkenny (GO Ms 684). Those for Aglish were published in the *Irish Ancestor* 1977

The 1851 Census

The 1851 census was taken on 30th March 1851. The information given for each individual in the original returns was the same as in 1841, with an extra column for those deaf and dumb or blind. Ability to speak Irish and English, or Irish only was also to be indicated. The additional table concerning absent family members was similar to that in 1841. That concerning household members who had died since 6th June 1841 differed only in that it asked the season and year of death. The originals survive for all or part of 13 parishes in Co. Antrim and for the townland of Clonee in Co. Fermanagh.

The 'Pre-1901 Census Material'catalogue gives the call numbers. Walsh Kelly's extracts for Aglish (all but Curraghmartin townland), Portnascully and Rathkieran (two full townlands) civil parishes in Co. Kilkenny are at the Genealogical Office (Ms 684). Those for Aglish are published in the *Irish Ancestor* 1977. There are extracts covering a significant area of north-east Cork at the National Archives (M.4685). They are headed 'Union of Kilworth' but they cover most of Kilcrumper, Kilworth and Leitrim civil parishes as well as four townlands in Macroney and one in Clondulane. The occupation of each head of household is given. Names and ages of all household members are stated as well as their relationship to the head of household. Those who emigrated later in the early 1850s have the date and destination added. The National Archives also has lists of heads of household for Cromac ward in Belfast (Cen 1851/19) and for the city of Dublin (Cen 1851/18/1–2). Both give the names alphabetically (with house number) under each street. In Belfast the streets are arranged in one alphabet while in Dublin they are subdivided by parish. Incidentally, at that time Cromac ward covered the municipal borough east of the river and directly south of Donegall Square. These lists are of importance because they name the head of each family within a house. Neither the street directories nor Griffith's *Primary Valuation* would be as comprehensive.

CENSUS SEARCH FORMS

Legislation in 1908 introduced the Old Age Pension throughout the United Kingdom, with 70 as the age of eligibility. As civil registration of births was not introduced in Ireland until 1864, Irish-born applicants for the pension had to provide other evidence of age. The 1841 and 1851 (and in exceptional cases 1821) census returns were used for this purpose. Beginning in September 1908, census searches were conducted for individuals and Local Government Boards throughout the British Isles. Obviously, these searches were no longer possible after the original returns were destroyed in 1922. Two apparently unrelated processes were employed, involving two separate types of request form: the 'Green Form' and the 'Form 37'.

The Green Form

Green Forms were individual application forms completed with information submitted by or on behalf of the applicants. Each gave the applicant's name, contact address, stated age, parents' names and stated address at the time of the census. When the search was conducted the result was added in. This usually consisted of a brief note stating the child's name and age or 'not found'. Occasionally a more detailed abstract was written at the side or on the reverse of the form.

The Green Forms which are now available are held at the National Archives. They are from all parts of the country (including Northern Ireland) and are covered by the Census Search Forms catalogue which is on the open shelves. Each volume of the catalogue covers one or two counties. Each is arranged by barony, then civil parish, townland/street and finally surname of the family searched. You, therefore, have to know approximately where your family lived in 1841 or 1851. Where a second surname is given in brackets it is the mother's maiden name as stated by the applicant. If you order out a particular form (with the 'Cen/S/...' reference given in the catalogue and the corresponding shelf number) you will be given a box containing hundreds of forms. Interspersed among all the Green Forms you may see some that are pink. These are similar to them in almost every detail, but they were submitted exclusively by officers of Customs and Excise on behalf of applicants. Those which survive appear to date from 1910 and they are, of course, covered by the Census Search Forms catalogue.

Form 37

Form 37s were sheets submitted by local pensions offices on which information on several applicants was given; name, stated age, parents' names and stated address at the time of the census. When the search was conducted the result was entered in the right-hand column in the same manner as above, though usually there was no space for a detailed abstract. If the correct entry was found in either case, the Public Record Office (what is now the National Archives) could issue a certified copy of the relevant return. This might consist of a full transcript, including information from the additional tables concerning absent or deceased family members, or an abstract of the details relating only to the parents and the relevant child, i.e. the pension applicant.

The Form 37s which are now available are in two locations. A set of these from the Cavan Social Welfare office, concerning people born in Cavan and neighbouring counties, was deposited in the National Archives (M.3168/1–267). They date from 1908 forward. The 'M.3168' catalogue on the open shelves is, unfortunately, in numerical rather than alphabetical order, so it is laborious to check. PRONI has a similar set relating to Northern Ireland counties, obtained from local Customs & Excise offices (T.550/2–37). They are arranged roughly by barony within the various counties, making them difficult to search. They are, therefore, worth checking only as a last resort. There is a partial index to them on microfiche (Mic.9/1/1–9) but its references, which are to the Mormon microfilm copy, are difficult to equate to the originals. T.550/35 is a volume of miscellaneous documents. These are certified copies of Church of Ireland baptismal records (see Chapter 4); census searches in Great Britain for applicants who were born there but were subsequently resident in Ireland; and blind pension applications.

Miscellaneous Census Extracts

Various copies or extracts from census returns for 1821, 1841 and 1851 were presented to the Public Record Office (now the National Archives) after the originals were destroyed in 1922. These are available and they consist of certified copies made for pension applicants (or copies of such documents) and extracts of various kinds made by genealogists. The 'Census Records Miscellaneous Copies' catalogue at the National Archives, which is bound with the 'M.3168' catalogue mentioned above, is the only guide to them. Unfortunately, it is not arranged by surname or county but by accession number. You would have to search right through the catalogue on the off-chance of finding a relevant entry. There are also certified copies of census returns in PRONI (T.550/1). These are mainly from Co. Armagh, with a few from Co. Antrim, and they were made in the period 1916–22.

18th Century Census-type Records

Three significant census-type surveys were conducted in the 18th century and the results, arranged by parish, are available for considerable areas of the country. It is important to remember that this means the Church of Ireland parish of the time, which generally covered a larger area than the 19th-century civil parish.

The 1740 Protestant Householders' Lists

In March 1739/40 the Irish House of Lords requested the Lord Lieutenant to order a return of the names of all 'Protestant House-keepers' throughout the country. The survey was conducted by the Hearth Money collectors and the results were received by October 1741. The returns simply named all Protestant heads of household in each parish. The originals have not survived, so it is unclear whether the entire country was actually covered. The transcripts which are now available are only for certain parishes within Ulster and all emanate from the work of one genealogist, Tenison Arthur Groves. However, they are extensive. Some are in manuscript form but most are in typescript. There are several copies covering certain parishes, scattered among the various record offices.

A complete set is available in PRONI (T.808/15258) and there is a photocopy of it on the open shelves in the Search Room. The areas covered by the transcripts are the north-western part of Co. Antrim, all parishes of Co. Londonderry, the baronies of Inishowen East and West in Co. Donegal, the parishes of Derrynoose, Mullaghbrack, Shankill (and Lurgan) and Tynan in Co. Armagh, Kilbroney and Seapatrick in Co. Down, and Derryloran and Kildress in Co. Tyrone. Most of these are also available in Dublin. The Antrim, Londonderry and Donegal material is in the Genealogical Office (Ms 539; index in Ms 539A). The Armagh (with the exception of Mullaghbrack) and Tyrone material is in the RCB Library (Ms 23). The Down parishes are in the National Library (Ms 4173) and Derrynoose and Tynan are also there (Ms 4464).

The 1749 Elphin Census

This was a census of the diocese of Elphin (which covers almost all of Co. Roscommon and parts of counties Galway and Sligo), arranged by parish and townland. The fragile original is held at the National Archives (M.2466), but you will be given a microfilm copy (MFS 6). The information given is the name and occupation of each householder, the number of children under and over 14 and the number of male and female servants. In addition, each individual is identified as either Protestant or Papist. A surname index to this census, compiled by Peter Manning, has been published in two typescript volumes. It may be consulted at or purchased through the IGRS Library in London.

The 1766 Religious Returns

In March 1766 the Irish House of Lords requested the Church of Ireland bishops to direct their parish clergy to return 'a List of the several Families in their Parishes', distinguishing between Protestants and Papists, as well as a list of 'reputed Popish Priests and Friars'. All returns were submitted by January 1768. They varied in format. Many were mere numerical summaries. On the other hand, some gave the number of inhabitants in each house, named the householders townland by townland, and differentiated not only between Protestants (Anglicans) and Papists (Catholics), but also listed Dissenters separately. Most parish returns were between the two extremes, but several only named the Protestants.

Only a small number of originals have survived and they are in the National Archives (Parliamentary Returns 648–702, 773–4 and 1431). They relate to 32 parishes in Armagh diocese, 23 in Cashel & Emly diocese, two (Rathbarry and Ringrone) in Cork & Ross diocese and one (Killoteran) in Waterford diocese. It must be remembered that many of these are merely numerical. As with the 1740 Protestant Householders' Lists, there are transcripts of the returns for various parishes held in a number of locations. The vast majority of these were again the work of Tenison Groves. Transcripts are available for at least part of 21 out of the 32 counties. There are none for any part of Connaught or for counties Carlow, Clare, Kerry, Kildare, Laois and Monaghan. Cork and Louth are substantially covered.

The '1766 Census' catalogue (with handwritten additions) on the open shelves in the National Archives is a comprehensive guide to all parishes for which there are originals or transcripts available. It is arranged by diocese. These are held in the National Archives, the Genealogical Office and the National Library. The catalogue does not note all duplicates of the transcripts, whether in these repositories or elsewhere.

A number of parish returns have been published and these are as follows:

Co. Armagh: Creggan parish; *Louth Archaeological Society Journal*, Vol. 8, pp. 156–162

Co. Cavan: Kinawley, Lavey, Lurgan and Munterconnaught parishes (Protestants only); *Breifne*, Vol. 1, pp. 357–362

Co. Cork: Dunbulloge parish with extracts from St Peter's and Whitechurch; *Cork Historical and Archaeological Society Journal*, Vol. 51, pp. 69–77; Kilmichael parish; *Cork Historical and Archaeological Society Journal*, Vol. 26, pp. 69–79

Co. Fermanagh: Kinawley (Protestants only); *Breifne*, Vol. 1, pp. 357–362

Co. Limerick: Croagh, Kilscannell, Nantinan and Rathkeale parishes (Protestants only); *Irish Ancestor*, 1977

Co. Londonderry: Derryloran parish; *Seanchas Ardmhacha*, Vol. 4, pp. 147–170

Co. Longford: Abbeylara parish (Protestants only); *Breifne*, Vol. 1, pp. 357–362

Co. Louth: Ardee union (Ardee, Kildemock, Shanlis, Smarmore and Stickillin parishes); *Louth Archaeological Society Journal*, Vol 10, pp. 72–76; Creggan parish; *Louth Archaeological Society Journal*, Vol. 8, pp. 156–162 Ballymakenny, Beaulieu, Carlingford, Darver, Dromiskin, Philipstown (in Ardee barony), Tallanstown and Termonfeckin parishes; *Louth Archaeological Society Journal*, Vol. 14, pp. 103–117

Co. Offaly: Ballycommon parish; *Kildare Archaeological Society Journal*, Vol. 7, pp. 274–276

Co. Tyrone: Aghaloo and Carnteel, Derryloran, Dungannon (Drumglass and Tullyniskan) and Kildress parishes; *Seanchas Ardmhacha*, Vol. 4, pp. 147–170

Co. Westmeath: Russagh parish (Protestants only); *Breifne*, Vol. 1, pp. 357–362

PRACTISING RESEARCH TECHNIQUES

The 1901 edition of the *Townlands Index* shows that Caher, the townland in which Anne Forbes lived at the time of her marriage (see end of Chapter 2), is situated in the District Electoral Division (DED) of Kinneigh which, for the purpose of the 1901 Census, is numbered 115. No. 115 in the 1901 Census Catalogue for Co. Cork lists several townlands, arranged in numerical order. Caher is townland no. 6. We now have the essential references to retrieve the 1901 Census returns for the townland of Caher: 1901 Census/Cork/DED 115/6.

The return made for the Forbes family includes John Forbes (aged 64), his wife Julia (aged 52) and two servants. From information gathered from the Catholic baptismal register of Enniskean (see Chapter 4) and from the Land and House Revision Books at the

Valuation Office (see Chapter 5), John Forbes is identified as a brother to Anne Forbes, wife of Jeremiah Kehelly.

To retrieve the 1911 returns for the Forbes family of Caher you turn to the 1911 Census Catalogue for Co. Cork to find Kinneigh DED. This time it is numbered 116, but within it Caher is again shown as townland number 6, so we complete the Order Docket as follows: '1911 Census/Cork/DED 116/6'.

Three people are returned for the Forbes household: John Forbes (aged 74), his wife Julia (aged 61) and his niece Nellie Coakley (aged 20). Julia is stated as being married 43 years and as having no children born alive. This important piece of information suggests that John Forbes and Julia were married about 1868.

Although Julia's maiden name was not known, as suggested within the text of this chapter (and in Chapter 2), a return visit was made to the GRO to examine the Indexes to Marriages, 1867–1869, under John Forbes. Two references were noted, both for the year 1868; one was registered in the Superintendent Registrar's District of Bandon and the other in that of Dunmanway. Not knowing Julia's maiden name, there was no way of cross-checking the Index (as outlined in Chapter 2), thus photocopies of both entries were requested. These revealed that the marriage of John Forbes of Caher and Julia Coakely of Teenah is registered twice: they married on 25 February 1868 at the residence of the bride in the townland of Teenah, which is covered by the Superintendent Registrar's District of Dunmanway and, on the same day, their marriage was recorded as taking place in Enniskean Roman Catholic chapel, which is in the Superintendent Registrar's District of Bandon. (For a possible explanation, see Chapters 2 and 4).

Now knowing that she was Julia Coakely before marriage allows us to identify Nellie Coakley, aged 20, returned on the 1911 Forbes Census Return (see above), as Julia's niece rather than John's.

4 Church Records

ROMAN CATHOLIC RECORDS

Roman Catholic church records could play a pivotal and indispensable role in your ancestral research. Vast numbers of Roman Catholics left Ireland, voluntarily or otherwise, during the 19th century and for very many of them the baptismal or marriage register could be the only source in which their existence is recorded. Many of those who left, such as the rural and urban labourer, the cottier, the servant, the 'spailpeen' or migratory labourer, would not have held land, or a cabin or house tenancy and thus are not recorded in 19th century land or house holders records (Chapter 5); for very many, civil registration of births, marriages and deaths commenced too late or if not too late the events may have 'slipped through the net' and were never registered.

It can be more beneficial sometimes to start your research with the parish register even if your ancestor was born after civil registration commenced (see Chapter 2); for instance, if your ancestor had a relatively common surname and you know from where the family came, you probably would identify your ancestor and family more easily from the church register than from the indexes to the civil records at the GRO.

On the other hand, the civil birth record together with the church baptismal/birth record, sometimes can pose interesting questions: If, on retrieving both the civil birth record and the church birth/baptismal record, you find that the date of birth given on the civil record is several months later than that which is entered in the baptismal register, which one should you consider accurate?

The responsibility to register a birth with the District Registrar lay with the parents or a person present at the birth and a heavy fine was payable if the birth was not registered within three months. However, in many areas, it took several years to inform the public about the process of registration and, for many, the District Registrar's dispensary could have been a distance from home. When it came to registering, three months or more might have elapsed, so to avoid having to pay the fine some months might have been taken off the childís age. However, the child would have been baptised within a few days of birth.

The Rites of Passage

Up to the middle of the 19th century, baptisms, marriages and the waking and keening of the dead generally took place in the home. Notwithstanding the active discouragement of the bishops, it was not until the late 19th century that the parish church, particularly in rural areas, became the accepted location for such events. The child was baptised, within a few days of birth, either in the priest's house or, if the family could afford the priest's fee and subsequent festivities, in the family home.

This strongly held custom (up to the early 1960s), of baptising the child a few days after birth is supported whenever you read a baptismal register that also includes the birth date of the infant.

Marriages usually took place in the home (usually in that of the bride's) or in the priest's home during the late afternoon or early evening, One of the reasons why this custom of an afternoon marriage in the home persisted in certain areas, particularly in Munster, was that a large proportion of the priest's income depended on the monetary collection taken at the marriage festivities. Another reason, perhaps, may have had to do with the fact that the civil registration of Catholic marriages was legislated for until 1863. The 1844 legislation, which set up the civil registration of non Roman Catholic marriages from 1 April 1845, laid down that a religious marriage take place in a church during the morning hours and the responsibility of registering the marriage lay with the officiating clergyman. However, in 1863, legislation was passed to include the civil registration, from 1 January 1864, of Catholic marriages, and with the responsibility of registering the marriage falling to the husband. There was no stipulation that the Catholic marriage had to take place in the church.

The Canon law of the Catholic Church prohibited the solemnisation of marriages during Lent – the period including the 40 weekdays which precede Easter Sunday. Between the Epiphany, 6 January and Shrove Tuesday, which can fall between 3 February and 9 March, was a favoured period to marry.

The waking and keening of the dead usually took place, over several days, in the home of the deceased. The custom of laying out the corpse in the home over a two-day period or so and giving hospitality to all those who come to pay their respects before burial, was an integral part of rural and community life. Breaking with tradition and bringing the body to the parish church to repose came about, as you would expect and understand, sooner in urban areas.

The Church as Record-Keeper

A Catholic parochial administrative structure took shape by the middle of the 18th century in some urban areas, such as Dublin City; Kilkenny City, Cork City, Wexford Town, etc. Baptismal and marriage registers began to be kept and parish churches were furnished with baptismal fonts and eventually church baptisms became routine. Furthermore, some rural parishes with a tradition of scholarship and learning began to keep registers from the start of the 19th century.

The parish priest is the custodian of his parish records and practically all of the original registers are held in the parishes of their origin. However, the National Library holds microfilm copies of the majority of these registers.

Some comments with regard to Catholic parish church registers:

- Unlike civil registration, there is no uniform year for the commencement of Catholic parish registers.
- The majority of Catholic registers commenced during the first half of the 19th century; however, there are many parishes with registers that have much later starting dates.
- Some parishes, mainly urban, have registers with entries dating from the last quarter of the 18th century.
- Catholic parish records usually consist of baptismal and marriage registers.
- Burial or death registers are not usual and when they do exist it is usually for a limited or inconsistent number of years.
- Parish burial grounds were, by law, the property of the Church of Ireland (Anglican Church) but historically, many had belonged to the medieval monasteries and churches of the particular area or parish; thus, depending on the particular Church of Ireland parish rector of the time, *the burials of Catholics may be recorded in Church of Ireland burial registers.*
- Entries in parish registers are written in either Latin or English – once you familiarise yourself with the Latin forms that some Christian names can take and with the Latin terms or abbreviations used, it should not be a worry. *Surnames and place-names are not translated into Latin.*
- The actual register books are of different shapes and sizes, with handwriting ranging from the indecipherable to copperplate. The condition of any register can be uneven, with mutilated pages;

faded entries; missing pages and often with gaps of several years within the particular register. (This description can also relate to the church registers and records of any other denomination.)

- Entries in baptismal, marriage, death, or, combined baptismal and marriage registers, are usually presented in chronological order, that is, by year, month, date.
- By the beginning of the 1900s virtually all parishes had commenced using uniform or large pro-forma baptismal and marriage registers, which allowed for the inclusion of detailed particulars against each entry, entered clearly within uniform columns.

Searching Through Church Records

The National Library

The microfilm copies of the Catholic registers at the National Library have 1880 as the 'cut-off' date. A search aid – *List of the Roman Catholic Registers on Microfilm at the National Library* – which is available for consultation on the open shelves in the Reading Room, gives the name and contents of each microfilmed parish register, together with the microfilm 'call number'. The *List* is arranged alphabetically by diocese, within which ecclesiastical parishes are grouped. At the beginning of the volume there is an alphabetical list of the parishes together with the name of the diocese in which the parish is located. When you have identified the parish register you wish to examine, make a note of its starting date, of how complete and continuous the register is, if the register has gaps or missing years and, of course, note the microfilm call number(s), the P number.

There are usually more than the registers of one parish on the same microfilm reel and you may also find that the registers of the particular parish you require are spread over more than one microfilm reel.

LATIN WORDS

Some Latin terms and abbreviations used in Catholic registers:

- *Ego baptizavi/bapt/B.* = I baptised
- *fil(ius/m)* = son; *fil(ia/m)* = daughter
- *sponsoribus/sp/sps.* = sponsors, godparents
- *in matrimonium, coniunxi/conj* = joined in marriage
- *testimonii/test* = witnesses
- *gemini* = twins

Some Latin forms of forenames:

- *Anna* = Anne;
- *Cornelius* = Cornelius, Conor, Neil
- *Demetrius* = Jeremiah (Demetrius is a latinised form of the Gaelic name *Diarmaid* which had been incorrectly anglicised as Jeremiah), Jerome, Jerry, Dermot, Darby
- *Gulielmus* = William
- *Jacobus* = James, Jacob
- *Johanna* = Johanna, Hannah, Joan, Jane
- *Johannes, Joannes* = John
- *Honoria* = Hannah, Nora, 'Norry'
- *Margarita* = Margaret, 'Peg'
- *Maria* = Mary
- *Nigellus* = Neil
- *Timotheus, Thaddeus* = Timothy, Tadhg, Thaddeus, Thady

(*Continued overleaf*)

LATIN WORDS

Latin nouns change their endings according to their case: nominative, accusative, genitive and dative. Endings also change depending on whether the noun is singular and plural. Thus if you come across a clearly written entry in Latin you may notice changes to endings, such as:

- *Maria* (nom.), *Mariam* (acc.), *Marie* (gen.), *Marie* (dat.)
- *Gulielmus, Gulielmum, Gulielmui*
- *filius, filium, filii, filio, filia*
- *Johannes* (John), *Johannem, Johannis, Johanni*
- *Johanna* (Johanna, Joan), *Johannam, Johanne* (gen. and dat.)
- Sometimes it may be difficult to differentiate between *Johannem* and *Johannam* – the accusative cases of John and Johanna/Joan respectively, particularly if *filium* (son, acc.) or *filiam* (daughter, acc.) are not decipherable.

Even if you have the precise date of your ancestor's birth/baptism or marriage, when you come to examine the particular register cover a number of years before and after the date of the event, say, five years before and five years after the particular year. Personal dates were not a priority for our ancestors and furthermore, you will become familiar with the format and calligraphy of the particular register and maybe pick up a younger or older sibling or identify the marriage entry of a brother or sister. Remember to write out and keep in front of you, all possible variations of the surname and forename, and allow for a variety of phonetic spellings. Also, don't forget to have paper and pen/pencil: photocopies or printouts of Catholic parish register entries are not available.

If it happens that the parish register you wish to examine does not have records early enough for your search, consider examining the registers of neighbouring parishes, if their commencement dates are appropriate. Each county volume of the National Library's *Index of Surnames* (see p. 133) contains a map illustrating the civil parishes of the specific county together with a list of the approximate corresponding Catholic parishes. The map will help you to identify the surrounding parishes; then consult the National Library's *List* to find out the commencement dates of the registers in question.

Always consult Lewis' *Topographical Dictionary* (see Glossary) before you decide to order up a microfilm copy of a parish register; it could save you time by eliminating doubt as to whether you have identified the right parish. Under the entry for the appropriate civil parish, a description is given of the Roman Catholic boundaries, subdivisions and churches.

MICROFILM TIME-SAVER

When it comes to working with the microfilm and microfilm readers at the National Library it is worth remembering that it can happen that the film is wound on to the master reel in reverse – from beginning to end, which means that the end page of a register, and not necessarily the register you wish to examine – comes up first. Each register should be preceded by a large label with the name of the parish and a description of the contents, followed by the National Library copyright declaration. If you are unfamiliar with the workings of microfilm readers and the mounting of film reels, do not hesitate to avail of the assistance of the Library's staff.

Other Sources for Church Records

There are some parish registers and some early registers of other parishes that have not been microfilmed, but, in recent times, they may have been indexed by the Heritage Centre for that area.

The Public Record Office Northern Ireland (PRONI) holds microfilm copies of the Catholic parish registers for the nine counties of Ulster. The Mormons also have microfilm copies of most of the parish registers (see Chapter 10, LDS Family History Centre).

Indexing Centres throughout the island of Ireland are indexing church registers (of all denominations), civil records, census returns and other records of a genealogical nature, relevant to their respective county or counties. Some centres have completed the indexing of Catholic parish registers and have put the information on to a database (see Chapter 1).

How to identify your ancestor's parish

If You Know Your Ancestor's Townland and County of Origin

With the *Townlands Index* you should be able to identify the civil parish in which your ancestor's townland is located; you then need to establish the corresponding Catholic parish; you can achieve this by reading the civil parish entry in Lewis' *Topographical Dictionary* which includes a description of the Catholic parish division and the location of the church or chapels. In addition, examine the maps and list of civil parishes with their approximate corresponding Catholic parishes, attached at the beginning of each county volume of the National Library's Index of Surnames.

If You Know Your Ancestor's County but not the Specific Townland

Consult Chapter 5 which deals with the *Index of Surnames*; this index will enable you to isolate specific civil parishes, within the county, in which your ancestor's surname occurred. Then examine the appro-

Roman Catholic Dioceses

priate registers of the corresponding Catholic parishes. However, if you find that the surname was numerous throughout the particular county, there may be no other way but to examine one parish register after another. However, the Indexing Centre covering your particular county may have all or some of the registers indexed, which would at the very least reduce the number of registers that need to be individually examined.

DUBLIN CITY

Nineteenth-century Dublin City was covered by ten Catholic parishes; starting dates of their registers range from the first to the last quarters of the 18th century. Except for the registers of the parish of St Mary's (Pro-Cathedral), the registers of all the other city parishes, up to the cut-off year of 1880, are on microfilm in the National Library.

From the early 1850s the marriage registers of the parishes in the Diocese of Dublin give the names and addresses of the parents of both bride and groom. Because so many people from outside Dublin were drawn to the city, the inclusion of these addresses can immediately lead you to the original home county of the families in question.

Dublin Directories, such as *Dublin Almanac and General Register of Ireland* and Thom's *Irish Almanac and Official Directory* (see Chapter 9) can be of assistance if your ancestor's family had a trade, a business, a profession, or if your ancestor's address in the city or environs is known. The civil parish in which your ancestor lived can be identified and then with the help of the list on page 87 you should be able to establish the appropriate Catholic parish.

(Continued opposite)

On the other hand, directories are of little or no help in tracking down a labourer or unskilled worker, who, in all probability, often moved home or lodgings and probably shared rooms in a building with many tenants. So, are there any short-cuts other than examining all the city parish registers, parish by parish?

You could examine the microfiche copy of the *International Genealogical Index (IGI)* (see Glossary) for Dublin; note the Catholic parishes in which your ancestor's surname occurred and begin by examining the registers of those parishes. You could also examine the microfiche of the *Alphabetical List to Householders recorded in Griffith's Primary Valuation for Dublin City, dated 1849*; note the civil parishes in which the surname is recorded, identify the corresponding Catholic parishes and start off examining these registers.

Dublin City and County church registers are being indexed and computerised by three separate Indexing Centres; you could write to the centres, one at a time, so that they could examine their database, and if they all draw a blank you could take up the search and examine the microfilm copies of whatever registers have not been covered by the centres.

The registers at the National Library are microfilmed up to circa 1880. Records up to at least 1900 are being indexed by the Indexing Centres. The only way to have information extracted from the registers of St Mary's (the Pro-Cathedral) is through corresponding with the Reverend Administrator or his record searcher.

These suggestions made with regard to a Dublin City or County family search can be transferred easily to Belfast, Cork, Kilkenny, Limerick and Waterford cities and their hinterlands.

Mid-19th c. Dublin City Catholic Parishes	*Present-day address*	*Covers these Dublin City civil parishes*
St Agatha's	North William Street, Dublin 1	parts of St Mary's and St Thomas's
St Andrew's	Westland Row, Dublin 2	nearly all St Andrew's, St Mark's, St Anne's and part of Peter's
St Audoen's	High Street, Dublin 8	St Audoen's
St Catherine's	Meath St, Dublin 8	nearly all of St Catherine's
St James	James Street, Dublin 8	nearly all of St James'
St Laurence O'Toole's	Seville Place, North Wall, Dublin 1	parts of St Mary's and St Thomas'
St Mary's (Pro-Cathedral)	Marlborough St, Dublin 1	principally St Mary's, St George's and part of St Thomas'
St Michan's	Halston Street, Dublin 7	most of St Michan's and parts of St Mary's and St George's
SS Michael & John (no longer used as a church)	Lr Exchange St, Dublin 2	parts of St Nicholas Within, St Michael's, St Andrew's, St John's, St Peter's, St Bridget's and St Werburgh's

Mid-19th c. Dublin City Catholic Parishes	*Present-day address*	*Covers these Dublin City civil parishes*
St Nicholas	Francis Street, Dublin 8	St Nicholas Without, Liberties of Christ Church and St Patrick's, and principal parts of St Nicholas Within, St Bridget's, St Peter's and St Luke's
St Paul's	Arran Quay, Dublin 7	principal parts of St Paul's and St Michan's

What do Catholic Parish Registers Contain?

A Baptismal Record

A baptismal record usually includes: date of baptism, baptismal name of the child, parents' names – usually including the mother's maiden name and names of sponsors (godparents). Many registers include the name of the townland in which the family lived.

Records of baptism were not necessarily entered into the register on the day of the event. Indeed, up to the middle of the 19th century, baptisms, performed at different venues, on different days but entered into the register at the same time would have been probably the norm.

A Marriage Record

A marriage record usually includes the date of marriage, the name of the couple getting married, the witnesses to the marriage and sometimes the celebrant. Marriages usually took place in the parish of the bride; sometimes the entry might include her home townland and in exceptional cases, the groom's home parish or townland might be named. Bear in mind that, depending on the circumstances of the time and the parish in question, marriages probably were not entered into the register at the time of the event.

A marrying couple who were related within the fourth degree of consanguinity, that is, a couple descended from a common great-great grandparent (making the bride and groom third cousins), had to obtain special permission. This permission, or dispensation of consanguinity, to marry, and the degree of kinship, which is sometimes recorded with the marriage entry, can be a valuable piece of unexpected genealogical information. The information may be recorded as follows:

- *in 3 [tertio] et 3 grad[io] consanguineo* = full 2nd cousins
- *in 4 [quattuor]et 4 grad[io] consanguineo* = full 3rd cousins
- *in 3 et 4 grad[io]* = 2nd cousins once removed.

ACCESS TO REGISTERS

To examine the microfilm copies of the registers of the dioceses of Cloyne (east and north-west Cork), Limerick and Kerry, you need prior written permission from the respective bishops so that the National Library staff can release the microfilms to you. Generally, this permission is given by return of post or fax and if requested the diocesan authorities will fax the permission directly to the National Library.

(Continued opposite)

(However, the registers of most of the Catholic parishes of County Cork North West (Diocese of Cloyne) and of County Kerry East (Diocese of Kerry) are published in the volumes of *O'Kief Coshe Mang, Slieve Lougher and Upper Blackwater*, ed. Albert E. Casey (1963–68, USA). These volumes, numbering 15, are available in libraries and repositories in Ireland and overseas and are individually indexed. What is more the cut-off date of many of the published registers is *circa* 1900.

The Archbishop of Cashel and Emly (the Archdiocese of Cashel and the Diocese of Emly include most of Co. Tipperary and a few parishes in counties Clare, Cork and Limerick) does not allow researchers access to the National Library's microfilm copies of the parish registers of the dioceses. Information from the registers of these parishes, which number approximately 46, is obtained only from the Tipperary Heritage Unit, where computerised indexes are held (see Chapter 11). We do not wish to sound negative or discouraging, but by presenting some of the potential difficulties you may find beforehand, we hope to give you the opportunity to prepare well the groundwork and then to spend your valuable time actually researching. It is important to give yourself plenty of time to familiarise yourself with the layout of a repository, with the process of identifying and retrieving documents, microfilms or microfiches and then with the reading and interpretation of records.

Practising Catholic Church Records Research

According to her civil marriage record, Anne Forbes was married in the Catholic Church of Enniskeane; at the time of her marriage she was living in the townland of Caher. The *Townlands Index* lists seven

Caher townlands in Co. Cork; however, accepting that Enniskeane was her home parish, Caher in the civil parish of Kinneigh, is the townland in which Anne Forbes lived. The same result is obtained by using the guidelines, laid out in the chapter.

The National Library's *List of Microfilm copies of Roman Catholic Registers* details the contents of the registers of Enniskeane, Diocese of Cork and Ross – and includes the microfilm reference or call number – - P 4798. The baptismal registers of the neighbouring parish of Desertserges, together with the marriage register of the combined parishes of Enniskeane and Desertserges, are also on the same microfilm reel.

The first baptismal record entered in the register is dated 24 November 1813 and the register appears to be continuous. Thus, the baptismal entry of Anne Forbes should be recorded in the register. As we learned in Chapter 1, we know from her marriage certificate that her father's name was Edward Forbes; her death record (as Anne Kehelly), states that she died on 11th October 1926 aged 76 years, which would indicate that she was born *circa* 1850, as we found out in Chapter 2. However the Census Return for 1901 gives her age in 1901 to be 60 years, which would make *circa* 1841 the year of her birth which we discovered in Chapter 3. To cover both possibilities the baptismal registers were examined for the years 1830 to 1850 and all Forbes entries were noted.

The entries in the registers of Enniskeane are written in English, but two potential problems arose. First, the baptismal entries do not include the townland or place of residence of the parents; and second, 41 Forbes baptismal entries were extracted, involving a total of eleven distinct families and the fathers of five of these families were named Edward! However, the baptismal register, for the period in question, records only one entry for an Anne Forbes: her father was Edward (or Ned as was recorded); and the year of her baptism – 1841 – establishes as correct her age (60 years), as recorded in the

1901 Census Return (after all she did not have a direct input into what is entered on her death certificate!).

The baptismal record of seven siblings of Anne were also identified, including that of her brother John, who was baptised 27th December 1836 (see Chapters 3 on the 1901 and 1911 Census Returns, and Chapter 5).

NAME SPELLINGS

The baptismal records of the eight children of Edward Forbes and Norry Carthy, retrieved from the Enniskeane register, highlight the much-repeated guideline to disregard any set views that you may have about the spelling of both forenames and surnames: Forboes/Forbus/Forbes/Firbush; Carthy/Carty/McCarthy; Edward/Ned; Norry/Honora.

CHURCH OF IRELAND RECORDS

From early in the 16th century until 1869 the Church of Ireland or the Anglican Church was the State or Established Church in Ireland. The commencement dates of many Church of Ireland records are much earlier than those of the Catholic Church. There are some parishes with registers extant from the latter half of the 17th century, but the majority commence between the 1770s and 1820.

Legislation, which was passed in 1869 disestablishing the Church of Ireland, became effective on 1st January 1871. The records of the Church of Ireland were then deemed public records and as such were to be lodged in the Public Record Office (now the National Archives) – baptismal and burial records up to 1870 and marriage records up to 1845, the year civil registration for non-Roman Catholic marriages commenced. Legislation was passed in 1875 and 1876 to enable this order to be effected. Those parishes which had suitable and safe storage could retain their registers and parishes which were subsequently able to provide such suitable storage could recall their parish registers from the PRO.

By the early 20th century the registers of about a thousand parishes, which amounted to over a half of all the Church of Ireland parishes of the country, had been deposited in the PRO. In June 1922, during the Civil War, the Four Courts and the record treasury of the Public Record Office were destroyed and among the many original records destroyed were the Church of Ireland registers. However, the original registers of somewhat less than 50 per cent of the parishes were still in the custody of their respective clergy; transcripts of some original registers had been made and retained by parish clergy before sending the originals to the PRO. Genealogists and historians, researching at the PRO prior to 1922, had extracts from various registers; and, during the early years of this century, *The Parish Register Society of Dublin* published many early registers, mainly of Dublin City. Thus, some gaps have been filled, but it has resulted in Church of Ireland registers and other records being held in more than one repository.

The Representative Church Body Library holds a substantial archive of registers and other church records, such as vestry and account books, of parishes no longer active, or which have been amalgamated. The collection is being added to continuously.

What do Church of Ireland Records Contain?

The principal records of genealogical interest are baptismal registers, marriage banns, marriage registers, burial registers and vestry books.

Baptismal Records

Baptismal records include: the date of baptism, the child's Christian name, the father's name, the mother's Christian/forename name (the mother's maiden name is seldom included) and the name of the officiating clergyman; the address of the father may also be given as can the father's occupation.

Marriage Records

Early marriage records may include simply the date, the names of the couple marrying and the clergyman performing the ceremony. Later on, addresses and witnesses names were included. From 1 April 1845 state registration of non-Roman Catholic marriages commenced, and from that date the information entered in Church of Ireland marriage registers is identical to that which is contained in the records held at the General Register Office (see Chapter 2).

The Church of Ireland was the State Church and for a marriage to be deemed legal and valid the clergy of the Church of Ireland had to be the officiating clergy. Prior to 1782 it was not legal for Presbyterian ministers to perform marriages and up to 1844 it was not legal for them to perform 'mixed marriages' (marriages between a Presbyterian and a non-Presbyterian), although many Presbyterian clergy ignored the law. Marriages of Presbyterians and other Protestant denominations were often recorded in Church of Ireland registers and, in most cases, there would be nothing entered in the register to distinguish between a mixed, non-Church of Ireland Protestant marriage or a non-mixed marriage.

Marriage Banns

The 'calling of the banns' to notify the intention to marry was 'called in' or read during service on three consecutive Sundays at the respective parishes of the individuals concerned. Records of these marriage banns were sometimes made and where they exist the information entered states the names and parish addresses of both parties and sometimes the individual dates of the 'calling of the banns' may be included. As banns were called or read in the parish of each party, they can help in pinpointing the date and the particular parish in which the marriage took place.

Marriage Licence Bonds

A licence to marry could be purchased as an alternative to the 'calling of banns'. Before the bishop of the diocese in which the marriage was to take place issued the licence, the groom (usually) and another person (usually a relative of the bride) lodged a sum of money as surety that there was no 'just cause or impediment' to the marriage. The bond was usually taken out in the diocese of the bride. The original Diocesan and Prerogative Court Marriage Licence Bonds, which were lodged in the Public Record Office, were destroyed in 1922. What survive are the Indexes, arranged by diocese, and some abstracts.

Several Indexes to Diocesan Marriage Licence Bonds have been published, such as the Marriage Licence Bonds for the Diocese of Dublin, which form part of the *Index to Dublin Will and Grant Books, 1270–1800; 1800–1858*, Deputy Keeper of Public Records of Ireland Reports, No. 26 (1895) and No. 30 (1899). The Genealogical Office holds manuscript volumes of abstracts to Prerogative Marriage Licences 1630–1858.

Burial Records

Burial records include the name of the deceased with the date of death or burial; age and residence sometimes may be included.

Church of Ireland burial registers may include Catholic individuals and families and indeed families of other religious denominations. This is particularly the case in Dublin and other large urban areas. The church and the surrounding burial ground, although under the aegis of the Established Church, can have Catholic burials and burials of other denominations. *All parishioners had the right to be buried in the parish graveyard.*

Vestry Books

These contain the recorded details and minutes of the civil responsibilities of the parish, such as road maintenance, the caring of foundlings (abandoned infants), cess or local tax collection and the management of the local constabulary and fire brigade. If the Vestry Book of your ancestor's parish is extant, it would be worth consulting.

Miscellaneous Extracts (Members of the Former Established Church Only)

The Old Age Pension, eligible from the age of 70, was introduced in 1908, but as civil registration of births did not commence in Ireland until 1864, applicants for the pension had to find other evidence of age (see Chapter 3, Census Search Forms). The Church of Ireland baptismal registers, lodged in the Public Record Office (now the National Archives), also were used to provide evidence of eligibility. Applicants, applying for a certified copy of their baptismal record, completed the Search Forms with their name, contact address and maiden name (in the case of a married woman applicant), both parents' names, parish church in which the applicant was baptised and year of birth/baptism. After the search was carried out, the result and maybe some observations were added. It would appear that these applications were made between 1915 and 1922.

The catalogue *Parish Registers & Related Material*, available on the open shelves at the National Archives, lists these individual Search Forms in alphabetical order by parish only, not by surname. Also listed in a section of the same catalogue is T.550/35, a volume of miscellaneous extracts, which includes certified copies of Church of Ireland baptismal records returned to the PRO after 1922.

Searching Through Church of Ireland Records

There are five catalogues all of which you may need to consult in order to ascertain the existence (or otherwise), and the whereabouts of the parish register you wish to examine:

1 The National Archives Catalogue 'Church of Ireland Parish Registers and Related Material' – only available in the Reading Room of the National Archives.

2 The National Archives Catalogue 'Church of Ireland Parish Registers' available in the National Archives; a copy is also available in the Reading Room of the National Library.

3 *A Table of Church of Ireland Parochial Records and Copies* (ed. Reid, 1994), available in the National Archives, National Library and other libraries.

4 *Guide to Church Records: Public Record Office of Northern Ireland* (PRONI 1994); this published guide, although covering the whole island, relates only to what PRONI holds.

5 A regularly updated list prepared by the Representative Church Body Library, which can be purchased for a nominal amount. As churches close and parishes amalgamate, original registers and records are deposited with the RCBL.

Church of Ireland records can be found in:

- Local custody
- National Archives (formerly the Public Record Office)
- Representative Church Body Library
- Public Record Office Northern Ireland
- National Library
- Genealogical Office

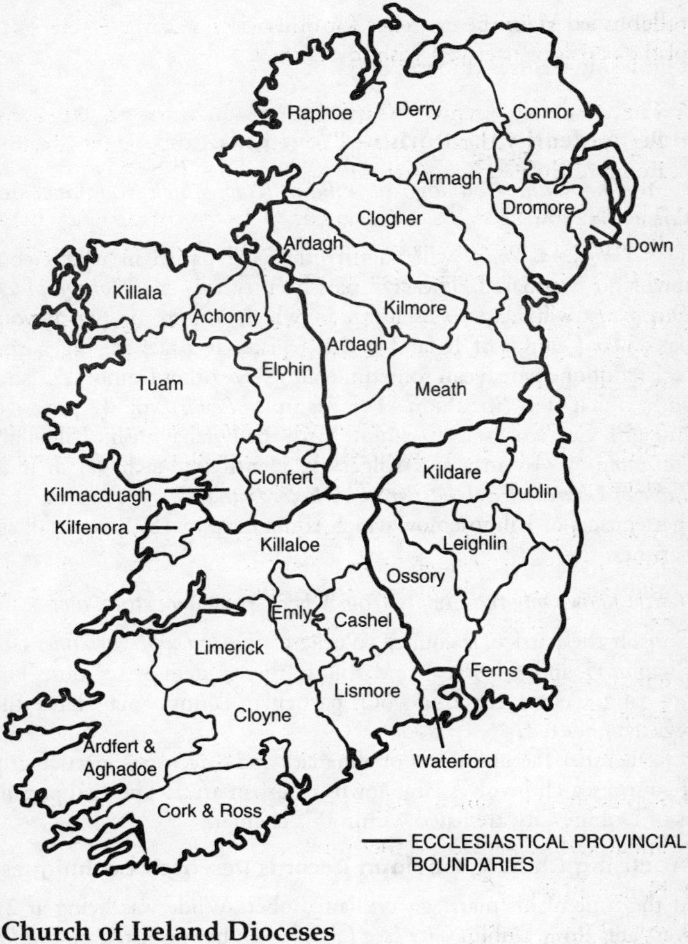

Church of Ireland Dioceses

- Published Volumes
- Indexing Centres (Indexes only).

How to Identify the Parish of Your Ancestor

If You Know the Townland or Village from Which Your Ancestor Came

The *Townlands Index* will identify the civil parish in which your townland is situated. The civil parish entry in *Lewis' Topographical Dictionary* will help to establish in which 'union' or parish your particular Church of Ireland parish register is attached; the parish register of one parish can sometimes also serve other (minor) parishes with which it is 'in union'. For example, *Lewis'*, vol. 1, page 41: Ardagh, Co. Mayo is in union with Ballynahaghlish, Kilbelfad, Kilmoremoy, Attymas and Kilgarvey; identifying each parish in *A Table of Church of Ireland Parochial Records and Copies* confirms that the registers of Kilmoremoy, which commence in 1801, serve all six parishes.

If You Know Only the County from Where Your Ancestor Came

Consult the particular county volume of the *Index of Surnames* (see Chapter 5 and Glossary) and follow the guidelines set out. The Indexing Centre covering your particular county, may have the registers indexed.

Remember the usefulness of almanacs and directories, particularly if your research involves large towns or urban areas. The civil parishes of Dublin City are listed within this chapter.

Practising Church of Ireland Records Research Techniques

At the time of his marriage William Robert Wilde was living at 21 Westland Row, Dublin City (see Chapter 2); he was listed in *Dublin*

Street Directories from the early 1840s onwards. Under the alphabetical street listing of the 1846 *Thom's Directory*, Westland Row is described as lying between Great Brunswick Street (present-day Pearse Street) and Park Street, East (present-day Lincoln Place) and situated in the civil parish of St Mark. Catalogues 1, 2, 3 and 5 previously referred to, list the original registers of St Mark's parish as extant and located in the Library of the Representative Church Body. The baptismal and marriage registers commence in 1730 and the burial register in 1733.

Oscar Fingal O'Flahertie Wilde was baptised 26th April 1855; he was born on 16th October 1854; note that the baptismal register includes the date of birth, but not his mother's maiden name.

PRESBYTERIAN RECORDS

The Irish Presbyterian Church is not a parish-based organisation, but instead is organised by congregation. The Presbyterian Church in Ireland, which has its origins in Scottish Presbyterianism, was established by the early 17th century and its numerical strength lay in the Province of Ulster, where Scottish Presbyterian tenants came to settle. However, during the Cromwellian period (mid-17th century), English Presbyterians established a small number of congregations, most of which were located in the southern part of the country, for example, Clonmel, Athlone, Limerick, Dublin and Mullingar.

During the 18th century, there were several internal divisions within the Presbyterian Church which saw the creation of the 'Non-Subscribers', the 'Seceders' and the 'Covenanters'. In 1840, the General Assembly of the Presbyterian Church in Ireland was formed with the coming together of the Synod of Ulster and the Secession Synod.

Presbyterians were dissenters and suffered many of the disadvantages that were the lot of Catholics. Strictly speaking, until 1782 it was not legal for Presbyterian ministers to perform marriages and it was only in 1844 that it became legal for Presbyterian ministers to perform 'mixed marriages' – a marriage between a Presbyterian and a non-Presbyterian. Thus, during the 18th and early 19th centuries, many Presbyterian marriages and indeed also baptisms were recorded in the registers of the Church of Ireland. Most congregations did keep records, some dating from the later quarter of the 18th century. However, the vast majority of the records date from after 1819, the year in which Presbyterian ministers were required, by their synods, to commence keeping marriage records.

What do Presbyterian Records Contain?

Presbyterian records include baptism and marriage registers, communion rolls and session minutes. Burial or death registers are rare.

Baptism Records

An early baptismal entry would consist of the date of baptism, the name of the child and the parents' names. In the 19th century, the mother's name before marriage, the date of birth, sponsors' names and possibly the address of the parents began to be included.

Marriage Records

An entry in an early marriage register consisted of the date and names of the couple marrying and possibly the name of the father of the bride. Subsequent to 1819, when the Presbyterian Synod decreed that marriage registers were to be kept by each minister, the information to be included was the date of marriage, the names of the bride and groom, the congregation to which each was attached and the names of at least two witnesses. However, this rule was not always adhered to.

MARRIAGE REGISTRATION

Remember, from 1st April 1845, civil registration of all Protestant marriages (including Presbyterian) commenced (see Chapter 2).

Session Minute Books and Stipend Rolls

The Session was the Congregational Court, which administered church justice on such as matters relating to irregular marriages, blasphemy, drunkenness, fornication, etc. It was necessary to give notice to the Session of a forthcoming marriage, thus, if the marriage register for a particular congregation does not exist and the Session Minute Book does, the Session Book could prove helpful. The Session Minute Book might also include a reference to a letter or certificate of transference having been requested or issued to a member leaving the particular congregation. A reference might be recorded of such a certificate or letter having been received from the holder who subsequently became attached to the particular congregation.

Early Stipend rolls are usually lists of the payer (usually the head of the family) and the payment made and recorded. These rolls or lists were either entered into separate books, or included in Session Minute Books. From the 1850s–60s onwards the Rolls consist of printed books recording the name of the payer (head of the family group), address, the stipend or payment made and sometimes the number in the family.

Communicants' Roll Books

These list the names of the congregation and whether they took Communion at the traditional occasions; information such as married, transferred to —, unwell, etc., may also be included.

Where can Presbyterian records be found?

- The majority of original Presbyterian records are held locally by the respective ministers.
- The Public Record Office Northern Ireland (PRONI) holds the largest single collection of Presbyterian Church Registers; they are available on microfilm and the collection is continuously being added to. The registers are listed in the *Guide to Church Records at the Public Record Office, Northern Ireland* (Belfast 1994) together with the call number and a list of the records of which copies have not yet been made.
- The Presbyterian Historical Society, Belfast, holds original records including records of some congregations of the Republic of Ireland, no longer in existence. A set of PRONI's microfilm copies are also available. *The History of Congregations of the Presbyterian Church in Ireland*, published by the Presbyterian Historical Society (Belfast, 1982) is a helpful publication in assisting to identify where a Presbyterian congregation is or was.

Remember to examine the appropriate Church of Ireland parish records when searching for a record of your Presbyterian ancestor. *Lewis' Topographical Dictionary* can also help to identify whether and where a Presbyterian Church and Congregation existed in a particular civil parish.

Thom's Irish Almanac and Official Directory, which was first published in 1844, included from the 1846 edition, a complete list of Presbyteries, their congregations, ministers, and the post towns and an alphabetical list of ministers in the General Assembly. The Annual Directory of The Presbyterian Church in Ireland includes the names and addresses of all Presbyterian ministers.

Methodist Church Records

Wesleyan Methodism, founded in England by Rev. John Wesley in the early 18th century, was a spiritual movement within the Established Anglican Church and as such spread throughout Ireland. John Wesley first came to Ireland in 1747 and by the time he died in 1791 had made at least 20 visits, travelling around the country preaching and establishing Methodist Societies. Methodists, most of whom were Anglican (though some were Presbyterian), remained in full membership with their original Protestant denominations.

In 1816 the Methodists split. The Primitive Wesleyan Connexion continued to baptise, marry and bury within the Church of Ireland; the Wesleyan Methodist Connexion started to perform these rites for themselves. Although there is a baptismal register dating from 1816 for Dublin, generally, baptismal registers tend to date from the 1820s. The two Methodist bodies united in 1878 and formed the Methodist Church in Ireland. A further two small Methodist Connexions were in existence in Ireland: Methodist New Connexion and Primitive Methodist Connexion. The administrative records of Methodist New Connexion and of Primitive Methodist Connexion are located at The John Rylands University of Manchester, Manchester, England.

What do Methodist Church Records Contain?

Baptismal Registers

Baptismal information can include the dates of birth and baptism, the child's name, parents' names and residence, the occupation of the father (sometimes) and the name of the officiating preacher. There is a 'consolidated' baptismal register for the period 1817–1850, covering the entire country, except for Dublin. The register is on microfilm at PRONI.

Register of Members and Classes

A Class with its Leader is the basic unit of the Methodist Society and considerable importance was given to the gathering and recording of information about members. However, not many survive.

CHECKING REGISTERS

Until 1816 Methodists were usually baptised and married within the Church of Ireland. When you have identified your Methodist ancestor's place of origin, don't forget to examine the Church of Ireland registers, if they exist.

Marriage Registers

Marriages were not widely performed by the Methodists until the 1840s and where they do exist, the entries are usually to be found at the back of the baptismal registers. From April 1845, Methodist marriages were registered by the state.

Where Can Methodist Church Records be Found?

- Local custody: most of the registers are in local custody and finding the relevant register can prove difficult. When preaching houses or chapels ceased, their registers were passed on to the next Circuit; then the registers were sometimes renamed. In urban areas it happened that for particular chapels, although their location did not change, the Circuits to which they were attached did, and this could mean that baptisms, performed in the same chapel over a period of years, could be entered in different registers. An example is the Baptismal Register of the Kilrush area of Co. Clare; this register is now held in Co. Tipperary!
- The Public Record Office Northern Ireland (PRONI) has the most

extensive collection of registers and records, particularly in connection with the Circuits in Northern Ireland. These records, which are catalogued by name of Circuit, with the distinction being made between Wesleyan and Primitive Wesleyan, are listed in PRONI's *Guide to Church Records*.

- The Wesley Historical Society (Irish Branch) at Aldersgate House, 9–11 University Road, Belfast, has a substantial collection of both manuscript and printed material, together with microfilm copies of the registers made by PRONI.

Thom's Irish Almanac and Official Directory from the year 1846 contains an alphabetical list of Wesleyan Methodist Ministers and the years they began to travel; also included are the names of the Districts, the Congregations within each District and their Ministers and preachers. The Directories also include an alphabetical list of the Primitive Wesleyan Methodist Ministers. Minutes of Conference list the names of the Circuits each year; these are printed and are available at the National Library.

QUAKER RECORDS

The Religious Society of Friends, known familiarly as the Quakers, came to Ireland in the middle of the 17th century and from the beginning they carefully kept and preserved their records. The nucleus of Quakerism is the meeting-house, where one or more congregations gather for worship. Minutes of the Meetings were kept and the Registers of the Monthly Meetings contained the records of births marriages and deaths. Quaker records are continuous, extensive, indexed and are located in two principal repositories. From early in the 18th century marriage records were forwarded to the relevant Provincial or Quarterly Meeting and were entered into a separate marriage book from which an Index to all Quaker marriages was created.

What do Quaker Records Contain?

Birth Records

Birth records include: date and place of birth, the surname and forename of the child, parents' names and place of residence, and the place or name of the Monthly Meeting. Quaker children are not baptised.

Marriage Records

Marriage records include: the date of the marriage and the name of the Monthly Meeting where the marriage was performed, the name and place of residence of the bride, the groom and their respective parents.

Death or Burial Records

Death or burial records include: the date of death, the name, age and possibly the residence of the deceased; if the deceased was married, widowed or the names of his or her parents; and the name of the Monthly Meeting at which the death was recorded. Deaths recorded in the Monthly Meeting Minutes were abstracted and printed in *The Annual Monitor*, which was published annually from 1813.

Where can Quaker Records be Found?

- Dublin Friends Historical Library, Dublin
- Religious Society of Friends, Archives Committee, Lisburn, Northern Ireland
- The National Library holds microfilm copies of many of the birth, marriage and death records, arranged under the name of the area of the Monthly Meeting.
- The National Archives holds copies of some of the births, marriages and deaths records.

BAPTIST CHURCH RECORDS

The Baptists came to Ireland in the middle of the 17th century, probably with Cromwellian soldiers and settlers. The Baptists in Ireland were never numerous, probably never numbered in thousands. Each Baptist church is independent and each kept its own minute book, which could include biographical annotations, such as marriage and death notices of specific church members. What records exist are held in local custody and it can prove difficult to gain access.

A microfilm copy of the combined birth, marriage and death register, dating from 1837, of the now-extinct Lower Abbey Street, Dublin congregation, is held at the National Library. The Baptist Union of Ireland Offices, 117 Lisburn Road, Belfast, hold some records. *Thom's Directory* from 1846 lists the Baptist pastors, the places and counties in which churches were located.

BAPTIST MARRIAGES

Remember copies of Baptist marriages from April 1845 are to be found at the General Register Office.

HUGUENOT CHURCH RECORDS

Huguenots were members of the Reformed Church (Protestant) in France. Although Huguenots had settled in Ireland from the later half of the 16th century, the majority came as a result of the revocation of the Edict of Nantes in 1685, which reimposed penal laws against their freedom of worship. Portarlington, Queen's Co. (present-day Co. Laois); Youghal, Co. Cork; Waterford City; Cork City; Lisburn, Co. Antrim and Dublin City were the principal areas in which they settled.

The government of the day gave financial support to those Huguenots who agreed to subject themselves to the canons of the Church of Ireland – they were the Conformist Huguenots. The Huguenots who did not conform were known as non-Conformist Huguenots and they had to financially support their own clergy and chapels.

Dublin had four Huguenot churches: two Conformist – the Lady Chapel in St Patrick's Cathedral and the Chapel of St Mary, Meetinghouse Lane off Capel Street; and two non-Conformist – the Chapel of St Brigide's, which was located in Peter Street and the Chapel of Lucy Lane (present-day Chancery Place).

The original registers of both Conformist churches were lodged in the Public Record Office and were subsequently destroyed in 1922. However the Huguenot Society of London had published the registers: Volume 7 of the *Publications of the Huguenot Society of London* contains the registers of:

- St Patrick's: baptisms 1668–87; marriages 1680–1716; burials 1680–1716
- St Mary's: 1705–16; 1705–15; 1705–15
- United Churches: 1716–1818; 1716–88; 1716–1830.

The original registers of the combined non-Conformist Dublin churches – baptisms 1701–31; marriages 1702–28; burials 1702–31; 1771–1831, which were also destroyed in 1922, were published in Volume 14 of the *Publications*. The registers of St Peter's were lost as a result of vandalism in the late 18th century and other misfortunes in the 19th century. The original Huguenot registers of Portarlington are extant and have been published in Volume 19 of the *Huguenot Society of London Publications*.These volumes are available at the National Library and at the National

Archives. The Irish Huguenot Archive is located at the Representative Church Body Library.

HUGUENOT REGISTERS

Baptism, marriage and burial records of many Conformist Huguenots are to be found in Church of Ireland registers. Also they were often married by Church of Ireland licence; thus the relevant Index of Marriage Licence Bonds should be consulted (refer to section on Church of Ireland records).

JEWISH RECORDS

In the early 19th century the Jewish population in Ireland numbered some hundreds; then in the late 19th century and beginning of the 20th, Jews arrived from the states of Eastern Europe, mainly Lithuania. These Jews settled mainly in Limerick, Cork, Dublin, Waterford, Drogheda, Belfast and Derry. In 1911 there were approximately five thousand Jews in Ireland; at present, Jews number less than two thousand.

The earliest Jewish communities in Ireland were formed in Dublin and in Cork and they established their own cemeteries. The Dublin cemetery at Ballybough is still in use. The Irish Jewish Museum, in Dublin, holds the Registry Book of the *Hebrew Congregation of the Dublin Synagogue*, which was located in Mary's Abbey, off Capel Street. The register includes 336 birth entries between the years 1820 and 1879 and 40 death entries between the years 1842 and 1879. This *Registry Book* is published in *The Jews in Ireland from the earliest times to the year 1910*, by R. Hyman (London 1972). Most of the Jews who came to Dublin in the late 19th century settled in the vicinity of Portobello, Lennox Street and the South Circular Road.

OTHER RECORDS

Congregationalist Records

The Congregationalists or Independents emanated from the English Congregationalist movement and they were established in Ireland at the latter end of the 18th century. PRONI holds the original records for the following four Dublin congregations: Zion Chapel in King's Inns Street, York Street, Oriel Street and Kingstown (now Dún Laoghaire). PRONI also holds Limerick records. The congregation of Salem chapel, Kilmainham, Dublin, still functions and the records are in local custody. PRONI's *Guide to Church Records* lists the Congregational Chapels of Belfast and their records.

Lutheran Records

Schulze's register of baptisms and marriages, which are records of the Dublin Lutheran church, are available at the General Register Office (see Chapter 2).

Moravian Records

The surviving Moravian Congregation in Ireland is at Gracehill, Co. Antrim. The starting date of their baptismal marriage and death records is 1750. There were Moravian congregations in Corofin, Co. Clare; Cootehill, Co. Cavan and in Dublin. No records survive for Corofin. Dublin records include baptisms, 1748–1977; marriages, 1799–1854 and 1866–1980; burials, 1765–1979. The original records of Dublin and Cootehill are held at the Gracehill Moravian Church. Microfilm copies of the records are held at PRONI.

5 19th-century Householders' and Landholders' Records

In the absence of comprehensive 19th-century census returns, two property surveys have become important in tracing what might be termed 'ordinary' families. These are the Tithe Applotment and Griffith's *Primary Valuation*. Tied to the latter are a number of related valuation records. These are dealt with here first.

GRIFFITH'S *PRIMARY VALUATION*

One of the most widely known and frequently used sources in Irish genealogy is Griffith's *Primary Valuation*, a list of property occupiers as of a particular date between 1848 and 1864, depending on the part of the country you are dealing with. Its importance lies in its accessibility and in the fact that it records almost every head of household in Ireland directly after the Famine and at the beginning of the period of highest emigration. Its full title is the *General Valuation of Rateable Property in Ireland* but it is referred to as the *Primary Valuation* or, more commonly, Griffith's *Primary Valuation*. Sir Richard Griffith was the commissioner under whose supervision it was conducted. The survey had its roots in an Act of 1826 which allowed for a uniform valuation of property throughout Ireland for levying of county cess charges and Grand Jury rates. It was to run in tandem with the Ordnance Survey, then beginning in Ulster. Numerous amendments to the Act were passed as the work progressed. The first, in 1831, excluded from survey houses under the annual value of £3. A further amendment in 1836 excluded houses under £5. Beginning in 1836, the results of this *General Valuation of Ireland* or 'Griffith's First Valuation' were published in the *Dublin Gazette*, but only the total value of land and houses in each townland was stated (not the occupiers' names). By 1848 the results for all parts of the country except Dublin city and Munster had been published.

The Poor Relief Act of 1838, which established Poor Law Unions, allowed for a separate survey to be conducted where necessary for levying the poor rates for the upkeep of the new workhouses. Rather than simply requiring an overall valuation of each townland, this was to be based on individual holdings, so it was found that the survey then in progress under Griffith was inadequate. The appendices to the *Report on the Poor Law Act Valuation* contain lists of £10 electors and of many property occupiers from various Unions. However, the Poor Law Act Valuation was not published as such. Instead, under the provisions of a further Act of 1846, Griffith was commissioned to conduct a comprehensive valuation to include the names of property holders. This was to be the basic or 'primary' valuation from which the information required for both the county cess or Grand Jury rates and the poor rates were to be calculated.

The first volume of the *Primary Valuation* eventually published was for the barony of Balrothery West in Co. Dublin. It was printed on 15th June 1847 but was reissued after amendments on 15th May 1848. It was followed by volumes from various parts of the country. There was no systematic county-by-county publication, though the very early portions were mainly from Cos. Dublin and Kilkenny. Initially the barony was the unit for each volume but it was later replaced by the Poor Law Union (see Glossary), which was used in the vast majority of cases. Where the Union straddled a county boundary the sections were published separately. Most volumes appeared during the 1850s. The last counties to be completed were those in Ulster. The final volume to be published was for the portion of Armagh Union within Co. Armagh. It was printed on 1st December 1864.

In the survey, properties are listed in rural areas under their townlands. Each townland is recorded in the relevant civil parish in the relevant barony (or in exceptional cases District Electoral Division) in the relevant Poor Law Union. Even towns are arranged by the townlands over which they extended and are usually subdivided by street. In cities the streets are arranged by civil parish and sometimes by ward.

There are eight columns of information in the survey, as follows:

- Lot number
- Townland/street name; Ordnance Survey map sheet number; name of occupier
- Name of immediate lessor (or landlord)
- Description of property, e.g. house, offices (sheds), mill, forge, yard, garden, land, bog, mountain
- Area in acres, roods and perches
- Rateable annual value of land
- Rateable annual value of buildings
- Total valuation.

SAME-NAME PROBLEMS

Occasionally the occupier's name is followed by another name in brackets, for instance 'John Sullivan (Patrick)' or 'John Sullivan (Black)', or simply 'John Sullivan (jun.)'. This is merely to differentiate between two people of the same name. When the brackets contain a forename this is usually, but not necessarily always, the individual's father's name (see Chapter 1, Naming Patterns).

Theoretically, all households were covered by the valuation. However, a certain proportion of the more humble dwellings in rural areas definitely missed the net. In cities many families were not recorded because they were not the sole occupants of a house. For example, in some Dublin streets whole rows of houses were listed simply as in tenements, the individual heads of family not being recorded. In other cases, houses were merely described as occupied by lodgers.

As a genealogical source, Griffith's *Valuation* is disappointing on its own. It only shows at a particular date the name of the property occupier (the head of family, and *not* all family members). However, it gives an insight into the family's social background. A farm of thirty acres or upwards was relatively comfortable, depending on the quality of the land. A house valued at 5s. was a poor dwelling and one of £10 was a substantial building. Griffith's *Valuation* can also be a useful reference for background information when checking civil or church records. For instance, if you were searching for a Forbes from Caher it would be useful to know whether there were several Forbes families in the townland or only one, so you could judge the relevance of any entries you might find.

'IN FEE'

When you see 'In Fee' in the Immediate Lessor column it means that the occupier was the outright owner of that property. It usually means that that person was also the landlord for the entire townland. This is important to note, as you will need to know the landlord's name when looking for estate papers (see Chapter 6, Identifying the Landlord).

Where to Find Griffith's *Valuation*

Griffith's *Valuation* is available on microfiche in the major record repositories, not only in Ireland, but in Australia, Canada, Great Britain, New Zealand and the US. It is generally accompanied by a guide in book form giving the fiche references for each civil parish, arranged by county. Once you know the county and civil parish your ancestor's townland (see Glossary) is in, it is easy to locate it in the record. If you only know the county your ancestor was from, you should find the indexes to Griffith's and the Index of Surnames useful.

Indexes to Griffith's

Apart from the Index of Surnames (see below and Glossary), there are indexes specifically relating to Griffith's *Valuation* for certain counties. Most of these are on microfiche and are produced by All-Ireland Heritage or Andrew J. Morris. They give full names rather than just surnames, so that you can for instance pinpoint the Forbeses with the forename Edward or John. Like the Index of Surnames, they are indexes to householders, rather than property occupiers. The distinction is simply that they do not record every separate land holding of a particular individual, only the one containing his or her house. This makes them a more accurate guide to the actual number of people of a particular name, but do remember that your ancestor might have held or sublet other property in another townland and street.

The All-Ireland Heritage indexes state the civil parish, townland, Ordnance Survey map reference and page number within the relevant volume of Griffith's. They are available for Belfast and Dublin cities and Cos. Carlow, Cork (including Cork City in a separate alphabet), Fermanagh, Limerick, Longford, Monaghan, Tipperary and Waterford. The Andrew J. Morris indexes state the civil parish, Poor Law Union and page number within the relevant volume of Griffith's. In addition, they include tables of the most common forenames and surnames in the county. They are available only for Cos. Mayo and Wicklow. David Leahy's *County Longford Survivors of the Famine* is another index to Griffith's for Longford. As well as occupiers it covers immediate lessors. It includes tables of the most common surnames, the most extensive immediate lessors, and houses valued over £35. These details may be of assistance in identifying your ancestor's landlord (see Chapter 6, Estate Papers). An index to Griffith's *Valuation* is now available on CD-ROM from the Genalogical Publishing Co. in Baltimore, USA.

Valuation Office Revisions

While Griffith's *Valuation* relates specifically to dates between 1848 and 1864, the valuation records have been updated ever since. These revised records are available for consultation, though only in manuscript form, as are most of the accompanying maps, so it is possible in most cases to trace the occupancy of a property right through. For instance, you could begin with the person listed in the original published valuation and trace forward to the 20th century, or begin with the head of household you find in the 1901 or 1911 Census and trace back.

The revision books, or 'cancelled books', have printed pages similar to those in the published valuation, but with a large observations column on the extreme right. On to these pages the records were handwritten. If and when a change occurred to any part of an entry, the specific detail was simply crossed through and the new information inserted above or below it. The date of this change was entered in the observations column, usually in an abbreviated form (e.g. '88' would represent 1888). It should be remembered that while the records were theoretically updated annually, the change may not have been noted for a few years. It will also be found that changes up to the early 1860s are often undated.

Such changes might simply concern the acreage or the valuation of buildings, if they were structurally altered, or the name of the landlord. These are interesting in themselves, but the most significant changes would concern the occupier's name. If replaced by someone of the same surname the most likely explanation is that the former occupier had died. It is then worth searching for a death record at the General Register Office (see Chapter 2). If replaced by someone of a different surname it is likely that the family had moved elsewhere or emigrated, but it is also possible that the new occupier was a married daughter or a son-in-law. Incidentally, if a John Sullivan was replaced as occupier by his son John, the entry would not be altered unless there was another person of the name in the townland from whom he had to be distinguished, as mentioned in the panel on page 121.

With subdivisions or amalgamations of holdings the lot numbers also changed over the years, so you should not assume that Lot 6 in the early 1900s is the same property as Lot 6 in Griffith's *Valuation.* Over a period there may be several changes to the details concerning any given holding, so the pages often become cluttered with revisions. At first sight such conglomerations can look like an unintelligible mess. However, the changes were made in different colours of ink, so that with the dates from the observations column it is possible to pick your way through them chronologically. Were they to continue entering revisions into the one book for a long period it would simply be impossible to make sense of the colour code. For that reason, the revision books were periodically cancelled and the up-to-date details transferred to new books. Each revision or 'cancelled' book has an index of townlands or streets at the front. There is sometimes also a list of revision dates written in the various colours of ink.

In the books covering the first two decades of the 20th century you may see that most of the occupiers in an entire townland became outright owners ('In Fee') at the same time, with the initials 'L.A.P.'

for 'Land Act Purchase' stamped on each entry. Most tenant farmers acquired their land under the provisions of the late 19th-century Land Acts.

The cancelled books are held in two separate locations. Those for the 26 counties now within the Republic are in the Valuation Office in Dublin (see Chapter 10). There the cancelled books are bound together chronologically into large volumes, the oldest books being at the back of the volume. If you are researching from Griffith's *Valuation* down to the present day, you would begin at the back of the earliest volume and work forward through the individual books. As always when handling manuscripts, do be careful with these precious records. The most recent books are still in use and these must be requested at the front office. The related maps are also held in the Valuation Office and many are very fragile. These are Ordnance Survey sheets on to which the boundaries of properties were drawn. As with the revision books, changes to the size or numbering of properties were indicated on the maps. They were periodically cancelled, with the cancellation date written on the reverse side. Using the revision books in conjunction with the maps you can usually pinpoint an exact property.

The cancelled books for the six counties now in Northern Ireland are held in PRONI in Belfast. The books there are *not* bound into large volumes. They each have an individual call number within the series VAL 12B and may be called up separately. Unfortunately, they are only available up to the early 1930s. The corresponding revision maps are in the series VAL 12D and these too are available up to the early 1930s.

Valuation Office Surveyors' Notebooks

While the revisions of Griffith's *Valuation* reflect the situation after publication, the surveyors' notebooks compiled in preparation for it can in many cases provide information on a number of years directly before it. However, those that have survived are not comprehensive and they are scattered between three repositories. In the Valuation Office they are designated 'Perambulation Books' and in PRONI they are called 'Field Books'. Those in the National Archives are subdivided as 'Valuation Office House Books', 'Field (land) Books', 'Tenure Books', 'Quarto Books' and 'Miscellaneous Books', but in many cases they are arbitrarily labelled. Occasionally you will find a 'House Book' and a 'Field Book' stitched together and labelled as one or the other. It is, therefore, best to check all available notebooks for your ancestor's parish.

It is important to remember that Griffith's *Valuation* was in effect the result of three surveys: the original commenced under the 1826 Act, the unfinished Poor Law Act Valuation and the final combined work. Because Ulster was the first area to be surveyed in the original and the last to be completed in the final work, there is a significant time lapse between the two sets of notebooks for that region. This has given rise to the mistaken belief that there were two distinct valuations for the entire country.

The notebooks are arranged by civil parish or by town. There may be a number of revised books for any one parish or town. Sometimes two or three books are bound into one. On the other hand, in some cases there is no book available at all. The notebooks had different functions. Some were concerned only with the type of soil while others dealt with acreage, buildings or tenure (the conditions by which the occupiers held their property). The most useful are those giving details of buildings or tenure. As already noted, from 1831 houses under the value of £3 and from 1836 those under £5 were exempt in the original valuation. The notebooks compiled under those provisions are, therefore, restricted to larger buildings. However, the books compiled after the mid-1840s should cover all buildings. The original survey was not concerned with individual holdings, but simply with the value of properties. For that reason tenure books date only from the 1840s and they are not available for all parts of the country.

The notebooks concerning buildings or 'House Books' generally state the occupier's name, the quality classification, and the length, breadth and height of each building (including outhouses), as well as the proposed valuation. The quality classification gives an indication of the type of structure. Houses are designated as 1st Class (slated with walls of stone or brick and lime mortar), 2nd Class (thatched with similar walls) or 3rd Class (thatched with walls of stone and mud mortar, or simply of mud). They are also lettered A (new), B (medium) or C (old). There are sometimes additional observations in the margin regarding the condition of the house, the terms of the lease and, within towns, the type of business conducted on the premises. The 'Tenure Books' generally state the occupier's and immediate lessor's names, the acreage, the rent charged and the terms of tenure, whether 'at will' (at the landlord's pleasure) or by lease (with its date).

These surveyors' notebooks may contain numerous amendments. As with the revision or cancelled books, if a change of occupancy occurred the original occupier's name was crossed through and replaced by the new one, though the date of the amendment is not always discernible. In each of the repositories you will be handling the originals so, as always, be gentle.

Those held at the Valuation Office are only for counties now within the Republic and would seem to be exclusively from the final combined survey. They are arranged by county, barony and civil parish, and there is a checklist of parishes covered. The notebooks in PRONI are for counties now in Northern Ireland, but there are two sets. Those from the first survey or the 'Townland Valuation'

(1828–40) are in the series VAL 1B. Those from the final combined survey (1856–64) are in the series VAL 2B. As we already said, the notebooks held at the National Archives are subdivided (sometimes randomly) as 'V.O. House', 'Field', 'Tenure', 'Quarto' and 'Miscellaneous Books'. There is a catalogue on the open shelves for each set, arranged by county. There are 'House Books' from all counties in the Republic and from two parishes in Fermanagh. There are 'Field Books' from all counties throughout the island. The 'Tenure Books' are from only ten counties and the 'Miscellaneous Books' from fifteen, all within the Republic. The 'Quarto Books' are from twelve counties, including Antrim.

TITHE APPLOTMENT BOOKS

The Tithe Applotment, like Griffith's *Valuation*, is a source generally used as an inadequate substitute for the lost early 19th-century census returns.

The History of Tithes

Tithes were a church tax on one's annual income from farming, nominally (but not necessarily) comprising one tenth of the value. From the time of the Reformation they were designated for the upkeep of the Church of Ireland clergymen in each parish. However, in some cases they were rented by the Crown to a layman who was entrusted with appointing a clergyman and paying his salary. Often this position of trust was abused and only a small portion of the money was paid to the clergyman. As the Church of Ireland was the state or Established church, parishioners were liable for tithes, irrespective of their religious denomination. Throughout the 18th century both Catholics and Protestant Dissenters resented this tax. Their resentment was heightened by the fact that from 1736 grazing land, which constituted most of the property directly in the hands of landlords, had an exemption. Tithe payment was one of the causes of widespread agrarian disturbances in the 1760s.

The tradition of tithe charges varied from place to place. Depending on the parish, tithes were imposed on certain crops and not on others. It was even the case that in two parishes under the same Church of Ireland minister potatoes were tithable in one but not in the other. Originally tithes could be paid in kind but their transfer into a cash payment began in the 1820s. The Tithe Composition Acts of 1823 and 1824 allowed for the substitution of a set charge on land for the traditional tithes on various crops. The composition was to be based on the average tithes paid over the seven years prior to 1st November 1821 and subject to variations in the price of wheat or oats. The decision to adopt composition was a matter for the minister and those parishioners paying County Rates. They nominated two commissioners who jointly conducted the applotment of the parish. However, until 1832 composition was neither compulsory nor permanent. In 1830 the prelude to the 'Tithe War' began with Catholic parishioners in Graiguenamanagh, Co. Kilkenny, withholding their tithes. In 1831 their lead was followed in most parts of south Leinster and Munster, the situation errupting into violence and resulting in many deaths.

In 1832 a further Act was passed making the composition permanent and extending it to parishes which had not yet adopted it. It also transferred liability from tenants at will (those without leases) to their immediate lessors (or landlords) as of 1st November 1833, but allowed the landlords to add the amount to their rent. It also exempted those who took new leases after the passing of the legislation. Popular feeling against tithes was finally ended by an Act of 1838 abolishing composition and substituting a rent charge payable by the landlord.

What Will You Find in the Tithe Applotment Books?

Tithe Applotment Books are available for most parishes outside of cities. They exist because of the composition between 1824 and

1838, though some are dated as early as the late 1810s and some as late as the 1840s. They vary in format but they are usually arranged by townland, stating the acreage held by each farmer and the tithes due. Many also indicate the quality of the land and the annual value. As tithes were related to the Church of Ireland administration, the Tithe Books were generally compiled by Church of Ireland parish or union of parishes rather than by civil parish. It should also be remembered that in most cases they pre-date the Ordnance Survey, so they often contain placenames which were not later used as official townland names.

It is important to remember that the Tithe Books are surveys of land and do not cover all households. Labourers and tradesmen and those who did not have land holdings will not be found. It is only in exceptional cases that town dwellers are included. Where a number of tenants held land in common, often only one of them is named in the Tithe Book and the others are concealed behind terms such as 'and Partners' or 'and Co.' Of course, the books for parishes which adopted composition after the 1832 legislation will very likely not include tenants at will or the recipients of new leases.

LISTINGS IN THE TITHE APPLOTMENT

If your family were recorded in Griffith's *Valuation* but not in the Tithe Applotment, it does not mean that they were not living there at the time. Unless they held a substantial farm in Griffith's, there is no reason to assume that they will certainly be recorded in the Tithes.

The land measurement used in Griffith's *Valuation* was the imperial or English acre. That used in the Tithes was the plantation or Irish acre. In many cases this explains the difference in the size given for one family's holding in the two surveys. However, in many cases the holdings were actually larger in Griffith's. This might be explained by depopulation during and shortly after the Famine.

Where to find Tithe Applotment Books

The Tithe Applotment Books are available on microfilm at the National Archives, National Library and Gilbert Library in Dublin. Those for the nine counties of Ulster are also available at PRONI.

Tithe Defaulters

The 'Tithe War', mentioned above, was basically an organised large-scale refusal to pay tithes. This resulted in Church of Ireland ministers in many parts of Leinster and Munster being almost entirely without this source of income during 1831. The Clergy Relief Fund, established by legislation in 1832, was for those effected by this protest. To avail of the fund each minister had to complete an application, appending a schedule containing the names of tithe payers within his parish who defaulted during 1831. In all, 499 such schedules of defaulters were submitted, of which 127 still survive. Each schedule gives the defaulters' places of residence and the amount due for 1831. Most also state the location of the land in question, which sometimes differed from the residence. More significantly, about half of the schedules state the defaulters' occupations. Many constitute a complete or near-complete list of tithe payers for a parish.

Where such a schedule survives it can be useful to compare it with the relevant Tithe Applotment Book, especially if there is a lapse of a few years between the two. This might allow you to determine that an occupier was replaced in the intervening period by a family member, perhaps his widow or his son. The surviving lists are held at the National Archives in the Official Papers, Miscellaneous Assorted (CSO OPMA) series. Fifty-three of them relate to parishes in or partly in Co. Kilkenny. A further 30 relate to parishes in or partly in Co. Tipperary. The other counties for which there is partial coverage are Carlow, Cork, Kerry, Laois, Limerick, Louth, Meath, Offaly, Waterford and Wexford. A complete list of the surviving schedules, giving the relevant OPMA references, was published in the *Irish Genealogist* in 1990. Another article on this source appeared in *Irish Roots* magazine (1997; no. 1).

THE INDEX OF SURNAMES

The Index of Surnames is a typescript index to names listed in the Tithe Applotment and Griffith's *Valuation*. Arranged in 35 volumes, it is also sometimes called the 'Householders' Index'. Three volumes cover Co. Cork, two Co. Tipperary and each other county has one volume. It should be noted, however, that the Co. Dublin volume does not cover the city. The index is divided into two sections. The first is a general alphabetical list of surnames stating the baronies in which they occurred. The second is an alphabetical list by civil parish within each barony). The initial 'G' indicates that the surname occurred in Griffith's *Valuation* and the accompanying number indicates how many households of that name appeared. 'T' indicates that the surname occurred in the Tithe Applotment but the frequency is not given. In relation to Griffith's *Valuation* this index is not as straightforward as the All-Ireland Heritage, Andrew J. Morris and David Leahy indexes mentioned above.

However, the Index of Surnames is of particular assistance when researching an uncommon name. A quick survey of the 35 volumes will show the general distribution if it is very unusual. Within a county the index will narrow down the scope of a search and allow you to concentrate on the most likely areas if you intend to search baptismal registers. The frequency of entries in Griffith's will also dictate which areas to try first. The Index of Surnames is of less use with a common surname but, if you already know where your family was from, knowing exactly how common the name was can be of help in determining the relevance of references you might find when searching the church register. Certainly, if you have the surnames of a husband and wife married in Ireland about the mid-nineteenth century, a search of the Index of Surnames for both their names can often be a good indication of the best locations on which to concentrate your research.

Where to Find the Index of Surnames

The Index of Surnames is available in the National Archives, National Library and PRONI in book form. It is also on microfiche and very often is found in repositories which hold microfiche copies of Griffith's.

PRACTISING RESEARCH TECHNIQUES

Griffith's *Primary Valuation* for the relevant part of Co. Cork was published in 1852. We have already established that the Forbes family lived in the townland of Caher, in the civil parish of Kinneigh, barony of East Carbery (W.D.), Co. Cork, (see previous chapters). The Index of Surnames for Co. Cork South-West, under the civil parish of Kinneigh shows that (i) there are four Forbes householders recorded in Griffith's *Primary Valuation*; (ii) Forbes is entered in the Tithe Applotment Book; (iii) at the top of the page, the publication year for that section of Griffith's was 1852; (iv) and there are two Tithe Applotment Books, one for the year 1827 and one for 1834. However, the Alphabetical list of Householders in Griffith's *Primary Valuation* for Co. Cork (*All Ireland Heritage* Fiche) is more straightforward. It lists all the Forbes in the county, identifying the civil parish and the townland for each: twelve Forbes householders are listed for Co. Cork (Cork City not included), including Edward Forbes of Caher. The reference numbers for the relevant fiches were found in the Fiche Catalogue for Griffith's and were written in on an Order Docket.

Edward Forbes held lot number 2/a from Thomas K. Sullivan (the immediate lessor and in fact the owner and landlord of Caher townland), a house and offices (sheds) with 76 acres 0 roods 6 perches of land in partnership with Jeremiah Crowley; Edward's total valuation was £16.10s.0d. It was also noted that Edward Forbes held a further 46 acres 3 roods 15 perches (lot no. 3/a) and furthermore he was the immediate lessor of three houses (2/c; 2/d; 3/b).

The revision or cancelled books show that prior to 1864 changes (or rationalisation) in farm holdings had taken place; Edward Forbes had one holding (number 3/a), house, offices and 46 acres 3 roods 33 perches of land; the valuation was £21.10s.0d. By 1864, Edward's name was replaced with that of Honoria (his wife's name was Honoria/Honora/'Norry').

In 1884 Honoria was replaced by John (her son). In 1914 John Forbes became outright owner of his land ('in fee'), arising out of the Land Act Purchases (L.A.P.). In 1924 John Forbes' name was crossed out and replaced with that of Michael Murphy. (We know from John Forbes' 1911 Census Return that he and his wife Julia Coakley had no children.)

The Tenure Book for the parish of Kinneigh is extant and Caher townland was surveyed by John McManus and dated 18 December 1847. With regard to the Forbes family, interesting information was gleaned from the revisions and 'observations' column: Joseph, Edward and John Firbush/Forbes held their houses and land, by virtue of 'an old lease of 4 lives, all living, but mislaid, dated about 1819'.

The Tithe Applotment Book for the parish of Kinneigh, dated 20 October 1827, records Edward Forbes in Caher townland as holding a total of 22 tithable acres, with an annual tithe 'composition' or payment of £0.14s.5$^{1}/_{5}$d. (Joseph and John Forbes, together, are also listed, having a total of 90 acres with an annual tithe of £2.12s.3d.) T. K. Sullivan, the landlord is named as 'liable for whole of Caher'.

6 Deeds and Estate Papers

Once you have exhausted civil records, census returns, church registers and the more general 19th-century householder/landholder records, there are few sources left that might throw light on 'ordinary' families. At this point it would be worthwhile to investigate the possibility of there being records for the estate of your ancestor's landlord.

Up to the end of the 19th century, the ownership of property in Ireland was in the hands of the aristocracy and gentry, or of middle-class speculators. Practically everyone else rented their property from one of these landlords. In the case of the minor gentry, many of them were not the outright owners of the greater part of their estates, merely holding long leases from wealthier landlords. The property encompassed in any one estate might have consisted of anything from a few townlands to hundreds of thousands of acres spread over several counties.

Estate papers might include copies of leases or lists of tenants which could provide new names for your family tree as well as adding to your knowledge of the family's circumstances. You should bear in mind, however, that a large percentage of tenants did not hold leases. Their tenancy was from year to year or 'at will', meaning that there was no written agreement and that they continued their occupancy at the landlord's pleasure. Of course, if your ancestors were themselves of the landlord class, estate papers would be an invaluable source.

The records of the Registry of Deeds can be bracketed with estate papers because they frequently concern transactions between landlord and tenant. As they are more easily accessible in most cases than the records of individual estates, they will be dealt with here first.

REGISTRY OF DEEDS

The Registry of Deeds (see Chapter 10) was established in 1708 as part of the mechanism introduced by the Penal Laws. These laws restricted the religious, political and business practices of people of denominations other than the Church of Ireland. They also placed obstacles in the way of Roman Catholic land-owning and lease-taking. The Registry of Deeds was set up primarily to ensure that land already transferred to Protestant ownership did not slip back into Catholic hands.

You might expect that copies of all property transacted since 1708 would be found at the Registry of Deeds, but registration was not compulsory. It is impossible to determine what percentage of deeds were registered, but it is likely that the majority were not. As well as that, the restrictions placed on Catholic ownership by the Penal Laws meant that few transactions involving Catholics were registered before the legislation was relaxed in the last thirty years of the 18th century. From 1772, Catholics could take leases of 61 years on bog land for reclamation. The first Catholic Relief Act, in 1778, allowed them to take leases for up to 999 years. It also ended the compulsory gavelling of estates, by which a Catholic could not bequeath his property as he saw fit. Instead, it would be divided equally between all his sons, unless one of them converted to the Church of Ireland. After the 1778 Act, Catholics could inherit in the same way as Protestants. Finally, from 1782, they could purchase land, except in parliamentary boroughs.

Of course, all of these circumstances concerned propertied Catholics. It is important also to remember that if your ancestor was a servant or a labourer or a farmer with a small land-holding (irrespective of religious denomination) there is little likelihood of there being a record of them in a deed of any description, unless as a witness. This particularly applies to the 18th century.

The types of transactions registered at the Deeds were mostly leases, sales, mortgages, marriage settlements and wills. A cursory look at the various indexes to prerogative and diocesan wills (see Chapter 7) would show you that the percentage of wills on record at the Deeds is quite low. Nevertheless, those registered there amount to 2,115 up to 1832, after which there are few if any registered. According to the eminent genealogist Rosemary ffolliott, the most likely reason for registration was if a member of the testator's family was purposely omitted from the will with the intention of disinheriting them. *Registry of Deeds: Abstracts of Wills*, published in three volumes by the Irish Manuscripts Commission, and edited by P. Beryl Eustace (Vol. 3 with Eilish Ellis), contains summaries of all wills up to 1832. The volumes cover the periods 1708–1745, 1746–1785 and 1785–1832. Each contains full indexes to persons and places.

What Will You Find in a Deed?

The basic information contained in a deed, other than a will, is its date, the names (and usually addresses and occupations) of the parties involved, details of the transaction, the terms of the transaction and the names (and usually addresses and occupations) of the witnesses. If the transaction concerned property, size and location of the property are usually stated. Often the location is more precisely described by the names of the occupiers of adjoining properties being mentioned. For registration, a copy of the deed, called a 'memorial', was made, witnessed and sworn. The memorial might have been slightly abbreviated, substituting a term like 'as therein more fully described' for a lengthy passage in the original. At registration, which might be several years after the transaction, the memorial was deposited in the Registry of Deeds, where its details were transcribed into a large tome. This transcript is what you will be working on when you visit the Deeds. It is, in fact, a copy of a copy of the original document.

Apart from the physical difficulty of hauling those large tomes off their shelves, the main problem about working at the Deeds is interpreting the legal jargon and abbreviations in the transcripts. At first sight they may look completely incomprehensible. Actually, in extreme cases it is difficult for anyone to determine exactly what was happening. However, once you have read through a number of them you will recognise the repetitive phrases and begin to pick out the important words.

A very simple deed would involve two parties. The grantor, who would normally be named first, would be making over a property (usually a lease or mortgage of it) to the grantee. The document might relate how the grantor came into possession of the property. It would certainly state that the grantor was now granting it to the grantee. Usually the property's location would be stated. Then, beginning with a phrase such as 'to hold unto [the grantee] for', the terms of the transaction would be stated. This might be for a number of years or for the duration of the lives of a number (usually three) of individuals. The annual rent might then be stated along with the days on which it was to be paid. The 'lives' were usually relatives of the grantor or the grantee, but they were sometimes well-known people, such as members of the Royal Family. The grant was for the longest of the three lives. At the death of each of those named, a new life could usually be added on payment of a renewal fee.

It is often difficult to determine whether the property was being sold, leased or mortgaged. A phrase such as 'grant bargain sell assign transfer and makeover' could feature in any such transaction. However, the term 'subject to redemption' is a tell-tale sign that you are dealing with a mortgage. More complicated deeds may involve several grantors, all with an interest in the property, and a number of grantees.

Marriage settlements, or marriage articles, were a feature of the Deeds from the very early years. They were, in modern parlance, prenuptial agreements which protected the husband's property while making provision for the wife, and any children they might have, in case she should be widowed. As with leases, the poorer members of society would not have had any such written agreement. The essential parties in a marriage settlement were, of course, the intended husband and wife. The bride's father or brother or widowed mother would usually be involved as well, since they were providing her dowry. The groom's father might also be involved, especially if an annuity was being charged on his property for the bride in the event of her husband dying. Most marriage settlements also involved two independent parties to act as trustees for whatever agreement was being made. Usually one was connected with the bride's family and the other with the groom's. The agreement was normally entered into on or just before the day of the wedding. It might be registered once the event took place, but sometimes this was not done until several years afterwards. The date of registration is, therefore, very important as well as the date of the settlement.

Another type of deed to be found, during Penal times, particularly in the mid-18th century, concerned Protestant discovery. Any Catholic who was in possession of property contrary to the law (for example, holding a lease for longer than 31 years or paying a lower rent than legally permitted) could be 'discovered' against by a Protestant, who could then claim the property. Large numbers of such discoveries were registered at the Deeds. While many were no doubt genuine discoveries, at least some were skilful steps for fooling the system. Such discoveries would involve a friendly Protestant presenting a bill to the court, claiming the property, and then registering a deed to the effect that he was holding it in trust for the erstwhile owner. It has been found that one circumstance in which this ploy was used was when a proprietor was in the process of converting to the Church of Ireland, for whatever reason, and wished to protect property for which he had title as a Catholic.

HOW TO FIND A DEED

There are two keys to the records at the Deeds, the Index of Grantors and the Lands (or Placename) Index. There is no index to grantees. It is, therefore, often difficult to locate transactions in which your ancestor was on the receiving end. In the case of a lease, for instance, the tenant is the grantee. In such instances you would need to know the landlord's name (see below) in order to use the Index of Grantors, or the townland, small town or street in order to use the Lands Index. However, if your ancestor was mortgaging property, he or she would be the grantor. Remember, by the way, that until the late 1800s women could own property only if they were unmarried or widowed. In the case of a marriage settlement, both bride and groom (as well as their fathers, if involved) were grantors and the trustees were the grantees.

INDEX OF GRANTORS

The format of the Index of Grantors changed several times over the years. Up until 1832, the Index gives the same basic information: the surname and forename of the grantor, the surname of the corresponding grantee (or the first grantee if there were a number) and the reference number (volume/page/memorial number). In the first period, 1708–1729, the index is arranged in one alphabet. The same format applies for each of the periods up to 1785, but from 1786 through to 1799 there is a separate alphabet for each year. You could easily miss this if you get used to the earlier structure. For 1800–1809 it reverts to the consolidated index. From 1810 to 1832 there are again yearly indexes.

The system changed considerably in 1833. From then onwards there is one alphabet for each period and the information given is the surname and forename of the grantor, the surname and forename of the grantee (or the first one), the location of the property involved and the reference number (year/volume/memorial number).

LANDS INDEX

The format of the Lands (or Placename) Index was unchanged until 1828. Up to then it was arranged in volumes by county or city. However, within each volume the entries are only alphabetical as far as the initial letter. Therefore, if you are looking for Caher, you have to work your way through all the places beginning with 'C', looking out for strange spellings of the relevant placename. The information given may be similar to the following:

Smith & ors. to Murphy & anr. 771 583 521911

In this case Smith is one of a number of grantors (ors. = others) and Murphy is one of two grantees (anr. = another), so your ancestor might well have been involved in a transaction without being named in the index. It is important to work your way right through the pages covering the relevant initial letter, as the townland you are searching might be recorded in it a number of times. Usually there will be a clump of references opposite the townland name, referring to different memorials. Incidentally, the index volume covering Co. Cork in the period 1739–1779 is missing places beginning with the initials A, B and C.

References for corporate towns are contained in the volumes covering the relevant county, but they are listed separately, at the end rather than in the general alphabet. Cities are listed in separate volumes. In the case of Dublin the street names are in fully alphabetical order from 1793 to 1832, being arranged by parish in 1828–1832.

From 1828 the Lands Index is subdivided by barony, so that it is necessary to know in which barony within the relevant county your townland is located. There is also a 'No Barony' section for instances in which the memorial does not state the barony. After 1828, therefore, there are two indexes to check in each period. For 1828–1832, these are in the same book, but thereafter the 'No Barony' section is always in a separate volume and can easily be overlooked. Cities are not effected by this change in format.

AVAILABILITY ON MICROFILM

Both the Index of Grantors and the Lands Index were microfilmed and copies are available in the National Library, the Public Record Office of Northern Ireland and in the LDS Library in Salt Lake City. The transcripts were also microfilmed and are available (with some gaps) in Salt Lake City and at PRONI.

ESTATE PAPERS

The records of individual estates can be difficult to track down and there is no guarantee that they still exist in the case of your ancestor's landlord. Those that have survived vary from collections of family correspondence or accounts, which give little or no information on the employees or tenants, to detailed annual rentals, which record the names of all landholders on the estate. Sadly, the latter are rare, but where they do exist they sometimes pre-date church registers. One of the best examples of such records are those of the Coolattin estate of the Earl Fitzwilliam in Co. Wicklow, with comprehensive rentals dating from the early 1800s and records of head tenants from 1758.

In addition to the records of individual estates, there are two collections of material connected with estates which are worth considering, those of the land courts and of the Irish Land Commission, which are discussed below.

Identifying the Landlord

The first step towards investigating estate papers is, of course, to identify your ancestor's landlord. There is no single all-embracing way of doing this. However, we can give some suggestions. In most cases the landlord's name can be found by checking Griffith's *Valuation* (see Chapter 5). The person named in the 'Immediate Lessor' column in relation to your ancestor's property was the person from whom the property was rented and the person to check in the Index of Grantors at the Registry of Deeds. However, this person was not necessarily the owner of the estate. He or she might have been a prosperous tenant renting a number of properties from the landlord. Usually a townland was entirely within one estate, so it is relatively safe to assume that if you see 'In Fee' (see Chapter 5, p. 122) appearing in the 'Immediate Lessor' column, the person occupying that property was the landlord of the entire townland.

Of course, a landlord would not necessarily have occupied property in every townland on the estate so 'In Fee' might not appear at all in your townland. As well as that, as already noted, minor landlords were not the outright owners of all their property so 'In Fee' would not appear for property they occupied. In such cases it is a matter of examining the 'Immediate Lessor' column closely to determine from whom the prosperous tenants were all renting. In relation to Longford, the lists of the most extensive immediate lessors and houses valued over £35 in Leahy's *County Longford Survivors of the Famine* (see Indexes to Griffith's in Chapter 5) would be helpful.

Another useful source for identifying landlords is the *Return of Owners of Land of One Acre and Upwards*. This relates to ownership in 1876 and lists owners alphabetically under each county, giving their addresses and the extent and valuation of their lands. The one problem in using Griffith's *Valuation* or the *Return of Owners of Land* to identify the landlord is that in many cases you are looking at the name of a new landlord who purchased the property from the Incumbered Estates Court in the mid-19th century (see below).

An alternative approach would be to check your townland in the Ordnance Survey Name Books. These were compiled by the surveyors in the 1830s in an attempt to establish the origins of placenames in order to fix acceptable standardised spellings. In the process they noted other information such as historical sites, large houses, the quality of the land and its ownership. The landlords' names are, therefore, given in most cases and often their addresses. In cases where the landlords were themselves tenants of wealthier owners, sometimes both names are stated. The O.S. Name Books are arranged by county and then by civil parish. They are most easily accessible in the National Library, where some counties are in typescript form – check the Author Catalogue under 'Ordnance Survey Name Books' – and others are microfilmed copies of the originals – check *Hayes Manuscripts* under 'O'Donovan, John' in the Persons section.

Knowing the landlord's name is only the first step. You then have to find out who he or she was so as to trace whether estate papers are available. This is usually fairly straightforward. If the landlord was titled, like the Duke of Leinster or Lord Palmerston, there is no problem about identification, but do refer to *Burke's Peerage and Baronetage* to familiarise yourself with the family structure and to ascertain their surname. If the landlord was not titled the best place to start would be with *Lewis' Topographical Dictionary* (see Glossary).

In its article on each civil parish it usually lists the 'principal residences' with their occupiers' names. If you find the relevant person here you have an address to work on. Referring to one of the many editions of *Burke's Landed Gentry* should provide you with more background information. This is important particularly if there were a number of landed families of the same surname. In east Galway, for example, there were several minor landlords called Daly and French. The more you know about the landlord the easier it will be to locate the estate records.

In case of difficulty in locating your landlord, there are a few steps worth trying. Many families appeared in some editions of the *Landed Gentry* but not in others. If you have identified the landlord's residence in *Lewis* you could check *Burke's Guide to Country Houses*, Volume 1, Ireland, by Mark Bence-Jones. It will state the occupiers' surnames and the Burke publications they appear in. Of course, your landlord might have been head of a minor gentry family not covered by the *Landed Gentry*. If this is the case, the earliest edition (1860) of *Walford's County Families of the United Kingdom* would be worth trying.

Locating Estate Papers

Estate papers, if they have survived, may be in a number of locations and there is no one source for determining which. If they are not still in private hands, the three most likely places in which they might be deposited are the National Library, the National Archives and the Public Record Office of Northern Ireland. However, some are held in other locations throughout the country and records of many Irish estates are held by various repositories in Great Britain.

The best way to start your search is with *Hayes Manuscripts* (see Glossary). You can check it either in the Persons volumes under the landlord's name or in the Places volumes under the relevant county's estates section, which lists estate records chronologically. *Hayes* may help you in one of two ways. First, it states the repository in which a collection of estate papers is located, along with the relevant manuscript numbers if it is sorted and catalogued. Secondly, it refers to National Library reports on private collections. These reports were compiled in the mid-twentieth century and they briefly describe the types of records contained in the collections as well as stating their then location. Many of these collections subsequently found their way to a repository. The reports are in typescript form and available on the open shelves in the Manuscript Room of the Library.

Unfortunately, *Hayes* is not comprehensive and is very much out of date. It was published in 1965 and its *Supplement* appeared in 1975. Because of the increased use of computer technology in library services, it is unlikely that further supplements will be published. Many collections which were listed in *Hayes* as unsorted have since become available to the researcher. Similarly, collections which were not covered by *Hayes* have since come to light. With regard to the National Library's own acquisitions, the card catalogue in the Manuscript Room covers collections which were sorted between 1975 and 1989. Collections sorted since then are being listed on the Library's computer catalogue (see Chapter 10). Application should be made to Department of Manuscripts staff for advice on the Library's recent acquisitions and cataloguing in progress.

To identify estate papers deposited in the National Archives since the publication of the *Hayes Supplement* the first step is to consult the 'Maps & Rentals' card index in the Reading Room. This relates only to larger collections. It may be checked either by place (estate name) under the relevant county or by the proprietor's name. It may also be worthwhile to try the 'Miscellaneous' card index located beside it. These would pinpoint most of the significant estate papers containing rentals which are now held at the Archives. To leave no stone unturned you would have to work through the 'Lists' catalogue on the open shelves. This records Large Accessions (numbered 1000 forward) and Small Accessions (999s) in chronological order, giving the year and the donor's name. Any entries found in it can be checked in the appropriate Accession List for more detailed information. At the back of the 'Lists' catalogue is a descriptive schedule of Large Accessions, again in chronological order, which is updated at the end of each year. Its contents from 1980 forward may be searched on the Internet.

The Public Record Office of Northern Ireland maintains card catalogues in its Search Room to its various manuscript holdings. These are arranged by person and by place, and they are in the process of being computerised. Estate papers held by PRONI can be checked in these, either under the landlord's name or the name of the estate. Any references you may find relate to the typescript catalogues of listed collections which are also in the Search Room. The catalogues give detailed information on the contents of the manuscripts themselves and provide the reference numbers to be called up.

The only published guide to estate papers in Irish repositories which makes any attempt at comprehensive coverage is one which deals solely with the period 1840–1855. This is *Estate Records of the Irish Famine* by Andres Eiriksson and Cormac O Grada, published in 1995. It lists records held at the National Library, National Archives, PRONI and various university and local libraries throughout the island. While it is not all-embracing, it provides a key to a substantial number of estate papers. The records are arranged by county and then by the proprietor's name, stating the periods available, the record types, the repository and the manuscript numbers. In the case of deeds, wills or other legal documents, only the larger collections are definitely covered.

As we already mentioned, there are Irish estate records in repositories in Great Britain. In some cases this is because the landlord also had property in England, Scotland or Wales, or because Irish estates were inherited or purchased by people who lived there. The most effective way of trying to track down such records is through the National Register of Archives (NRA). This is maintained at the Royal Commission on Historical Manuscripts, Quality House, Quality Court, Chancery Lane, London WC2A 1HP. The NRA is similar to *Hayes* in intent, but is on a much larger scale and relates to manuscript sources for British history. Its province is collections of all sorts held in private hands or in repositories (such as local record offices and national and university libraries throughout the United Kingdom and abroad) other than those governed by the Public Records legislation. It is constantly growing, but at present it includes 40,000 catalogues of manuscript collections and published guides to collections. These catalogues and guides are available in its Search Room and the key to them is a computerised database. It can be searched in the office or over the Internet.

LAND COURTS

The Incumbered Estates Court (IEC) was established by an Act of 1849 to facilitate the removal of property from the hands of bankrupt or nearly bankrupt proprietors. An estate could be auctioned at the request of the owner or on the petition of a creditor. In 1858 the IEC was replaced by the Landed Estates Court (LEC) which was additionally empowered to sell unincumbered properties. Following an Act of 1877 the LEC became part of the Chancery Division of the High Court under the new name of Land Judges' Court. The Land Judges' Court continued its functions into the twentieth century.

The National Archives holds conveyances relating to the period

1861–1881, the catalogue for which is arranged by name of purchaser. It also holds deeds and other instruments of title lodged with the courts. These are contained in boxes running to No. 1748, but there are many gaps in the series. A two-part catalogue arranged by box number states the owner, the lands, the court and the types of document.

The most accessible records of the various land courts and the most useful for descendants of tenants are the 'rentals'. Basically, these are printed sales catalogues for the information of prospective buyers. They itemise the various properties for sale within each lot, stating the name of the occupier, the type of premises, the acreage (if including land), the rent and a description of the terms. This last section might confirm that your ancestor was a tenant at will or it might give the date and terms of the lease by which the property was held. In the case of a lease for lives, the 'lives' may be named. The lease may well have been to the then occupier's father or grandfather. Sometimes the preamble to the rental gives similar information concerning leases for entire lots. In most cases there are detailed maps of the properties for sale.

Obviously every estate in the country was not sold by the land courts, so you are not necessarily going to have to look at these records. However, hundreds of estates were auctioned. The problem is that there is no one complete set of rentals. The National Archives and National Library each has two partial sets and PRONI has one. The 'O'Brien Rentals' in the Archives are the second most extensive set available (148 volumes, 1850–1885) and the easiest to check, because there is a placename index to them on the open shelves. The index is labelled 'LEC Rentals' and is in four large volumes, one for each province. Each is subdivided by county, civil parish and townland. If volume and rental numbers appear opposite the townland name you can order them up. The index appears to be incomplete. There is also an index labelled 'LEC Rentals Dublin City'. This, too, is incomplete. The Archives' second set of rentals is in the Quit Rent Office records and does not have an easy-access finding aid.

Of the National Library's two sets, the more important one is that acquired from the Irish Land Commission in the 1970s, which is referred to as the 'Green Set'. It is the largest collection available (173 individual bindings, some bindings containing two individually numbered volumes, 1850–1896). However, the index volume only runs to 1874 and it may be ordered up as the Index to the Incumbered Estates Court 'Green Set'. This is in manuscript form and arranged alphabetically by proprietor's name, giving the month and year of sale and location of the estate. Note that it has two alphabetical sequences under each initial letter. The other set, referred to as the 'Library Set', contains 56 volumes from the period 1850–1864. Its index is available at the Reading Room counter and has the same basic format as the 'Green Set' index. There are four additional volumes with the 'Library Set' from 1866–1867, which are not indexed. For both sets, order the volumes by quoting the month and year. However, the 'Library Set' is in a fragile condition and will only be produced in exceptional circumstances. PRONI has over 80 volumes of rentals from the IEC. These are not confined to Ulster counties. They are in the series D.1201.

IRISH LAND COMMISSION

The Land Commission was created by the 1881 Land Act and its powers were expanded by subsequent legislation. Initially it was to determine fair rents, but soon its main purpose was established as assisting tenants to purchase their property. The Congested Districts Board, set up in 1891, had a similar function. In 1923 the Free State government abolished the Congested Districts Board and transferred its functions to the Commission, while giving it general powers of compulsory purchase.

The records of the Land Commission are currently stored in the same building as the National Archives. They are very much on restricted access and you would have to put a very strong case to the Keeper of Records, Irish Land Commission, Bishop Street, Dublin 8, to be allowed conduct a search. However, the National Library holds a 35-volume catalogue containing summary descriptions of documents relating to the various estates the Commission dealt with. There are card indexes to these, arranged by proprietor's (or vendor's) name and by county and barony. There is a separate card index to the copies of wills contained in the Land Commission records (see Chapter 7).

PRACTISING RESEARCH TECHNIQUES

Thomas Kingston Sullivan was Edward Forbes's landlord (according to Griffith's *Valuation*) and was also landlord and probably overall owner of the townland of Caher, parish of Kinneigh, Co. Cork in 1852 (refer to Chapter 5). The Tenure Book, dated 1847 indicates that Joseph, John and Edward Forbes/Firbush held their property subject to 'An old lease of 4 lives all living but mislaid, dated about 1819'. Also, on the same page [the place] Bandon is inserted under Thomas Kingston Sullivan's name.

Registry of Deeds: Edward Forbes, although his life was one of the '4 lives' referred to in the 'old lease', would not be expected to have been a principal grantee in a registered memorial (see p. 136, Registry of Deeds). However, there could be a registered memorial reciting how his landlord, Thomas Kingston Sullivan, came into possession of Caher townland or indeed a registered memorial if he leased or mortgaged a part of the townland. With these possibilities in mind, the Indexes of Lands for Co. Cork were examined from the year 1708 to 1839 under Caher. No references to Sullivan or Forbes were found, as grantor or grantee against the townland of Caher.

A few comments: Caher in Kinneigh civil parish in the barony of Carbery East (West Division) is the townland in which Edward Forbes lived and, thus, the place in which we have a particular interest. However, there are seven townlands of that name in Co. Cork, two of which are in the barony of Carbery East (W.D.). With a relatively common name like Sullivan and the paucity of information included in the indexes, it could have been difficult to identify references pertaining to 'our' townland. Furthermore, the Co. Cork Lands Index for the years 1739 to 1779 are missing all place or townland names beginning with A, B, and C (see p. 136, Lands Index).

John O'Donovan's Ordnance Survey Name Book for Kinneigh parish, which were compiled in the latter half of the 1830s (see p. 145), includes an interesting description of Caher townland, parish of Kinneigh:

> Situated in the S.W. side of the parish and is bounded E. by the townlands of Lissacroneen and Conagh, N. by the latter and Teenagh, S. by Forth Robert and Connorville and W. by the parish of Fanlobbus'.
> Descriptive Remarks: This townland contains [gap] acres of which about 1/8 are bog and rough ground and the rest arable – Soil light and gravelly without limestone in it, producing potatoes and oats wheat and flax – The proprietors Arthur O'Connor of France and Thomas K. O'Sullivan Bandon Esqrs have it let to 12 tenants 6 at will and 6 with leases of 3 lives (under whom are (?15) workmen with a house and garden each) at 14d per acre in farms of (?10) to 24 acres. County cess 7d per acre half yearly and tithes (? 1s.) per acre. Bog of fuel is in plenty.

Considering the information entered in the Tenure Book and the above 'descriptive remarks', there is little doubt but that one of the '6 tenants with a lease of 3 lives' was Edward Forbes. John Forbes, Edward's son, married Julia Coakely at her home on 25 February 1868; she lived in the townland of Teenagh (see p. 73, Practising Research Techniques); John O'Donovan's Name Book describes clearly their situation one to the other: Caher is partly bounded on the north by Teenagh.

According to the *Return of Owners of Land of One Acre and Upwards in Ireland*, published in 1876 (see p. 145), Thomas Kingston Sullivan of Bandon, Co. Cork, was the owner of 3,264 acres 0 roods and 20 perches, with a valuation of £1,397.10s. – quite a sizeable acreage!

The 1894 edition of *Walford's County Families of the United Kingdom* (see p. 146) includes a wide-ranging entry relating to Thomas Kingston Sullivan, The Retreat, Co. Cork (only a fraction of which is summarised here): he was the youngest son of John Sullivan, Esq., merchant, of Bandon, Co. Cork, who died 1825, by Mary, daughter of the late Thomas Kingston, Esq., Lislee Court, Co. Cork; he was born in 1815. Mr Sullivan was admitted a solicitor in 1841; Residences: The Retreat, Bandon; Marina House, Kenmare, Co. Kerry.

If Thomas Kingston Sullivan was a solicitor he should be listed in the publication *King's Inns Admission Papers 1607–1867* (Dublin 1982) (see p. 190, Legal Profession). He and his two sons, John and Josias Tresilian Sullivan, are listed.

Thomas Kingston Sullivan, second son of John Sullivan, Bandon, tanner, deceased, and Mary Kingston, was over 16 years old when he applied for admission as an apprentice to an attorney in Easter Term 1832; he was educated in Bandon and the affidavit was made by his mother.

John Sullivan, first son of Thomas Kingston Sullivan, The Retreat,

Bandon, solicitor and Jane Trisilian; aged 24 on 20 April 1865; educated Trinity College Dublin; Michaelmas Term 1860. Middle Temple, Michaelmas Term 1863. Michaelmas Term 1865.

Josias Tresilian Sullivan, son of Thomas Kingston Sullivan, The Retreat, Bandon, solicitor; under 17 years old when he applied in Trinity Term 1861; the affidavit was made by his father.

John Sullivan of Bandon, Thomas Kingston Sullivan's father, who was deceased by 1832, had been a tanner (information required for Thomas' petition to be taken on as an apprentice), not a trade or business associated with the established landed gentry class. How had Thomas Kingston Sullivan acquired such a large acreage of land by 1876? There is plenty of scope for further research.

7 Wills and Testamentary Records

It is not a simple nor is it an easy task to present the background to testamentary records in Ireland, nor is the procedure and method of searching for a will straightforward. Two dissimilar testamentary systems operated in Ireland – ecclesiastical before 1858 and civil from 1858 forward. But most importantly and devastatingly, with the destruction during the Civil War of the Public Record Office in 1922, the vast majority of all the records, including testamentary, were destroyed.

First of all, let us take a look at the historical background to the administration of testamentary affairs in Ireland, and at the reason why it is that we usually have to resort to a will abstract, a will substitute or even an index entry, in place of an original will, when researching our family history.

WILLS

Wills are formal documents whereby a person leaves instructions as to how her or his property and possessions should be disbursed after death. Wills can contain much valuable genealogical information and can also give us an insight into the social and economic background to our ancestor's family and period, and possibly to his or her extended family. However, making a will was not obligatory.

For a will to take effect, a grant of probate has to be made by the court; this legalises the will and empowers the executors to administer the estate. If a person dies without leaving a will, letters of administration of the estate can be granted to an administrator (usually the next-of-kin), who enters into a monetary bond, guaranteeing that the estate will be administered properly.

The minimum information, contained in a will, for which a grant of probate would be made, would be as follows:

- Name and address of the testator (the person making the will)
- Name(s) of the beneficiaries (the person(s) to whom a bequest is made) and probably their relationship to the testator
- Name(s) of the executor(s) (the person(s) appointed by the testator to give effect to the will after his or her death)
- Names of the witnesses to the testator's signature (up to the early 1800s witnesses were often related to the testator)
- the date the will was signed
- *the date the will was proved by the court
- *the certified value of the 'estate' (the effects or belongings of the testator)
- *The name and address of the person(s) to whom probate was granted

* separate documents which should be attached to a probated will

Who Made a Will?

Generally speaking, up to the end of the 19th century, those who did leave a will were a minority of the population, and most of that minority were male. These men were propertied or prominent members of society, or substantive farmers, merchants or traders; or members of the professions. Only a small number of women left a will: widows and unmarried spinsters had a certain amount of discretion in the disposal of property but married women had no property rights at all.

Prior to the beginning of the 20th century, it was not usual for the small tenant farmer, cottier or labourer (from whom many of us are descended) to leave a will. However, the Land Purchase Acts of the end of the 19th and beginning of the 20th centuries enabled the small tenant farmer to purchase his holding and together with economic and educational opportunities opening up for some sections of the population, people from a broader social base were leaving wills.

Testamentary Jurisdiction

The administrative history of testamentary affairs in Ireland can be divided into two periods: pre-1858, with testamentary affairs under the jurisdiction of the ecclesiastical courts which, from 1536, meant the episcopal diocesan courts of the Established or Anglican Church; and from 1858 when the state abolished the ecclesiastical courts and established the Probate Court, consisting of a Principal Registry and eleven District Registries to cover the entire country.

From 1858 Forward

From 1858 the administration of testamentary affairs is straightforward and the relevant indexes and calendars can be easily identified; thus, we shall approach the modern period first.

The Court of Probate and Letters of Administration Act (Ireland), 1857, abolished the ecclesiastical courts and transferred testamentary jurisdiction for the whole of Ireland to a newly created civil court. The Probate Court consisted of a Principal Registry and 11 District Registries. The Principal Registry, located in Dublin, took over the responsibilities and powers of the Prerogative Court (see Pre-1858, following) as well as serving the large catchment areas of Cos. Dublin, Meath, Kildare, part of Offaly (then King's Co.) and Wicklow. The rest of the country is served by 11 District Registries, namely: Armagh, Ballina, Belfast, Cavan, Cork, Kilkenny, Limerick, Londonderry, Mullingar, Tuam and Waterford.

The Principal Registry and each District Registry made transcripts of the wills proved, and of the letters of administration granted, through their respective Registries.

With the establishment, in 1867, of the Public Record Office (now the National Archives), all original wills and testamentary records were to be deposited in the PRO after a time-lapse of 20 years. The PRO also held the (transcript) Will and Grant Books of the Principal Registry, but the District Registries retained their own respective transcript books. These transcript volumes are now deposited in the National Archives. However, it is worth noting that some of the District Registry transcript books are incomplete or contain gaps.

Since its inception in 1858 the Probate Court (the Principal and District Registries) has indexed and published annual calendars of all testamentary records processed through the Court. These annual 'Calendars of Wills and Administrations', which are in alphabetical order, contain a complete record from 1858 and cover all Ireland up to 1917 and from 1918 for what is now the Republic of Ireland. Each entry in an annual Calendar of Wills and Administrations includes the name, address and occupation of the deceased; the date and place of death; to whom probate or administration was granted (with the relationship to the deceased very often stated); at what Registry probate or administration was granted; and the net value of the effects or estate. The Calendars are held at the National Archives as is a composite index to the Calendars for the years 1858–1877 (only).

The Calendars of Northern Ireland Wills and Administrations (from 1918) are held in the Public Record Office of Northern Ireland (PRONI) where there is also a set of the Calendars for the whole of Ireland up to 1917.

PRONI also holds:

- original Wills and Grants of Administration, which had been held in the Belfast, Londonderry and Armagh Registries and were not sent to the PRO before 1922;

- Will books for the District Registries of Armagh, Belfast and Londonderry from 1858 onwards;
- the Grant Books from the Registries of Armagh, Belfast and Londonderry from 1886 onwards; (the Armagh and Belfast – *not* Londonderry – Grant Books from 1858 to 1885 are held in the National Archives; see below).

Pre-1858

From 1536 all testamentary affairs came under the jurisdiction of ecclesiastical courts of the bishops of the Established (Protestant) Church. Each diocese had a Consistorial or Diocesan Court through which the will of the deceased was proved and probate granted or, if the person died intestate, letters of administration could be granted. (The granting of marriage licences was also the responsibility of the ecclesiastical courts; see Chapter 4.)

If the deceased had property, valued over £5, in a second diocese, the will had to be proved, or letters of administration granted, through the Prerogative Court.

The Prerogative Court was the supreme court in ecclesiastical and testamentary affairs in Ireland and was under the jurisdiction of the Archbishop of Armagh. From 1644 the archbishop was empowered to appoint a judge to act on his behalf. However, the court did not have a permanent abode, which meant that the records were not necessarily kept in the one place, and this in turn led to the mislaying and loss of documents. In 1816 the Court was allocated a permanent building at the King's Inns, Dublin.

If the deceased left property in a second diocese and if the two dioceses were combined under one bishop, (such as, the combined dioceses of Cork and Ross; Limerick, Ardfert and Aghadoe; Cashel and Emly, etc.), probate of the will or administration of the estate would be granted through the relevant Consistorial (Diocesan) Court and not through the Prerogative Court.

The Prerogative Court of the Archbishop of Canterbury (England) was superior to the Prerogative Court of the Archbishop of Armagh. If the deceased had property in England the will would be proved, or letters of administration granted, in the Prerogative Court of Canterbury and a copy of the will would be resealed in the Prerogative Court of Armagh.

Indexes to pre-1858 testamentary records

With the establishment of the PRO in 1867 the testamentary records of the Consistorial and Prerogative Courts were deemed to be public records and were gathered and deposited in the PRO. During the course of the gathering in of these records, it became apparent that the records of the Consistorial Courts and those of the Prerogative Court were far from being complete: with regard to the Consistorial Courts documents were found to be very sparse prior to the 1780s and, as already noted, the records of the Prerogative Court were also incomplete.

With the testamentary records lodged with the PRO, their transcription into books was undertaken – Prerogative Will Books, Consistorial (or Diocesan) Will Books and Grant of Administration Bond Books. Separate alphabetical indexes to these individual Consistorial Books were then compiled, such as Index to Cashel and Emly Wills 1616–1858, Index to Cork and Ross Wills 1548–1858, Index to Waterford and Lismore Wills 1648–1858 and Index to Ardagh Administration Bonds; as well as Indexes to Marriage Licence Bonds, such as the Index to Raphoe Marriage Licence Bonds, etc.

The Prerogative Will Books were indexed in two parts: the first up to 1810; and the second from 1811 to 1857. Wills and grants of administration proved at the Prerogative Court were usually the wills of the wealthier sections of the population or of those whose residences or business concerns straddled more than one diocese.

Many of these original indexes were published, such as Indexes to the Dublin Grant Book (which also includes marriage licence bonds) 1270–1800; 1800–1858 (*Appendix to Deputy Keeper of Public Records of Ireland Reports*, No. 26 and 30); and *Index to Prerogative Wills of Ireland 1536–1810* (ed. Vicars, Dublin 1897).

DESTRUCTION OF ORIGINAL TESTAMENTARY MATERIAL AND THE AFTERMATH

The Four Courts complex, within which the PRO was located, is situated on the immediate north-west side of the River Liffey in Dublin City. In June 1922, during the Civil War, the buildings were destroyed and with them the vast majority of the records deposited in the PRO, including:

- Pre-1858: all original wills of the Consistorial and Prerogative Courts, except for one Consistorial will and eleven Prerogative wills;
- Pre-1858: practically all the Will and Grant Bond Books of the Consistorial and Prerogative Courts;
- All original wills and grants of the Principal and District Registries from 1858 up 1903/1900;
- From 1858, most of the Will and Grant Books of the Principal Registry.

Following the devastation and destruction of so much in 1922, the PRO (now the National Archives) set about replacing, with substitutes, as many as possible of the lost records. Copies of wills, will abstracts and transcripts were sought from, and given by, individuals and legal firms; and notes from research carried out by historians and genealogists at the PRO prior to 1922 were donated or acquired. For example, in 1810 Sir William Betham (1779–1853), had been commissioned by the Irish Record Commissioners to locate and identify the Prerogative Wills of Ireland and to superintend the compilation of an alphabetical index to the testators of these wills. While this work was in progress, Betham personally abstracted genealogical information from a large proportion of the pre-1800 Prerogative wills and from about 5000 pre-1802 Prerogative grants of administration. He subsequently compiled sketch pedigrees from these notes. The original note books were acquired by the PRO. Betham's sketch will pedigree volumes are held by the Genealogical Office and copies are held by PRONI. Gertrude Thrift (1872–1951), a professional genealogist who carried out research at the PRO prior to 1922; Philip Crossle (1875–1953); Ignatius Jennings (d. 1928); Tennison Groves (1863–1938) and Edmund Walsh Kelly (1857–1940) are some of the genealogists and historians whose notebooks and testamentary research materials were acquired by the then PRO and which help to alleviate the great loss of 1922.

Searching for Surviving Testamentary Material

The functions of the PRO (established in 1867) and those of the State Paper Office (established in 1702) were incorporated in new legislation – The National Archives Act, 1986, which was enacted in 1988.

In 1990 the National Archives (formerly the Public Record Office) transferred from the Four Courts complex to premises south-west of the city centre at Bishop Street, Dublin 8. The testamentary collection is constantly being added to. The National Archives probably will be your first and principal port-of-call when looking for a will. It holds the largest collection of original wills and will substitutes, such as transcripts, abstracts and manuscript indexes. It also displays on open shelves, published volumes of testamentary indexes and abstracts held in other repositories. Among the testamentary card indexes available in the Reading Room is the alphabetical Card Index to Testamentary Records. This card index lists surviving original pre- and post-1858 wills and certified copies, as well as the wills included in the surviving Will Books of the Principal Registry.

The Public Record Office of Northern Ireland also holds an extensive collection of testamentary records with particular relevance to the nine counties of the province of Ulster and these are listed on card index.

From 1858 Forward Search

As already indicated, a Calendar of Wills and Administration entry includes:

- the name, address and occupation of the deceased;
- the date and place of death;
- the name/s and address/es of the person/s to whom probate, or, administration, was granted;
- often stated is the relationship of the latter to the deceased;
- the date of probate;
- at what registry probate or administration was granted;
- and the net value of the estate.

The Calendars are intact from 1858, the year of inception; for the initial few years wills and administrations are calendared in separate volumes; and remember, there is a composite index to the calendars for the years 1858–1877 (only).

The following are the post-1857 testamentary records held at the

National Archives:

- surviving and incomplete Will books of the Principal Registry, such as Will Book G–M for the year 1874; A–Z for the year 1878; G–M for 1891; and A–F for 1896 (consult Card Index to Testamentary Records);
- the Will Books of the District Registries of Ballina, Cavan, Cork, Kilkenny, Limerick, Mullingar, Tuam and Waterford (indexed in the annual Calendar). Although books survive for each Registry, some are not continuous and thus do not contain copies of all the wills processed through the particular Registry;
- original Wills and Administrations proved at the Principal Registry from 1904 onwards (indexed in the annual Calendar);
- 1878, 1883, 1891 and 1893 surviving Grant Books for the Principal Registry;
- most of the Grant Books from 1858 for the District Registries;
- Grant Books for Armagh and Belfast Registries up to 1885; those thereafter are in PRONI;
- Original Wills and Administrations proved at most of the District Registries from the year 1900 onwards (indexed in the annual Calendar);

The procedure to follow, when searching for a Will or Grant of Administration, after the year 1857 is:

- Examine the annual alphabetical Calendar of Wills and Administrations for the specific year; for a number of years; or in a blanket search, depending on the information you have regarding the approximate date of death. (Remember, there is a consolidated index for the years 1858 to 1877).

- If you identify your ancestor's entry in the Calendar before 1900, and if the will was proved at a District Registry (for example, at the District Registry of Cavan or Waterford), complete an Order Document with the name of the District Registry and the date of probate to retrieve the specific Will Book.
- If the will was processed through a District Registry after 1900, you can call up the original will, grant of probate and schedule of assets;
- If the will was processed through the Principal Registry before 1904, check the alphabetical Card Index to Testamentary Records. If it is not listed it means that the National Archives does not hold a copy.
- If the will was processed through the Principal Registry from 1904, you can call up the original will, grant of probate and schedule of assets.

Remember, no will would have been processed if the deceased died intestate. If letters of administration (of the estate of the deceased) were sought and granted, your search will be for the Grant of Administration. Each entry in the Calendar states whether it was a will that was probated or whether letters of administration were granted.

ALLOW STAFF ENOUGH TIME

To call up an original will or a certified copy, the Reading Room staff needs at least one day's notice, as they are held off-site. However, Will and Grant of Administration Books are accessible on receipt of the Order Document.

Pre-1858 Search

As already indicated, the National Archives is the largest holder of testamentary records and indexes in Ireland. Many printed indexes, abstracts and catalogues of wills lodged in other repositories or libraries are available on the open shelves in the Reading Room. This can allow you to carry out quite a far-ranging search while in the one repository.

Before looking for a will, will transcript or abstract, you will need, first of all, to establish whether there was a will or intestacy (grant of administration). At this stage of your research you probably will have some understanding as to your ancestors' material or social background which, in turn, should allow you to assess what of the following sources may be of assistance.

Your first step in your research in the National Archives is to examine the Indexes to Prerogative and Consistorial Wills and Grants. Listed here are most of the testamentary and associated indexes available for consultation at the National Archives:

- Index to the Prerogative Wills of Ireland, 1536–1810; 1811–1858. The first part of this index was published and is also available on the open shelves: *Index to the Prerogative Wills of Ireland, 1536–1810*, ed. Vicars (Dublin 1897);
- Index to Prerogative Grants 1811–1858. This index is laid out in chronological order under the initial letter of the alphabet. [NB: there is an annotated version of this index: part 1, covering the period 1811–1834, lists the year and whether the grant involved a will or intestacy; part 2, covering the years 1835–1858, includes the date of death (Ref: 999/611).]
- The Indexes to the Wills of the Consistorial Courts. Virtually all of these indexes survive, although some are in a fragile condition. The

indexes list, in alphabetical order, the testator's name, address, occupation (sometimes) and the year in which probate was granted; they are available on the open shelves. Also, many have been published. However, there are two separate Diocesan Will Indexes, which, if required, need to be called up. The first, Index to Meath Diocesan Wills 1635–1838 (Ref: T/7431), was compiled by Betham but is held separately from the notebooks. The second, Ferns Wills Reconstruction Index 1800-1857 was compiled by Ian Cantwell (Ref: 999/493).

- The Indexes to the Administrations Bonds of the Consistorial Courts. These are indexed in chronological order under the initial letter of the alphabet (not in strict alphabetical order) and contain the name and address of the deceased, sometimes the occupation, and the year in which the bond was made (many have been published).

Published Volumes of Testamentary Indexes

Prior to the destruction of the Public Records in 1922, some testamentary indexes were already in print:

- Vicars' *Index to the Prerogative Wills of Ireland 1536-1810.*
- 'Index of Dublin Diocesan Will and Grant Books to 1800' (includes MLBs), (*Appendix to the 26th Report of the Deputy Keeper of the Public Records*, Dublin 1895).
- 'Index of Dublin Diocesan Will and Grant Books, 1800–1858' (includes MLBs), (*Appendix to the 30th Report of the Deputy Keeper of the Public Records*, Dublin 1899).
- Five volumes of Irish Will Indexes, incorporating 15 Dioceses, were published by Phillimore & Co., London, between 1909 and 1921; unfortunately, the cut-off year for the majority of these indexes was

1800 rather than 1858: Dioceses of Ossory, 1536–1800; Ferns, 1601–1800; Leighlin, 1652–1800; Kildare, 1661–1800; Cork and Ross, 1548–1800; Cloyne, 1621–1800, Cashel and Emly, 1618–1800; Waterford and Lismore, 1645–1800; Killaloe and Kilfenora, 1653–1800; Limerick, 1615–1800; Ardfert and Aghadoe, 1690–1800 (see second entry in the list following); Dromore, 1678–1800; Peculiar of Newry and Mourne, 1727–1858; Derry, 1615–1858; Rahpoe, 1684–1858.

- The Index of Kildare Consistorial Wills 1661–1858 and Index of Kildare Consistorial Administration Bonds 1770–1848 were published in the *Journal of the Kildare Archaeological Society* (1905 and 1907).
- In more recent times Indexes were published by *The Irish Ancestor*, (1969–1986), and the 15 volumes of Casey's *O'Kief, Coshe Mang, etc.* (1962–65) (see Glossary) include testamentary indexes and abstracts, mainly pertaining to Cos. Cork and Kerry.

A select list of some other testamentary index publications:

- Ardagh 1695–1857 (Suppl. *Irish Ancestor*, Dublin 1971);
- Ardfert and Aghadoe 1690–1858 (Vol. 5, *O'Kief, Coshe Mang, etc.*, ed. Casey, 1962);
- Clonfert Wills 1663–1857; Clonfert Administrations Bonds; (Suppl. *Irish Ancestor*, Dublin 1970);
- Cloyne 1547–1628; 1621–1858 (Vol. 8, *O'Kief, Coshe Mang, etc.*, Casey, 1968);
- Cork and Ross 1548–1858 (Vol. 6, *O'Kief, Coshe Mang, etc.*, Casey, 1963);
- Leighlin Administrations (Suppl. *Irish Ancestor*, 1972).

At this juncture, it is worth highlighting three separate pre-1858 testamentary record collections held in the National Archives, bearing in mind that they are not complete. The first is Betham's pre-1800 Prerogative Will and Grant notebooks. The pre-1800 will abstracts can be identified by consulting Vicars' *Index to the Prerogative Wills of Ireland 1536–1810* (Betham's Prerogative Will and Grant of Administration Pedigree Sketch Books are held by the Genealogical Office). The second is Indexes to Irish Will Registers and Irish Administration Registers 1828–1879. These indexes and registers were once held by the Commissioners of Inland Revenue in London. The yearly indexes list the name and address of the testator and that of the executor, or in the case of a grant the name and address of the deceased together with the name and address of the administrator. The indexes covering the years 1840–1857 are more detailed. (NB: These will and grants emanate from the Prerogative and Consistorial Courts of pre-1858 as well as from the Principal and District Registries of the Probate Court of 1858 onwards. The registers themselves are extant for the years 1828–1839 and consist of virtually full transcripts.)

Finally, there are the surviving Prerogative and Consistorial Court Will and Grant of Administration Books:

- Will Books for the Diocese of Down 1850–58;
- Will Book for the Diocese of Connor 1818–1820; 1853–58;
- Grant Book for the Diocese of Cashel 1840–45;
- Grant Book for the Diocese of Derry and Raphoe 1812–1821;
- Grant Book for the Diocese of Ossory 1848–1858
- Prerogative Will Book: 1664–1684; 1706–1708 (A–W); 1726–1728 (A–W); 1728–1729 (A–W); 1777 (A–L); 1813 (K–Z); 1834 (A–E);

- Prerogative Administration: Grant Book: 1684–1688; 1748–1751; 1839; Day Books, 1784–1788.

- Prerogative Administration Day Books: 1784–1788

If you identify a testamentary reference which interests you consult the Card Index to Testamentary Records at the National Archives; this card index, which has been referred to earlier in the chapter, is arranged in alphabetical order by surname, and is continuously being added to. It lists: (a) the surviving Prerogative and Consistorial Wills and Marriage Licence Grants (pre-1858); (b) the surviving Prerogative and Consistorial Will transcripts; (c) copies of wills deposited from solicitors' offices, businesses, etc.; and (d) miscellaneous wills, will abstracts, and certified copies. The card index does not list the testamentary abstracts made by Betham, Crosslé, Jennings, Thrift, etc.(see the list following), nor does it include testamentary material held outside the National Archives.

The finding aid to the Betham notebooks is listed as 'Betham and Thrift Abstracts' and is on the open shelves. Other Betham testamentary abstracts include: Kildare Wills 1661–1826; Dublin Marriage Licence Bonds 1638–1823 (surnames starting with the initials F–Y are listed only up to 1814); and Prerogative Marriage Licence Bonds 1629–1801.

The following are some further indexes to source material at the National Archives:

- Card Index to Crosslé will abstracts (mainly 17th and 18th centuries will abstracts, with an emphasis on material from north-west Ireland);

- Card Index to Jennings will abstracts (mainly Waterford wills and administrations);

- Card Index to Charitable Donations and Bequests, 1800–1858;

consist of an index to abstracts of wills from Charitable Donations and Bequests will extract books, and include the name of the testator (who bequeathed the money for charitable purposes), the name of the executor and the date of probate.

INDEXES AT THE NATIONAL ARCHIVES

There are also Indexes to Prerogative and Consistorial Marriage Licence Bonds at the National Archives as well as some abstracts from marriage licence bonds made by Betham. Similar to Will and Administration Indexes and abstracts, some of the Indexes to Marriage Licence Bonds and some abstracts from Consistorial Marriage Licence Bonds have been published. For example, abstracts from marriage licences of the Diocese of Ossory (virtually coterminous with Co. Kilkenny), 1739–1804 are published in *The Irish Genealogist* (1990); and Raphoe Marriage Licence Bonds, 1710–1755 and 1817–1830 are published as a supplement to the *Irish Ancestor*, 1969. While on the subject of marriage licences, the Genealogical Office also holds manuscript copies of Prerogative Marriage Licences, 1630–1830 (G.O. MS. 605–607), and Dublin Consistorial Marriage Licences (G.O. MS. 473–475).

We have already mentioned that the National Archives has, on the open shelves, several published indexes and reference books to testamentary material deposited in other repositories. For easy reference we shall list some of these volumes:

- *Registry of Deeds: Abstracts of Wills*, Vol. 1, 1708–1745 (ed. Eustace, Dublin 1956); Vol. 2, 1746–1785 (ed. Eustace, Dublin 1954); Vol. 3, 1785–1832 (ed. Ellis & Eustace, 1984). (See p. 175, The

Registry of Deeds.) Over two thousand Wills were registered at the Registry of Deeds.

- *Index of Will Abstracts in the Genealogical Office, Dublin* (P. Beryl Eustace, *Analecta Hibernica*, No. 17, Dublin, 1949). The Genealogical Office holds a substantial collection of mainly pre-1800 will abstracts. However, this Index does not list the Betham Will Sketch Pedigrees, which can be identified from Vicars' *Index to Prerogative Wills*. The G.O. typescript of the index contains abstracts not included in the printed one.
- *Guide to Irish Quaker Records 1654–1860* (ed. Goodbody, Dublin 1967) and *Quaker Records Dublin, Abstracts of Wills* (ed. Goodbody, Dublin 1957). As already mentioned in Chapter 4, members of the Society of Friends were meticulous when it came to recording births, marriages and deaths and to drawing up wills.
- *A Guide to Copies and Abstracts of Irish Wills*, Vol. 1 (ed. Wallace Clare, Dublin; reprint Baltimore, USA, 1972). This volume contains: (a) a list of copies and abstracts of Irish wills deposited in the library of the Society of Genealogists, London, and indexed by Rev. Wallace Clare in 1929 (most of the collection being abstracts presented by W. H. Welply, Belfast); (b) a list, made by Rev. Wallace Clare in 1929, of the copies of wills contained in the Prerogative Will Books, which were salved from the destruction of the PRO in 1922; (the references to these wills are also listed in the Card Index to Testamentary Records; see p. 171); (c) a list of a few early original wills deposited in England; (d) a list of copies and abstracts of wills contained in some archaeological and genealogical journals.
- *O'Kief, Coshe Mang, Slieve Lougher & Upper Blackwater* (15 vols., ed. Casey, Baltimore, USA 1961–67). These include testamentary

indexes and abstracts mainly, but not exclusively, covering the Dioceses of Cloyne, Cork and Ross. and Ardfert.

OTHER TESTAMENTARY ARCHIVES

Testamentary records are held in repositories and libraries other than the National Archives; what follows are the names of the principal repositories together with a sample of their respective testamentary records. The Public Record Office of Northern Ireland (PRONI) has already been referred to as an important repository for wills and will substitutes.

The Genealogical Office

The Genealogical Office has a substantial collection of mainly pre-1800 will abstracts, most of which are listed in G.O. Ms. 429, 'Index of the Will Abstracts in the Genealogical Office, Dublin' (presented by P. B. Eustace) was published in *Analecta Hibernica*, No. 17 (1949); this index does not list Betham's Will Pedigree series nor Betham's Abstracts from the Prerogative Administrations Intestate. (Vicars' *Index to the Prerogative Wills of Ireland, 1536–1810* fulfills the role of index to Betham's pre-1800 Will Abstracts.)

The National Library of Ireland

The National Library of Ireland has a wide-ranging collection of manuscript wills and will abstracts as well as microfilm copies of will collections from other repositories. However, they are not indexed as a separate unit or collection, so to retrieve a specific testamentary record or abstract you need to know what to look for in the catalogues.

The Library holds a card index of wills from the Irish Land Commission Records (mainly landlords' wills), and there are over 10,000 wills among these records, which accumulated as the result of the Land Purchase Acts of 1881–1909. However, access to these wills is restricted (see Chapter 6).

The Library also has a microfilm copy of The Carrigan Collection, 167 volumes of historical and genealogical material collected by Canon Carrigan for his History and Antiquities of the Diocese of Ossory, published 1905, the original of which is in St. Kieran's College, Kilkenny. The Collection contains over 900 17th- and 18th-century wills, transcribed before the originals were destroyed in 1922. An index to these wills was published in *The Irish Genealogist* (Vol. 4, No. 3, 1970). Volume 5 (1972) of the same journal contains abstracts of about 200 Ossory Diocesan Administrations, dating from 1660 to 1803, of which under 30 pertain to the Diocese of Leighlin from 1702 to 1802.

The Lane-Poole papers contain will abstracts, mainly of the 17th and 18th centuries and mainly covering Co. Wicklow. These were published in volume 8, number 4 (1993) of *The Irish Genealogist.*

The Registry of Deeds

Over 2000 wills were registered in the Registry of Deeds between the year of its establishment, 1708, and 1832. Abstracts of these wills were published in three volumes by the Irish Manuscripts Commission (refer to p. 131, Registry of Deeds).

The Royal Irish Academy

The RIA does not have a separate list or index of will abstracts. It holds some early 17th- and 18th-century wills, though its collection is not extensive. The Upton Papers, which mainly relate to Cos. Cavan, Longford and Westmeath, are available on microfilm at the National Library; the Mac Swiney Papers (Cos. Cork and Kerry); and Westropp volumes (Co. Clare and Limerick) form the basis of the Academy's testamentary abstracts.

Libraries

The Library of Trinity College, Dublin, which has a valuable collection of early manuscript wills, also holds the Stewart-Kennedy Notebooks. These contain some 500 17th- to 19th-century will abstracts pertaining mainly to families in the Dioceses of Down and Connor; PRONI has a copy and the National Library has a microfilm copy.

The Representative Church Body Library has a substantial collection of will abstracts made by W. H. Welply, which includes 1500 wills and about 100 administrations. An index to the Welply Will Abstracts in the RCBL was printed in volume 7, nos 3 and 4 of *The Irish Genealogist* (1988–89).

The Library of the Society of Friends (Quakers) holds abstracts of over 250 wills. They are listed in *The Guide to Irish Quaker Records 1654–1860* (ed. Goodbody, Dublin 1967) and in *Quaker Records Dublin, Abstracts of Wills* (ed. Goodbody, Dublin 1957). A small number, from Lisburn, Northern Ireland, were published in volume 2 of *The Irish Genealogist* (1950).

Armagh Library houses the Johnson collection of will abstracts.

The Irish Genealogical Research Society, London has an extensive library of printed volumes. The Society has a card index of will abstracts and copies held in the library. The journal of the Society, *The Irish Genealogist* (1937 forward), is a useful source to consult. Also held in the library are Irish Wills from the Swanzy Collection, which comprises 511 wills in all: 132 Diocesan and 379 Prerogative Wills. An Index of Persons, containing full names of all those named in the will abstracts, has been compiled by the Society's member Peter Manning; it is available for consultation and can also be purchased.

The Society of Genealogists, London, has a substantial collection of printed volumes of Irish Testamentary indexes and abstracts. The Society also has a microfilm copy of Betham's, Will Abstracts,

Administrations, and Sketch Pedigrees. The Rosbottom Collection consists of 4000 Irish will abstracts.

Publications

Wills, will abstracts and indexes are also to be found in printed family histories, local histories and printed calendars of family collections, such as The Kenmare Manuscripts (Dublin 1942), The Inchiquin Manuscripts (Dublin 1961) and the Calendar of Ormond Deeds (Dublin 1934–1970). Journals, such as the *Journal of the County Kildare Archaeological Society, Journal of the Cork Historical and Archaeological Society, Journal of the North Munster Archaeological Society, Journal of the Royal Society of Antiquaries of Ireland,* etc. are also worth remembering as useful sources.

PRACTISING RESEARCH TECHNIQUES

Edward Forbes, the father of Anne Forbes who was the wife of Jeremiah Kehilly, died c. 1860s ('cancelled' or revision books, see p. 124). The composite *Index to the Calendars of Wills and Administrations 1858–1877* does not include his name nor do the annual Calendars from 1878 to 1885 record his will or administration entry, which would indicate that no will was sent for probate, nor were letters of administration sought (not an unusual occurrence). Edward was a small tenant farmer with a lease on some 46 acres of land, which was transferred to his wife Honora around 1863 ('cancelled' or revision books); he was of that majority section of the population who did not leave a will.

Neither was a will or letters of administration recorded for Honora Forbes, whose name was replaced in 1884 by that of her son John Forbes ('cancelled' or revision book).

However, Jeremiah Kehilly, Anne's husband, who died on 20 July 1906, did leave a will, probate of which was granted to his widow at the District Registry of Cork on 20 July 1906. His original will, grant of probate and schedule of assets, which had not been transferred to the then PRO prior to 1922, are intact and deposited at the National Archives.

Sir William Robert Wills Wilde, surgeon and antiquarian and father of Oscar Wilde, died 19 April 1876. The Calendar entry of his Will is quite informative. The probate was granted at the Principal Registry and we know that the Will Book of the Principal Registry, in which a copy was made, was destroyed in 1922. The Card Index to Testamentary Records at the National Archives does not include a reference to the will, which indicates that the original probated will did not survive the destruction of the Public Record Office in 1922 and that no substitute has been lodged at the National Archives.

8 Trades and Professions

There are many occupations in which your ancestors might have been involved. The vast majority of people in rural areas were employed in agriculture, whether as farmers or labourers. In rural Ulster, where the linen industry was strong, many were engaged in weaving or in related work such as flaxdressing, spinning, winding and warping. There are no occupational records concerning such work. Of the many other forms of employment which existed, few have left records which would throw light on family history and fewer still have left easily accessible records. This said, there are occupations for which the records are not only accessible but also informative. The following are the main areas for which worthwhile records exist.

ARMY AND MILITIA

The British Army

A very large percentage of the officers and private soldiers in the British Army were Irish. In the 19th century the army was one of the few options open to those for whom there was no work on the land or labouring in the towns. Army records are an invaluable source of information, particularly concerning the rank and file. These records are not held in Ireland, but in the Public Record Office at Kew in England. They are so vast that they would be the subject of a book in themselves. In fact, many books have been written on them and it would be worth your while reading the PRO Readers' Guide No. 2, *Army Records for Family Historians* by Simon Fowler, before tackling a search. A shorter introduction is provided in 'Records of the Irish in the British Army' by Stella Colwell in *Aspects of Irish Genealogy*, published by the First Irish Genealogical Congress.

In relation to commissioned officers, it is possible to trace their careers through the *Army List*, which has been published regularly since 1754. The annual *List* was replaced in 1879 by a quarterly, and there was a separate monthly one from 1798. In addition, the unofficial *Hart's Army List* was published from 1839 to 1915 and contained notes on officers' war service. Of course, you could also go through the service records at Kew. While this would be time consuming, the records would give a more complete picture of your ancestor's career.

For soldiers other than commissioned officers there is no choice but to check the service records. It is necessary to know the regiment in which your ancestor served. This is particularly important if he was discharged to pension in or before 1872 because the Soldiers' Documents (Attestation and Discharge Papers) are arranged by regiment up to that point. Of course, he might not have spent his entire service in one regiment but the minimum of information needed in order to trace him would be the name of the regiment he was in at a particular date.

Once you know the regiment he was in when he was pensioned, it is possible to identify him in the Soldiers' Documents (in WO 97), which will give his birthplace, age at enlistment and former occupation, service record and reason for discharge. If he was not pensioned, knowing the regiment he was in at a particular date during his service will make it possible to trace him through the quarterly Pay Lists (in WO 10–16). This would be time-consuming but rewarding. It would allow you to trace back to his enlistment, follow his movements if he changed regiments, and trace forward to his discharge or death. It would also establish his whereabouts throughout his career, helping you to track down birth records for his children.

The First World War Soldiers' Papers (in WO 364) concern those who were discharged at any point between 1914 and 1920. While most of the original records of service were destroyed during Second World War bombing, the records in this class are from other depart-

> **IDENTIFYING THE REGIMENT**
>
> You will very often get the regiment on a soldier's civil marriage record and even sometimes on the church record of the marriage. It might also be given on the birth record of one of his children. If you know where he was stationed at a particular date you may be able to identify his regiment by checking the relevant monthly Army List or the monthly returns (in WO 17 and WO 73 at Kew), both of which state the location of each regiment or battalion.

ments. They are made available on over 4500 reels of microfilm, arranged in alphabetical order, and they may include attestation and discharge papers, or medical or active service records. There is a class list which indicates the sections of the alphabet covered by each reel.

As stated in Chapter 2, the General Register Office in Dublin has records of birth, death and marriage concerning Irish subjects serving in the Army overseas. The GRO has a separate index to the deaths of Irish soldiers who died in the Boer War. First World War death records are held at the General Register Office in London, but the GRO in Dublin has a copy of the index.

The Militia and Yeomanry

The Militia was a type of auxiliary army or defence force recruited on a county basis, but while on active service its county regiments served throughout the country. Though there had been militia forces in Ireland intermittently from the 17th century, the Irish Militia was established in 1793 and was on almost uninterrupted active service until 1816. It was an infantry force and enlistment was compulsory, based on a ballot (or drawing of lots) involving all the able-bodied men in the county. However, substitution was allowed where a selected man could find someone to take his place. As sufficient numbers volunteered for service in 1793, no ballot was necessary in most parts of the country.

Ballot lists are not known to have survived. However, Muster Books (of those enlisted) and Pay Lists, arranged by county, are held at Kew (WO 13/2574–3370). These merely name the officers and men serving during particular periods, but they are available from 1793 forward. If an individual enlisted, deserted, transferred to the Army or died in the period of the list, this may be noted against his name. The other records held at Kew are miscellaneous Militia Records in WO 68 and 79 and Militia Attestation Documents in WO 96. These attestations are recruitment records, but they date only from the second half of the 19th century. Though it was disembodied in 1816, the Militia was embodied again at various stages and in 1881 it became attached to the regular Army, forming the third or in some cases fourth battalions of the relevant county regiments. Sir Henry McAnally's *The Irish Militia 1793–1816* (Dublin 1949) provides an in-depth historical background.

The Irish Yeomanry was established by Act of Parliament in November 1796. It differed from the Militia in that it served at home, enlistment was not compulsory and, except in times of disturbance, it was on part-time service with the officers and men being paid for a duration of no more than two days a week. However, the sergeant and trumpeter or drummer in each corps was on full pay. There are Muster Books for this force at Kew (WO 13/4059–4159). They are arranged by county and then by corps. They name the men and state the dates of service. Unfortunately, they are available only from 1823 to 1834, when the force was discontinued.

The Irish Army

The records of the Irish Army are not yet open to public inspection. However, enquiries concerning general army matters may be made to the Military Archives, Cathal Brugha Barracks, Dublin 6. Veterans of the republican movement from about 1913 to 1921, including the 1916 Rising and the War of Independence were granted pensions or medals by the Irish government. Next of kin may apply to the Veterans Section, Department of Defence, Renmore, Galway, for information on them. Records of Irish Army officers up to the mid-1940s are held by the Military Archives and, again, next of kin may apply for information. With regard to other ranks, the next of kin may contact the Enlisted Personnel Section, Defence Force Headquarters, Park Gate, Dublin 8.

CITY AND TOWN MERCHANTS AND TRADERS

The most straightforward way of identifying someone who was in business in a city or a substantial town is through the various trade directories (see Chapter 9). With the early directories you can be sure only of finding the more prosperous business people but as you progress forward through the 19th century the coverage increases. The various publications collectively referred to as the *Dublin Directory* contain an alphabetical list of merchants and traders each year from the 1750s onwards. Other cities were covered only by spasmodic publications in the late 18th century and throughout most of the 19th. However, the *Belfast and Province of Ulster Directory* appeared frequently, though not annually, from the 1850s forward.

With regard to towns, the trade directories covering the entire country are *Pigot's*, 1820 and 1824, *Slater's*, 1846, 1856, 1870, 1881 and 1894, and *Kelly's*, 1905. Only the larger towns are covered by the early ones but by 1894 practically every village is included. Of course, directories merely identify the type of business your ancestors pursued as well as tying them to a particular date and possibly providing a street address. The only accessible records other than these which are likely to provide information on merchants or traders are those relating to guilds and freemen.

Trade Guilds

In cities and large corporate towns the right to conduct business or practise a trade was reserved to members of the various trade guilds. Admission to a guild could be obtained by serving an apprenticeship to a member, but members' sons could also be admitted by birthright. It was additionally required that the applicant be a freeman but this changed in time and often people were admitted to membership before becoming freemen.

In relation to Roman Catholics, it is important to note that during and following the Cromwellian period they were deprived of the freedom (and guild membership) of many towns. They were again excluded from the 1690s onwards, not by statute initially but by by-laws drawn up by the individual corporations. In the long run it proved impossible to completely exclude Catholics from trade, so a form of associate membership of guilds was devised, allowing them to conduct business as quarter-brothers (paying fees to the guild four times a year). Even after the franchise was restored to Catholics in 1793 many guilds refused to admit them as full members. Legislation in 1840 removed the political power of the guilds and they were abolished in 1846. By and large, records of such guilds have not survived but the *Directory of Historic Dublin Guilds*, edited by Mary Clark and Raymond Refaussé (Dublin 1993) indicates what is available for Dublin and where it can be found. In relation to other locations it can only be suggested that *Hayes Manuscripts* and *Hayes Periodicals* (see Glossary) should be consulted. In relation to trade organisations of more recent years, the *Select Guide to Trade Union Records in Dublin* by Sarah Ward-Perkins (Dublin 1996) would be a useful starting point, and its contents are not confined to unions operating within Dublin.

Freemen

Freemen were those within a city or corporate town with privileges such as the right to vote and exemption from certain taxes. The basic requirement for admission to the freedom of a city or town was to have served an apprenticeship under a member of one of the trade guilds. Other residents of standing whose occupations did not fall under this category could be admitted on payment of a fee. Freedom could be inherited, with admission by birth or through marriage. Occasionally it was extended to non-residents as a type of honour. The 1840 legislation extended the franchise to male householders with a £10 valuation; the entire system was abolished in 1918.

The register of freemen for the City of Dublin is extensive, beginning in 1468, though there is a gap from 1485 to 1575. It gives each person's name, occupation, date of admission and right of admission. In the case of those admitted by birth it is possible to hazard a guess at which of their predecessors in the register might have been their ancestor, though in most cases the father's name is given. Likewise, the wife's name is usually stated in cases of admission by marriage. The surviving records pertaining to freemen of Irish cities and towns are held in various repositories. A comprehensive survey of them, giving the relevant references, is to be found in 'Sources for Irish Freemen' by Mary Clark in *Aspects of Irish Genealogy*.

Civil Service

The Society of Genealogists in London hold the Evidences of Birth papers from the Civil Service Commission. These relate to people who applied for civil service appointments of all grades from the mid-19th century forward. They each had to produce affidavits or a certificate as evidence of their date of birth. The birth dates range from the late 18th century to the early 20th century and the applicants concerned were born in various parts of the world. A high proportion of them were Irish. There are many thousands of documents which are contained in over 200 boxes. These are currently being sorted into alphabetical order and indexed, so they are not as yet available for research. When the project is finished they will be microfilmed by the Mormon church. When they do become available they will prove an invaluable source.

CLERGY

Biographical details of clergy of the three main churches – Roman Catholic, Church of Ireland and Presbyterian – can be obtained without great difficulty. Some information on Methodist ministers is also available.

Roman Catholic

Throughout most of the 18th century the Penal Laws placed severe restrictions on Catholic worship. For that reason priests were educated in seminaries in Continental Europe. Legislation in 1782 removed various restrictions on Catholic clergy and allowed for Catholics to teach. This made way for the opening in October 1793 of Ireland's first Catholic college for higher studies, St Patrick's in Carlow. Two years later St Patrick's Seminary in Maynooth, Co.

A PRIEST IN THE FAMILY

While Catholic priests did not marry, their career records can help to tie other family information together. For example, if researching a priest who died in the late 19th or early 20th century, there would be a strong chance of finding an obituary and account of his funeral in a local newspaper (see Chapter 9). Such accounts often include lists of chief mourners, stating their relationship.

Kildare was established. While students continued to go to the Continent in the 19th century, the majority attended Maynooth or one of the many diocesan seminaries which developed. Religious orders also had their colleges.

The records of Irish seminaries are by no means complete and most have not yet become accessible to the public. However, some valuable material is available in printed form. *Carlow College 1793–1993* by John McEvoy (Carlow 1993) contains an alphabetical list of over 3000 ordained students giving place of origin, years attending Carlow, year of ordination and subsequent allocations. In some cases dates of birth and death are stated. There is also a list of over 300 members of the teaching staff giving similar details. *Maynooth Students and Ordinations Index 1795–1895*, edited by Patrick J. Hamell (Maynooth 1982), is less informative. It merely states the diocese of origin, date of matriculation and, where applicable, date of ordination. However, it lists over 9000 names. Strangely, its includes ordinations up to 1902. *Maynooth Students and Ordinations 1895–1984*, edited by Patrick J. Hamell (Maynooth 1984), is rather convoluted and only covers ordinations from 1903.

The Missionary College of All Hallows 1842–1891 by Kevin Condon, C.M., contains a fully indexed list of 2013 students who matriculated during the period in question. All Hallows was run by the Vincentian Order to train student priests for missions throughout the world. Each entry gives the parents' names, including the mother's maiden name, and their address, date of matriculation, age or date of birth, the mission for which the student was being prepared and his subsequent allocations. Many also state where he was previously educated. Not all of these young men were later ordained as it is noted that quite a number of them 'went home'.

The *Irish Catholic Directory* has been published annually since 1836. The early editions list the clergy by diocese, stating the parish in which each was ministering. They also contain one-line obituaries for priests (and sometimes religious sisters) who died during the previous year. Following a priest's career through the Directory can, therefore, help locate a full obituary in a local newspaper. Ordinations only appear from the late 19th century.

Church of Ireland

The records of Church of Ireland ministers are comprehensively dealt with by the Leslie Biographical Index, so-named after its originator, Rev. James B. Leslie. It is a typescript record held and regularly updated at the Representative Church Body Library in Dublin. It covers all known clergymen and refers to further reading in one of the various Succession Lists. These are chronological rolls of clergy arranged by parish within each diocese and they give much information on their background and career. They are also maintained in typescript at the RCB Library but Leslie published those for the dioceses of Ardfert and Aghadoe, Armagh (as well as a supplement), Clogher, Down (with Rev. H.B. Swanzy), Ferns, Ossory and Raphoe. Those for Connor were published by the Ulster Historical Foundation in 1993. Leslie did not repeat dioceses for which records had already been published. These are covered by W. Maziere Brady's *Clerical and Parochial Records of Cork, Cloyne and Ross* (1864), Rev. J.H. Cole's *Church and Parish Records of the United Diocese of Cork, Cloyne and Ross* (Cork 1903) and William H. Rennison's *Succession List of the Bishops and Clergy of the Dioceses of Waterford and Lismore* (1922).

Presbyterian

The Fasti of the Irish Presbyterian Church, 1613–1840, compiled by Rev. James McConnell and Rev. S.G. McConnell and edited by F.J. Paul and Rev. David Stewart (Belfast 1935), gives the biographical details of ministers of the main Presbyterian denomination, the

Synod of Ulster. It also contains a supplement listing 156 ministers who emigrated to America. In 1840 the Synod of Ulster united with the Secession Synod to become the General Assembly. *The Fasti of the General Assembly of the Presbyterian Church in Ireland*, compiled by John M. Barkley in three volumes (Belfast 1986–7), covers the clergy of the united church down to 1910.

Methodist

In relation to Wesleyan Methodist ministers and preachers, Rev. William Hill's *An Alphabetical Arrangement of all the Wesleyan Methodist Ministers, and Preachers on Trial, in connection with the British Conferences* (London 1885) gives the locations and corresponding dates for each individual throughout the early and mid-19th century. This may be checked at the Wesleyan Historical Society, Aldersgate House, University Road, Belfast. Brief notices of death for preachers are to be found in the *Minutes of Conference*. These are short annual reports dating from 1752 forward. They are bound into volumes, each with an index. The preachers are listed in the index under the heading 'died'. C.H. Crookshank's three volume *History of Methodism in Ireland* (Belfast 1885–6) also contains biographical material on preachers and other prominent Methodists up to 1859.

COASTGUARDS

The Coastguard was administered by various departments through the years. Consequently, there is no comprehensive index for those who served in it. However, all the available records are at the Public Record Office in Kew. Pensions paid to coastguards by the Admiralty in the years 1866–1926 are recorded in the Additional Pension Books (in ADM 23). Those paid by the Paymaster General, 1855–1935, are in Coastguard: Civil Pensions (in PMG 23). Regarding service records, it is necessary to know where an individual was stationed at a particular time in order to conduct a search.

Coastguard: Records of Service (in ADM 175) include records for stations in Ireland, 1816–1869, with gaps. The PRO's Records Information Sheet 8 covers the various Coastguard records.

LEGAL PROFESSION

Up to 1866, to join the legal profession, either as a barrister or an attorney (now called solicitor), it was necessary to gain admittance to the King's Inns Society. After that date the attorneys established the Incorporated Law Society of Ireland as their regulating body. Barristers practising in the Republic continue today under the authority of the King's Inns. According to the late P. Beryl Phair, almost all barristers were university graduates (see p. 203, University Students), while attorneys rarely were. From 1704 to 1792 Roman Catholics were precluded from entering the profession. They were still prevented from serving as judges until Catholic Emancipation in 1829.

Those admitted to the King's Inns as law students eventually became barristers, while those who were admitted as apprentices became attorneys. A law student had to submit a memorial giving various details, including his father's name, address and occupation, and usually his mother's maiden name. Later, to obtain his degree, he had to submit a second memorial giving, amongst other information, his age, along with a certificate proving that he had attended one of the English Inns of Court (Gray's Inn, Inner Temple, Lincoln's Inn or Middle Temple). The earliest of these admission papers now surviving date from 1723 and the collection is incomplete.

For admission as an apprentice to an attorney, an applicant had to make a petition stating the name, address and occupation of his father, and his mother's maiden name. He also had to produce an affidavit stating that he had attained the age of 16. Having served his apprenticeship, he had to enter into a bond on admission to the

King's Inns as an attorney. Papers relating to apprenticeship date from 1793, but many are missing. The available bonds are mainly for the period 1785–1804.

The relevant information from all surviving admission documents in the King's Inns relating to barristers and attorneys up to 1867 is published in the *King's Inns Admission Papers 1607–1867*, edited by Edward Keane, P. Beryl Phair and Thomas U. Sadleir (Dublin 1982). The additional information which is included, particularly on those admitted outside the periods of the surviving documents, is taken from a variety of manuscript sources. Similar publications are available for the four English Inns of Court referred to above. For those admitted to the profession in Ireland after this time, application would have to be made to the King's Inns Library, Henrietta Street, Dublin 1, or the Law Society of Ireland, Blackhall Place, Dublin 7.

For the later careers of both barristers and attorneys, the only straightforward sources are the lists of those practising in Dublin contained in the *Dublin Directory* (see p. 225, Trade Directories). These lists appear regularly from 1761. They give addresses, so it is quite easy to trace an individual forward. The lists of barristers include the date of being called to the Bar. From a later date judges are also listed in the Dublin Directory. However, *The Judges in Ireland* by F.E. Ball (London 1926), is the main source for them from earliest times to 1921.

MEDICAL PROFESSION

Medicine is a profession which evolved over the years until it reached its present form in the latter half of the 19th century. Before that it had a chequered history and for a long time there was only partial regulation of medical practice.

What is now the Royal College of Physicians of Ireland (RCPI), received its charter in 1667 and was re-incorporated in 1692 as the

King and Queen's College of Physicians in Ireland, named after William and Mary. Similar establishments existed in Edinburgh, Glasgow and London. Physicians were often university graduates. From 1576 Dublin surgeons were controlled by the Guild of Barber-Surgeons. Apothecaries were also included until they founded their own guild in 1747. By the mid-18th century surgeons had acquired more status, and in 1784 the Royal College of Surgeons in Ireland (RCSI) was established by charter. Again, there were similar institutions in Great Britain. In 1791 the Apothecaries' Hall was incorporated. It had its equivalent in the Society of Apothecaries in London. Many Irish medical men also received training in institutions on continental Europe.

By the 1840s there were seventeen institutions throughout the British Isles which had authority to confer degrees or licences to practise in the fields of medicine, surgery, pharmacy and midwifery. Thirteen of these were in Great Britain. These consisted of the English and Scottish universities, the colleges of physicians and surgeons in Edinburgh, Glasgow and London, and the Society of Apothecaries. The remaining four were all in Dublin – Dublin University (Trinity College – TCD), the King and Queen's College of Physicians (RCPI), the RCSI and the Apothecaries' Hall. As well as these, the Lying-in (now Rotunda) Hospital was authorised to certify practitioners in midwifery. There were many other colleges in which medical students received at least part of their education, such as the Royal Belfast Academical Institution and the Cork Medical Schools.

In the mid-19th century, a physician had to have a university degree (see p. 203, University Students) or a licence from one of the colleges of physicians, but many held both. A surgeon needed the qualification of one of the colleges of surgeons. That of the RCSI was a 'diploma'. An Irish apothecary had to obtain a licence from the

Apothecaries' Hall. Licentiates of the London Society of Apothecaries could not legally practise in Ireland, except in county infirmaries. An accoucheur (or practitioner in midwifery) had first to be a physician, surgeon or apothecary, before obtaining the additional qualification.

Regarding physicians, the RCPI has registers of fellows and members from the late 17th century but they are unindexed and give little information beyond a name and a date. There are early records of the Guild of Barber-Surgeons in the Manuscripts Department of Trinity College Library (Ms 1447), but they would not be worth pursuing unless you were fairly sure that an ancestor was a member. As both surgeons and apothecaries could become freemen, it would be much easier to begin such a search with the register of freemen for Dublin (see p. 183, City and Town Merchants and Traders).

A very useful source for early medical men is *Eighteenth Century Medics* by P.J. and R.V. Wallis (2nd enlarged edn 1988 Newcastle-Upon-Tyne). However, it is not easy to use, because of the abbreviated format in which its information is arranged. It is based on subscription lists as well as apprenticeship and licence records held at the Public Record Office in Kew, and includes medics of all descriptions. Its coverage of Irish men would appear to be confined mainly to those named in subscription lists.

For practitioners in Dublin, the *Dublin Directory* contains lists of physicians and surgeons from 1761. Some of those in the early 1800s state where those outside the respective Irish colleges received their qualifications. Many of them were from Edinburgh, but they were also from places on the Continent, such as Leyden and Rheims. Apothecaries are included under Merchants and Traders, so they are named as early as 1751, though the 1768 edition has a separate list of them. There are also separate lists in the 1820s. In the 1840s there are lists of apothecaries throughout Ireland. All of these give addresses. Likewise, the provincial directories name medical men in the towns they cover (see p. 225, Trade Directories).

The *Irish Medical Directory for 1843*, compiled by Henry Croly, was the first publication of its type dealing with the profession in Ireland. It contains alphabetical lists of graduates in medicine from TCD, members and licentiates of the RCSI, licentiate apothecaries and practitioners certified by the Lying-in Hospital. Its rolls of fellows and licentiates of the King and Queen's College are not alphabetical. All these lists also include addresses. The *Directory* also names medical men attached to county infirmaries, fever hospitals and dispensaries in lists arranged by county and subdivided by town, as well as medical officers at workhouses, arranged by union. Finally, its 'General Registry of Medicine' names practitioners throughout Ireland. This is arranged by county and subdivided by town.

Croly published a second *Irish Medical Directory* in 1846, along the same lines. This was followed by the *Medical Directory for Ireland*, which first appeared in 1852. While it retains most of Croly's features, it adds an alphabetical arrangement of the names of all medical men (though apparently not apothecaries) with their addresses, qualifications, official posts and publications. There is also a section on known Irish and British medics on the Continent, as well as some obituaries. This *Directory* was published annually until 1860 and then again from 1872 up to the end of the 19th century. At the same time Irish medics were also included in the *British Medical Directory* and the *Medical Register* (which merely lists names and addresses). They continued to be listed in these throughout the 20th century.

Finally, there is T.P.C. Kirkpatrick's biographical file on Irish medics, containing newscuttings and notes on various practitioners up to the mid-20th century. It is held at the RCPI, Kildare Street, Dublin 2. There is an index to it there and at the National Library.

POLICE

Career records of policemen are relatively straightforward. In 1786 a police force was established for Dublin city. Throughout the country there were individuals called barony constables who operated on a part-time basis and were paid by the local authorities. In 1814 the armed Peace Preservation Force was formed. In 1822 the County Constabulary came into existence, with an Inspector-General in each province. These two forces were amalgamated into the Irish Constabulary by an Act of 1836. From 1867 it became known as the Royal Irish Constabulary (RIC). The RIC was not responsible for the policing of Dublin. It still had its own force and by another Act of 1836 it was reconstituted as the Dublin Metropolitan Police (DMP). While the RIC was armed, the DMP was not.

The RIC was disbanded in August 1922. Its functions within Northern Ireland became the responsibility of a new force, the Royal Ulster Constabulary (RUC) which was established by an Act in May 1922. Within what is now the Republic it was replaced by the Garda Síochána, which was not established until August 1923. In April 1925 the DMP became the Dublin Metropolitan Division of the Garda Síochána. Further background can be found in Jim Herlihy's *The Royal Irish Constabulary: A Short History and Genealogical Guide* (Dublin 1977).

A list of those in the forces before the Irish Constabulary was established who received superannuation awards was published in the *House of Commons Sessional Papers 1831–1832*, XXVI. Other sources of potential relevance, though they would involve a lot of painstaking research are the Chief Secretary's Office Registered Papers and Official Papers (see p. 208). The records of the RIC are held in the Public Record Office in Kew. The General Register (HO 184), which gives career details, is arranged chronologically in order of service number and covers the period 1816–1922. It is, in fact, a register of constables of the Peace Preservation Force, the County Constabulary and the RIC. It is available on microfilm in a number of locations, such as the National Archives (MFA 24), PRONI and the LDS Family History Library.

The information given about each recruit consists of age, height, native county, religious denomination, date of marriage if during service, wife's native county, by whom recommended to the force, previous occupation, date of appointment, allocations (counties only), dates of transfer, promotions and reductions, length of service, date of death or retirement, and pension or gratuity. There is also a column stating the counties in which he or his wife were connected. This is not always completed. The most important information is the name of the person recommending him. As this was usually a magistrate or a clergyman it often gives a lead in identifying the relevant area of the native county (see reference to Thom's *Directory*, p. 226).

There is an index to this General Register which accompanies it on microfilm. It is divided in two (pre- and post-1867) and is alphabetical only to the initial letter. The reference it gives is the service number. There is a separate Officers' Register, 1817–1921, which has a similar arrangement and is also on microfilm. A microfiche index to the General Register has been produced by Hervey Bay Indexers in Queensland, Australia. Unfortunately, it quotes the LDS FHL microfilm number as a reference instead of the service number, making it cumbersome to use in conjunction with microfilm copies outside LDS centres.

Pensions and allowances granted to personnel or to their widows and children from the 1870s are also available at Kew (PMG 48). These usually include the address of the recipient. The PRO's *Records Information Sheet 11* gives further details on these.

The General Register of the DMP is held by the Garda Archives in

Dublin Castle, Dublin 2, but it is available on microfilm at the National Archives (MFA 6/3). It covers both officers and men and dates from July 1837 to January 1925. It is arranged by service number and has an index giving both name and county of origin. However, like that of the RIC, it is alphabetical only as far as the initial letter. The information given is similar to that in the General Register of the RIC, but it omits religious denomination and marital details and adds parish of origin and information on previous service in other forces.

Information from the records of deceased members of the Garda Síochána may be obtained by next of kin through the Garda Archives. In relation to the RUC, the records are retained by the Personnel Branch, RUC Headquarters, 'Lisnasharragh', 42 Montgomery Road, Belfast, BT6 9LD. They will provide information on written application from next of kin.

POST OFFICE

It is theoretically possible to obtain pension records of all postal employees throughout the British Isles from 1860. Prior to that date the only people for whom you are likely to find any career records are those in higher grades, such as post masters or packet-boat captains, and such records would typically consist of a one-line entry giving the year of appointment and the grade. All postal records down to 1922 are held at the Post Office Archives and Records Centre, Freeling House, Mount Pleasant Complex, London, EC1A 1BB.

At Freeling House the Pension and Gratuity Book for each year from 1860 to 1940 contains a roughly alphabetical list of all employees obtaining a pension during the year. It is, therefore, necessary to know approximately when the person retired, but as 60 was retiring age it is possible to make a fair guess. The next of kin of those who died during service could apply for a gratuity, and they would also be listed in the annual book. Once you identify someone in the book it is possible to call up the relevant Treasury letter, which will give the pensioner's age, date of birth, career record, salary and sometimes an account of bad conduct. A further series of pension records runs up to the 1950s.

Of course, the records from 1922 would include post office employees working in Northern Ireland, but not those working in what is now the Republic. For them it would be necessary to apply to the Personnel Unit of the Department of Public Enterprise, 25 Clare Street, Dublin 2. There they have personnel files on 150,000 Posts and Telegraphs workers.

Freeling House also has other records concerning the Irish postal service. The Letter Books: Ireland, 1784–1829, (POST 15/154–7) are transcripts of letter books once held in the Chief Secretary's Office, Dublin Castle (see p. 208), but which no longer survive. While they contain only a small number of specific references to employees, they have good indexes. From 1831 the Irish postal service was amalgamated with that of Great Britain and there was no longer a Postmaster General for Ireland. The Irish Minute series runs from then to 1920, after which all minutes are contained in a general series. Copies of all minutes to the Postmaster General concerning Ireland from the Secretaries in Dublin and London are contained in POST 36. These include references to appointments, dismissals and resignations of employees. In the case of a sub-postmaster or mistress the name is usually stated, but not in the case of an assistant or a postman.There is a rough index to the minutes. The correspondence relating to these minutes were retained only when a case was important. This is contained in POST 31.

The Letter Books: Ireland (POST 15) and the rough index to the Irish Minutes (POST 36) are available on microfilm at the National Archives (MFA 43/1–13). The index is divided into periods of between four and twenty-four years and is then arranged under the names of the post offices, with sub post offices listed chronologically at the end of each initial. Working through the index in such cases can be tedious and time consuming.

ROYAL NAVY

As with the Army records, those of the Royal Navy are held by the Public Record Office in Kew and they are so extensive that they cannot be fully covered in one chapter. The PRO has published a handbook on these records, *Naval Records for Genealogists* by N.A.M. Rodger (2nd edn 1988). Again, similar to the Army, there are different sets of records for officers (in this case commissioned and warrant officers) and men (in this case termed ratings).

There are printed sources in relation to officers. Seniority lists appear in *Steele's Navy List* from 1782 and in the official *Navy List,* published quarterly from 1814. Service records of commissioned officers living in 1846 are published in W.R. O'Byrn's *Naval Biographical Dictionary.* Comprehensive records of service are available for officers only from the mid-19th century, though there are various earlier service records. Service Registers are available for the most part from the 1840s. These usually contain a record of an officer's career right through to his retirement or death. They are mostly in the series ADM 196. Before the introduction of superannuation, late in the 19th century, half pay was often a form of pension. The other pensions paid by the Admiralty or by charitable foundations were primarily for those wounded in service or for the widows and children of those killed in service.

Comprehensive records of service for ratings date from the 1850s and from 1873 there are Service Registers (ADM 188) similar to those for officers. Prior to that the main sources for the careers of ratings are Ships' Musters, which date from 1667, but it is necessary to know the name of the ship and an approximate date before trying them. From 1764 the musters are likely to give a man's age and place of birth. As with officers, before the introduction of superannuation pensions were usually only paid for those wounded or the dependents of those killed. However, the Royal Greenwich Hospital provided a home for pensioners from 1705, as well as maintaining out-pensioners, widows and orphans.

The PRO's *Records Information Sheets 2* and *125* provide an introduction to Service Registers, half pay records, pensions, and Ships' Musters, as well as Ships' Pay Books, Certificates of Service, medals and records of the Royal Naval Reserve.

TEACHERS

Training for teachers was an uncommon practice until the 19th century, and even then it was not the norm. As late as 1870 only about a third of the teachers working in Ireland had received formal instruction. The first large scale scheme of training for teachers in primary schools was provided by the Society for Promoting the Education of the Poor of Ireland, more commonly called the Kildare Place Society. It was established in 1811 with the aim of providing elementary education without interference with the religious beliefs of the pupils. It opened its model school in Dublin for trainee teachers in the mid-1810s and up to 1831 had trained 2380 individuals, 482 of whom were women. It also supported schools throughout the country.

The Kildare Place Society instructed teachers of all Christian denominations. However, in the 1820s the Roman Catholic hierarchy raised objections to the practice in its schools of reading the Bible without interpretation. The controversy led to the setting up of an inquiry by the Commission of Irish Education. It recommended that government support for the Kildare Place Society be discontinued and that a new authority be set up. As a result, the Board of National Education was established in 1831. This Board, in conjunction with local clergy of the various denominations, began establishing National Schools throughout the country. In 1834 there were 9537 daily schools in Ireland. More than half of these were entirely supported by fees. A further 892 were in the National Schools system, 618 were supported by the London Hibernian Society and only 235 by the Kildare Place Society.

The Board of National Education established its Central Model School at its headquarters in Marlborough Street, Dublin. At the same time its agricultural department opened its first model farm school in Glasnevin, Dublin, which later became known as the Albert Agricultural College (see p. 203, University Students). The country was divided into districts, each with its own model school, and model farms were also set up around the country. It was only in the last quarter of the 19th century that the major training colleges for National School teachers came into existence. St Patrick's College, Drumcondra, Dublin was opened in 1875 for Roman Catholic men; what became Carysfort College opened in Baggot Street, Dublin, in 1877; and the Church of Ireland College of Education was established in 1884, succeeding the Church Education Society, which had taken over the Kildare Place Society's facilities.

Career records of teachers do not provide much genealogical information. The archives of the Kildare Place Society includes registers of trainee teachers from 1814 to 1854. Only the entries for males from 1825 forward are indexed. The information given consists of dates of entry and discharge, age, religious denomination, by whom recommended, school at which they were educated, by whom fees were paid, date of commencement of teaching, number of pupils taught, salary and type of certificate. These records are held by the Research Area of the Church of Ireland College of Education,

Upper Rathmines Road, Dublin 6, and may be viewed by appointment.

The Commission of Irish Education Inquiry produced a very valuable source in Appendix 22 of its *Second Report*. It contains lists of schools throughout the country in 1826–7, with the names of their teachers. *Schoolmasters and Schoolmistresses in Ireland 1826–1827*, by Dorothy Rines Dingfelder and E.J. McAuliffe (Chico, California, USA 1982) is an edited version of these lists in four volumes (one for each province), with a full names index for each county. The information in the original lists consists of the location of the school, the name of the master or mistress, the religious denomination of the establishment, whether it was a free or fee paying school, and the total annual income. Dingfelder and McAuliffe give the teachers' names, the religious denomination, the location, and the page number in the original.

Records of teachers in the National School system are not particularly informative and are fairly cumbersome. The main source is the series of Teachers' Salary Books, which are held by the National Archives. As they are in off-site storage it is necessary to order them up a day in advance. They are arranged by school, so you first need to know where the individual worked. If this is known, you can identify the school in a card index in the Reading Room. This will give the school's roll (reference) number and the number of the district it was in. The catalogues to Department of Education material (ED) on the open shelves include a section on Teachers' Salary Books (ED 4). In the period 1834–1844 the salary books are in volumes covering the entire country. From 1844 to 1855 they are in order of county and thereafter arranged by district. In each case the schools are recorded by roll number. The registers are for the most part annual, so it would be necessary to order up several in order to trace a career. The basic information given concerns the salary, but there are occasional comments. These would be of particular interest if given at the beginning and end of the teacher's employment.

There is a separate series of salary books relating to teachers instructing in model schools (ED 5). These give similar details. Information on specific teachers in other sections of the ED series at the National Archives is incidental and difficult to locate. For more background information on the schools system and its records the 'Byways' articles by Mihail Dafydd Evans in *Irish Roots*, 1993 Nos 1–3, are very helpful.

UNIVERSITY STUDENTS

Until the middle of the 19th century the only university in Ireland was Dublin University, more familiarly known by the name of its single college, Trinity. Most Irishmen who gained a university education up to then, other than those sons of prosperous Catholics who were sent before and during Penal times to continental Europe, would have attended Trinity or one of the two ancient English universities, Oxford and Cambridge.

Trinity College Dublin (TCD) was founded in 1592. Following the Penal Laws, Catholics were admitted from 1793. Women were first admitted to degrees in 1903. The available records concerning its students and graduates down to 1860 are published in *Alumni Dublinenses*, edited by G.D. Burtchaell and T.U. Sadleir (2nd edition Dublin 1935). The entries for 1846–1860 are in a supplement at the end of the book. The information given in most cases includes the date he entered, his age, county of birth, and father's name and occupation. Similar, but more extensive works are available on both Oxford and Cambridge, *Alumni Oxonienses*, compiled by Joseph Foster, covering 1500–1886, and *Alumni Cantabrigienses*, compiled by John Venn and J.A. Venn, from earliest times to 1900. The Manuscripts Department of TCD Library holds records of entry for students from 1860 up to the end of the 19th century. An accompanying index gives the year of entry for each student and identifying the relevant person is a matter of searching through the records for that year.

In 1845 legislation established the Queen's Colleges in Belfast, Cork and Galway. These opened to students in 1849, and in 1850 the Queen's University in Ireland (QUI) was founded, with power to confer degrees on students of the three colleges. The Queen's University was dissolved in 1882 and its functions were taken over by the Royal University of Ireland (RUI), which had been founded in 1880. Graduates of the QUI could automatically become graduates of the RUI. Degrees from the RUI were conferred on students of various institutions, not merely the three colleges. In 1908 the Irish Universities Act replaced the RUI with two new establishments, the Queen's University of Belfast (QUB) and the National University of Ireland (NUI), with its seat at Dublin. The Queen's College in Belfast came under the QUB, while those in Cork and Galway were renamed University Colleges and joined University College Dublin (see below) under the NUI. Graduates of the RUI could automatically become graduates of either the QUB or the NUI. Women students were first admitted to the Queen's Colleges in the late 1870s.

To complicate matters further, there was the Catholic University of Ireland, which opened in Dublin in 1854. This was established by John Henry (later Cardinal) Newman at the invitation of the Irish Roman Catholic bishops, but it had no authority to award degrees. In the beginning it had one 'house', St Patrick's, situated in St Stephen's Green, but others were later opened, all of them in Dublin. In 1881 St Patrick's House became University College Dublin (UCD) and its students, like those in other institutions, could take degrees of the RUI. From 1883 it was run by the Jesuits, until the

1908 Act brought it under the NUI. The Catholic University's Medical School in Cecilia Street remained separate until it became incorporated in UCD in 1909.

The *Royal University of Ireland Calendar*, published regularly up to 1909, contains an alphabetical list of living graduates (whether of the QUI or the RUI), stating their degrees and the years they were conferred. It also names those deceased graduates removed from the list since the last publication. The 1909 edition could, therefore, be regarded as giving an almost complete list of graduates. The *Calendar* also contains lists of honours graduates, arranged by faculty, degree course, and then year by year. These list degrees back as far as 1852 and in each case the college or institution at which the student attended is stated. It is possible, therefore, in many cases to work your way back from the alphabetical list of graduates to find the relevant college.

Each of the Queen's Colleges also regularly published a *Calendar*, naming graduates, though it is unclear whether those deceased were omitted. There are occasional brief annotations regarding the individual's later career, but otherwise they merely state the degrees and the years conferred. There is no such publication for the Catholic University or for UCD (prior to 1910–11). The various *Calendars* will not identify students who did not graduate, nor will they give genealogical information on those listed. Such information is contained in the record of each student's entry to the college. The availability of such records and access to them is different in each case.

The records for Belfast from 1849 to 1880 are held by the Archivist at QUB, Belfast BT7 1NN, and may be consulted under certain circumstances and by appointment. If the student did not graduate, it would be necessary to identify them in the Matriculation Roll Book in order to determine the relevant year. The records of entry themselves are now in the form of typewritten slips, which are kept in chronological order. They give the approximate year of birth, father's name and address, and where the student formerly received education. Those for Cork from 1849 to the early years of the 20th century are held by the College Archivist, University College, Cork, to whom enquiries in writing may be made. The Archivist will check the register of students if you have the approximate year. It gives the age, place of birth and former place of education, as well as the father's name and address and (in the early years) mother's maiden name. Those for Galway are still in the administrative section of University College Galway. They are not available for research.

University College Dublin Archives Department, Belfield, Dublin 4, holds the register of students for the Catholic University for 1854–1879, along with a typescript index. The Archivist will answer postal enquiries on the records. They give the age, place of birth and former place of education, the father's name and the house of the university to which the student was admitted. The Archives Department also holds incomplete registers of students at the Albert Agricultural College, which opened as an agricultural model school at Glasnevin, Dublin, in 1838 and the Royal College of Science for Ireland, which opened in Dublin in 1867. Both were absorbed into UCD in 1926. Neither register has an index, but postal enquiries will be answered. The register of students for UCD is not held by the Archives Department and is not currently available for consultation.

9 Miscellaneous Sources

CATHOLIC QUALIFICATION ROLLS

In 1774 an Act was passed allowing subjects of all religious denominations to testify their loyalty by taking an oath of allegiance to the king. Though it brought no concessions, over 1500 Roman Catholics took the oath in 1775 and 1776. The original lists of these individuals were destroyed in 1922, but a complete transcript made by Ignatius Jennings has been published as an appendix to the *59th Deputy Keeper's Report*. It states names, occupations and addresses. In 1778 the Irish Parliament began the relaxation of the Penal Laws in earnest, with the passing of the first Catholic Relief Act. Those Catholics who wished to avail of the provisions of this and subsequent Acts of 1782, 1792 and 1793 had to qualify by taking the oath. They could do this at the Four Courts (Chancery, Common Pleas, Exchequer or King's Bench), the quarter sessions for Co. Dublin or the assizes in any county. Those who would have had occasion to take the oath were primarily landed gentlemen, prosperous merchants or men entering the legal profession.

The original qualification rolls were destroyed in 1922. Two sets of indexes have survived at the National Archives and these more or less give the information which was contained in the rolls. Both are arranged by court in rough alphabetical order under the initial letter, stating the name, occupation and address of each individual, along with the date and the court. One is for the entire country, covering the period 1778–1790. The other is divided by province and begins in 1793. The entries run up to 1801 in the case of Munster. Entries giving Fermanagh and Monaghan addresses are reproduced in the *Clogher Record* Vol. 2 No. 3. A list of the merchants, manufacturers and traders from Dublin who qualified from 1778 to 1782 is published in *Reportorium Novum*, Vol. 2 No. 2.

CHIEF SECRETARY'S OFFICE REGISTERED AND OFFICIAL PAPERS

The Lord Lieutenant was the British monarch's representative in Ireland. His Chief Secretary was the official who was in charge of administration. While the Chief Secretary was nominally the Lord Lieutenant's subordinate, the junior post came to hold more influence with Parliament in London in the 19th century. The Chief Secretary's Office (CSO) became the focal point for communication between the London administration and government offices in Ireland on all types of business. For that reason the correspondence of the CSO was concerned with a broad spectrum of governmental matters, such as crown estates, policing, the postal service and public health. While much of it was of a very general nature, it could also contain quite specific references to individuals, for example concerning appointments to public offices or petitions from prisoners.

Many of the earlier records of the CSO were in the Public Record Office in the Four Courts when the complex was destroyed by fire in 1922. The others largely remained in the State Paper Office and were subsequently transferred to the National Archives. Miscellaneous items of incoming correspondence to the CSO in the period 1818–1924 were given reference numbers and recorded or 'registered' in a series of bound volumes. These volumes constitute the only comprehensive guide to this correspondence and are called the Chief Secretary's Office Registered Papers (CSO RP).

They have vast potential for research purposes, particularly in relation to local history. However, they are of such an esoteric nature that they should only be tackled by those with lots of patience and determination. Searching them without some definite subject of correspondence in mind (an appointment or pension application; a prisoner's petition; a public disturbance) would be a needle in a haystack situation. As well as that, there is no certainty that the original correspondence to which they refer will be available.

The system of recording incoming correspondence changed somewhat over the years, so that the CSO RP do not have a uniform organisation. Up to 1839 there are correspondence indexes, rather than registers, with supplementary indexes for certain topics. From 1840 forward the correspondence is registered in two sequences, each with an index. The system is far too complex to explain in a few short paragraphs. Its background and format are explained in a comprehensive article, 'The Registered Papers of the Chief Secretary's Office', by Tom Quinlan in the *Journal of the Irish Society for Archives*, Autumn 1994. This includes a full list of the registers and their indexes.

Another collection of incoming material to the CSO is referred to as the Official Papers (CSO OP). There are three series of Official Papers and their type of contents does not differ greatly from that of the Registered Papers. The first series is for the period 1788–1831, the second for 1832–1880, and the third is the Official Papers, Miscellaneous Assorted (CSO OPMA), 1780–1882, which includes the Tithe Defaulters' records mentioned in Chapter 5. There are card indexes to the first and second series, and a bound indexed descriptive list for the third. As with the Registered Papers, it would take some time to get familiar with these records. Their use in relation to transportation is dealt with in 'Sources in the National Archives for research into the transportation of Irish convicts to Australia (1791–1853)' by Rena Lohan, in the *Journal of the Irish Society for Archives*, Spring 1996.

CONVERT ROLLS

The 1703 'Act to prevent the further Growth of Popery' and other legislation passed from 1691 forward, collectively known as the Penal

Laws, denied Roman Catholics access to careers in a number of areas, such as the legal profession (see p. 190), and prevented them from purchasing land, obtaining long leases or inheriting in the normal course (see p. 136, Registry of Deeds). This effected wealthy or prosperous Catholics most particularly. In order to avoid the disabilities imposed by the Penal Laws, a Catholic had to obtain a certificate from the Church of Ireland bishop of the diocese in which he lived, testifying that he had conformed to the Anglican faith. In other words, he had to convert to Protestantism. He then had to have the certificate enrolled in the Court of Chancery. After 1782 it was permissible to furnish a certificate from a Church of Ireland minister rather than the bishop.

The Convert Rolls, as the records were known, perished in 1922 like so many other original documents. However, the Calendar of Convert Rolls survives. It is in two parts, 1703–1789 (with approximately 5,500 names) and 1789 forward (with about 380 names). Most conversions would have taken place up to the 1770s, after which the impediments regarding property were removed bit by bit (see Catholic Qualification Rolls above). Incidentally, it was also a requirement for a man wishing to hold office that his wife was Protestant. This was one of the reasons for women to have been enrolled. *The Convert Rolls*, edited by Eileen O'Byrne (Dublin 1981), provides all the information from the calendar, supplemented by other material, most notably from 'Lodge's Convert Book' which is held at the National Archives. The name of the convert, date of certificate and date of enrolment are given. An address or other additional information is given in about half of the entries. Sometimes an accommodation address of 'Dublin' is given for people from other parts of the country. O'Byrne appends two lists, one of converting priests, 1703–1738, taken from the Rolls and the other of about 200 people who took the oath of abjuration (converted) but who do not appear on the Rolls.

CONVICT TRANSPORTATION RECORDS

Until the mid-19th century one punishment for convicted criminals was to be sent overseas to a British penal colony. Originally this meant transportation to the east coast of North America or to the West Indies. America was no longer an option after the War of Independence in 1775 and the authorities turned their attention to Australia. The first fleet of convict ships arrived there in 1788. The first ship sailing from Ireland arrived with the third fleet in 1791 and the last arrived in 1853. Approximately 39,000 prisoners were transported to Australia direct from Ireland in that period. Of course, many Irish people were also sent from Great Britain for crimes committed there. Transportation continued from England until the 1860s. The last convict ship arrived in Western Australia in 1868, carrying 63 Fenians who had been convicted in Ireland but imprisoned in England.

Records in Ireland

There are no original records of an official nature surviving in Ireland in relation to those transported to America and the West Indies. *Emigrants from Ireland to America, 1735–1743*, edited by Frances McDonnell (Baltimore, USA 1992), reproduces the Report of the Irish House of Commons into Enforced Emigration to America, which was published in the *Journal of the Irish House of Commons* in 1796. It concerns an inquiry into abuses of the laws regarding the transportation of convicted felons and vagabonds over a seven year period. The enquiry also looked at the failure to keep adequate records of indentures entered into between merchants transporters and persons they transported as servants. The report contains the names of nearly 2000 convicts ordered for transportation at various courts throughout Ireland. The only information given is the date and place of conviction, and sometimes the crime. However, McDonnell provides a full name index.

The documents concerning those transported to Australia are in the records of the former State Paper Office, which are now held in the National Archives. Unfortunately, these records are incomplete, especially before 1836. The five main categories are covered by a computer index. These are as follows.

Prisoners' Petitions and Cases, 1788–1836 (PPC)

These are petitions for clemency submitted to the Lord Lieutenant by or on behalf of convicts. They were referred by him to the authorities connected with the case, through the Chief Secretary's Office. They can provide a picture of the prisoner's family circumstances as well as basic details about the crime and trial.

State Prisoners' Petitions, 1798–1799 (SPP)

These concern people convicted for involvement in the 1798 Rebellion and are similar to the PPC.

Free Settlers' Papers, 1828–1852 (FS)

These concern male convicts who requested that their dependents be given free passage to join them. They were entitled to apply for this having served four years of their sentence. The lists of convicts' wives and children who sailed for Australia between 1828 and late 1835 are published as 'Free Settlers in New South Wales', by Eilish Ellis, in the *Irish Ancestor*, 1979 No. 2 to 1984 No. 2.

Transportation Registers, 1836–1857 (GPO TR)

These are part of the Government Prisons Office papers. They are arranged by year and subdivided by sex, with entries arranged by county or city. The basic details given are age, date and location of trial, crime and sentence. They may contain additional information, such as the name of the ship on which the prisoner was transported. In some cases the prisoner died before embarkation. The registers for 1790–1835 have not survived.

Convict Reference Files, 1836–1856 and 1865–1868 (CRF)

These follow on from the PPC with regard to petitions but they may contain additional correspondence. The later ones concern some of the transported Fenians.

These five categories of records have been microfilmed. They and the computer index are available at the National Archives but also in Australia. For a more detailed account of them it would be worthwhile to read Jennifer Harrison's 'Australian Notebook' in *Irish Roots* 1995 No 4. There are further records dealing with these convicts in Australia and England (refer to the Australian sources in Chapter 1).

Other sources of potential relevance at the National Archives include the Chief Secretary's Office Registered Papers and Official Papers (see p. 208). The Government Prisons Office registers of incoming correspondence (GPO CR) and letter books of outgoing correspondence (GPO LB) may contain material of interest. The incoming records begin in 1850, while the letter books date from 1846. Finally there are Convict Letter Books (CON LB), which contain copies of outgoing letters from the Convict Department beginning in 1843. These various records demand careful attention, with no guarantee of success. For a detailed guide to the classes of records mentioned above, 'Sources in the National Archives for research into the transportation of Irish convicts to Australia (1791–1853)' by Rena Lohan, in the *Journal of the Irish Society for Archives*, Spring 1996, is an excellent source.

Newspaper Accounts of Trials

You would be very lucky to find mention of a trial in an 18th-century newspaper, but it is worth trying. The local newspapers which became plentiful in the 19th century (see p. 220, Newspapers) carried reports on trials in the county assizes, which were held in each location twice a year, or the quarter sessions, which were held four times a year. Where a local newspaper is available for the relevant date it is likely that you will find at least some mention of each trial. If you are lucky a detailed account will be published. Apart from bringing a momentous episode in your family history to life, it may provide enough clues to allow you to trace a marriage or baptismal record for the convict.

Prison Registers

The register of Kilmainham Gaol, dating from 1798, is held at the National Archives. It is complete up to 1823, after which there are some gaps. The catalogue labelled 'D/ Justice – Prison Registers' gives the location and remember that it is in off-site storage, so it must be ordered up a day in advance. The other prisons for which the Archives has registers prior to 1840 are Cork City Gaol, Cork County Gaol, Galway, Grangegorman Female Prison (Dublin), Limerick, Maryborough (now Port Laoise), Sligo and Trim. Many others begin after that date. The type of information you are likely to get on a prisoner, depending on the period and the institution, is when committed and from where (including transfer from another prison), crime, court, sentence, when discharged or transferred, and usually age.

FREEMASONRY

Freemasonry has certainly been in Ireland since the 17th century. The Grand Lodge of Ireland was established by 1725 and it controlled the various lodges throughout the country. Masonic rules did not exclude any man on grounds of religion and Roman Catholics comprised a significant part of the membership until the Catholic hierarchy made clear its disapproval in the early years of the 19th century. Irish Masonic lodges were not confined to Ireland. They were formed all over the world, many of them due to those serving abroad in the British Army.

The records of the Grand Lodge of Ireland are held at the Freemasons' Hall, Molesworth Street, Dublin 2, but they are accessible to the public only by appointment. It is important to understand the limitations of the records. If an ancestor had a Masonic certificate, giving the date and lodge number, there should be no problem about identifying him in the membership register. However, this would merely confirm what you already know and give the location of the lodge. If you are merely speculating that an ancestor may have been a Freemason, the records are not arranged in such a way as to facilitate a search and the results, if positive, would add little to your knowledge of his background.

The main documentation held by the Grand Lodge is the membership register, which records members of all lodges. It is arranged under lodge number and simply lists the members with the dates they joined. Any additional information is incidental. The earliest volume of the register now existing dates from 1760. There is also correspondence from the various lodges, mainly dating from the 1820s forward. The only section of it likely to contain information of a genealogical nature is that dealing with charity petitions. These petitions were for the consideration of the Committee of Charity. They give some background information on the petitioners and their cause of distress. In a number of cases people were helped to emigrate. However, these petitions are unindexed.

The minute books of some lodges are also held by the Grand Lodge. These could be worth investigating. The minutes of the Committee of Inspection, which supervised applications for membership, may give full addresses and occupations. Further reading would be advisable before embarking on a search in this area. 'The Records of the Freemasons of Ireland' by C.G. Horton in *Familia*, Vol. 2 No. 2 (1986), and 'Irish Masonic Records: A Protestant and Catholic Source' by Dwight A. Radford in *The Irish*

At Home and Abroad, Vol. 3 No. 4 (1995/1996), give a good background to the records. The latter includes a full listing of lodges within Ireland which were active in 1804, including those of various county militia units.

GRAVESTONE INSCRIPTIONS

Gravestones often provide data on three or four generations of a family and they are an invaluable source of information when they date back beyond the church registers. However, there are some limitations. Firstly, the very poor could not afford anything more elaborate than a metal cross or a crude stone to mark their family grave. Secondly, those who could afford gravestones did not always erect them. Thirdly, many gravestones have not weathered well and their inscriptions are no longer legible. That said, the possibility of the existence of a family gravestone should never be overlooked.

A problem when dealing with this source is that there is no certainty about which cemetery a family may have chosen to use. While Roman Catholic and Church of Ireland families observed parish boundaries when it came to baptism and marriage, their place of burial was not necessarily within the same parish, nor was it always the closest graveyard to their home. In many cases they would return to the family's traditional burial place even if it was some distance away. You can only be certain about the graveyard if you find a death notice or obituary in a newspaper stating where the deceased was buried (see p. 220, Newspapers). Otherwise it is a matter of searching the graveyards in the general area.

One book which may help in establishing the scope of your search is *A Guide to Irish Churches and Graveyards* (Baltimore, USA 1990), compiled by Brian Mitchell. This is arranged by civil parish within each county. It lists churches and graveyards, stating the townland or town and street in which they are located, along with the Ordnance

Survey map number and a reference to Mitchell's *A New Genealogical Atlas of Ireland* (Baltimore, USA 1986), with which it is meant to be used. The Derry Youth and Community Workshop's *Parish Maps of Ireland* would also be useful in conjunction with it, as they show the location of each townland, allowing you to see the relative proximity of places within parishes.

Published Inscriptions

In relation to most graveyards throughout the country the only way of checking inscriptions is to trudge through the long grass and weeds, looking at each stone in the hope of finding the surname you are after. However, inscriptions from a sizeable number of graveyards have been transcribed and reproduced in a variety of publications, including the journals of local history societies. No comprehensive list is available. The following are the most accessible transcripts concerning significant numbers of graveyards or covering large cemeteries.

The Journal of the Association for the Preservation of the Memorials of the Dead, Vols 1–13 (1888–1937)

Members of the association throughout the country transcribed gravestone inscriptions and their transcripts were published in the *Journal.* While thousands of names appear in them, the inscriptions are miscellaneous. Members noted old or interesting memorials rather than covering an entire cemetery. There is a consolidated full name index to the first seven volumes, along with an index to graveyards by county. For the remaining volumes you would have to examine the full name and graveyard indexes in each one.

O'Kief, Coshe Mang (see Glossary), Vols 6–8 & 11 (1963–1966)

Included in these volumes are inscriptions taken from a number of graveyards in Kerry and north-west Cork. Volume 11 also includes references from Abbeyfeale and Mountcollins, Co Limerick. They are covered by the extensive full name index in each volume.

Gravestone Inscriptions, County Down, Vols 1–20 (Belfast 1966–1989), edited by R.S.J. Clarke

These provide systematic coverage of the pre-1865, and in some cases the pre-1880, gravestones in each burial ground in the county. There is a consolidated surname index at the end of every fifth volume.

Memorials of the Dead, Cos Wicklow & Wexford, Vols 1–10, typescript compiled by Brian J. Cantwell

These provide a systematic coverage of the pre-1880 gravestones in each burial ground in both counties as well as memorial inscriptions in churches. However, there are omissions. Each volume has a surname index but Vol 10 contains a consolidated index. It is only available at the Genealogical Office, National Archives, National Library, Royal Irish Academy, Royal Society of Antiquaries and Trinity College Library in Dublin, at the Irish Genealogical Research Society Library in London, and in the relevant county libraries.

Gravestone Inscriptions, County Antrim, Vols 1–3 (Belfast 1977–1995), edited by R.S.J. Clarke

These are along the lines of the Co. Down volumes, but the work is still in progress.

Gravestone Inscriptions, Belfast, Vols 1–4 (Belfast 1982–1991), edited by R.S.J. Clarke

These again follow the Co. Down model and the work is in progress.

Dublin City and County Gravestone Inscriptions, Vols 1–6, typescript compiled by M.J.S. Egan

These are arranged in a format similar to Cantwell's, but each volume covers miscellaneous graveyards rather than a geographical area and it is necessary to check the graveyards individually as there is no index as yet. It has been made available on the same basis as Cantwell.

Memorial Inscriptions of Deansgrange Cemetery, Vols 1–2 (Dublin 1994–1996), published by Dun Laoghaire Genealogical Society

This on-going project has so far covered the south-west and lower north sections of what is one of the largest cemeteries in the Dublin area. Inscriptions are given in an abbreviated form and both volumes are indexed.

Cemetery Records

In rural areas cemetery registers, where they exist, date only from the 20th century and are generally held by a representative of the local authority. They are unlikely to contain details other than of the sale of the plot. However, the large cemeteries in cities, such as, Belfast, Cork, Dublin and Limerick, have very detailed records concerning the sale of plots and the names of those buried in them. They are generally still in the possession of the cemetery owners and most of them will provide information from the registers for a fee. The register of Mount Jerome Cemetery in Dublin, dating from 1836, is on microfilm with the LDS Family History Library in Salt Lake City and there is a copy in the LDS Centre in Dublin. This register has a comprehensive index. Information is also available from the cemetery office. Regarding cemeteries in Co Dublin, a useful publication is *Directory of Graveyards in the Dublin Area: an index and guide to burial records* (Dublin 1988).

HEARTH MONEY ROLLS

Hearth Money was a tax introduced by an Act in 1662 and it was still in operation in the 18th century. It was exacted for each hearth, fireplace or chimney in every house. At that time not all houses had a such a luxury, so the Hearth Money Rolls did not always include houses without a hearth. They were compiled by local surveyors on circuits called walks. They simply named householders within each townland or town, stating the number of hearths they had and the amount they should pay. While the tax was originally payable half yearly and then annually, the records which survived in the Public Record Office up to 1922 were almost exclusively from the 1660s. These were destroyed by the fire there in 1922.

Luckily, transcripts or abstracts of the rolls for many parts of the country had been made by various individuals prior to the destruction. These are now available in a number of locations and in many cases they have been published. There are copies of Hearth Money Rolls for parts of the following counties: Antrim, Armagh, Cavan, Donegal, Dublin, Fermanagh, Kilkenny, Londonderry, Louth, Monaghan, Sligo, Tipperary, Tyrone, Westmeath and Wicklow.

Almost all available copies are noted in 'Irish Census Returns and Census Substitutes' by Rosemary ffolliott in *Irish Genealogy: A Record Finder* (Dublin 1981) and their locations are stated. One omission is a transcript for Wicklow published by Liam Price in the *Journal of the Royal Society of Antiquaries of Ireland*, Series 7 vol. 1 (1931). This covers the entire county with the exception of a portion which was missing from the original. While it gives the numbers of houses in each location, it only names householders with more than one hearth. The other source for Wicklow mentioned in ffolliott's list, Genealogical Office Ms 667, covers only the eastern portion of the county, but gives the names of all householders named in the original, including those with no hearth.

NEWSPAPERS

Newspapers of the 18th and early 19th centuries bear little

resemblance to the publications we are used to today. Those that aspired to being more than just provincial newspapers, such as the *Freeman's Journal*, appeared only twice or three times a week. They contained as few as four pages in their early days and the content was sometimes little more than clumps of advertisements and short reports, many of them copied from other newspapers. Of course, sensational crimes and tragedies were given a mention and a number of notices of births, marriages and deaths were carried. Needless to remark, these only concerned the aristocracy, gentry and middle class unless the circumstances were out of the ordinary, but they were not only from the immediate hinterland in the case of provincial papers.

As the 19th century progressed the newspapers developed. National publications appeared daily and even weekly provincial papers became larger. The advertisements and copied reports continued to make up a substantial part of their contents, but they were supplemented by more local news. Reports in provincial papers on county assizes or quarter sessions (see p. 211, Convict Transportation Records) were often detailed.

Obituaries

By the late 19th century the birth, marriage and death notices were joined by much longer obituaries of prominent locals, such as clergymen, politicians, professional men and prosperous farmers or businessmen. As well as outlining the deceased's life, these usually gave an account of his funeral and named the chief mourners, stating their relationship. Similar articles for women were less plentiful. Obituaries appeared in local newspapers well into the 20th century. Unfortunately, no matter how prominent an individual may have been, an obituary in a Dublin newspaper is unlikely to include a list of chief mourners.

Identifying Newspapers

The drawback in using newspapers for genealogy is that you generally need to have a fairly precise date for an event before venturing to hunt for coverage, since indexes are limited. If you have the date of a marriage or a trial or a fatal accident you first need to find what newspapers were being published at the time in the relevant area. For this the essential source is *Newsplan: Report on the Newsplan Project in Ireland* (England 1992), compiled by James O'Toole. This lists all newspapers published in Ireland with their dates of operation. It indicates the hardcopy and microfilm holdings of them in the British Library Newspaper Library in Colindale, London (which has the most extensive collection of Irish newspapers) and the National Library in Dublin, as well as substantial hardcopy holdings in other Irish repositories. It also has chronological lists of newspapers arranged by town of publication and by county, so it is easy to identify which papers were in existence in an area at a given time. Remember, however, to check under the names of adjoining counties, as local newspapers never respected invisible county boundaries.

Newspaper Indexes/Abstracts

As already mentioned, there are only limited indexes to Irish newspapers. However, where available, they are worth checking on the off-chance of picking up a reference to a family member. Most of them would more correctly be described as abstracts, as they contain all the information in the original entry. The following are the main indexes/abstracts available. Remember that in most cases they refer to incomplete runs of the newspaper.

Impartial Occurrences (Dublin), January 1705–February 1706

Announcements of marriages and deaths, published in the *Irish Genealogist*, Vol. 5 (1975).

Belfast Newsletter (Belfast), 1738–1864

Index to biographical notices, held at the Linen Hall Library, Belfast. Up to 1800 it is in bound volumes in the genealogical reference area. From 1800 to 1864 it is a card index which must be ordered up. This is based on the Linen Hall's run of the newspaper, which is one of the best in existence. However, there are gaps before 1764 and it does not cover 1836 (refer to *Newsplan*).

Pue's Occurrences (Dublin), 1744–1749

Biographical notices, published in the *Irish Genealogist*, Vol. 9 (1996).

Index to Biographical Notices Collected from Newspapers, Principally Relating to Cork and Kerry, 1756–1827

Compiled by Rosemary ffolliott and published on microfiche. This is a monumental source covering Cork and Kerry references from surviving numbers of all Cork newspapers of the period as well as from a number of Dublin and provincial publications. It also covers genealogically informative advertisements.

Index to Biographical Notices in the Newspapers of Limerick, Ennis, Clonmel and Waterford, 1758–1821

Compiled by Rosemary ffolliott and published on microfiche. This is similar in format to the other ffolliott index and equally useful.

Freeman's Journal (Dublin), September 1763–September 1771.

A microfilmed card index is held at the National Library. It refers to a complete run of the newspaper and is arranged by Date, Subject, General (including surname) and Places (subdivided by county). There is no reference number; it may be requested by name at the Reading Room counter.

Faulkner's Dublin Journal (Dublin), 1765–1766

All biographical notices, published in the *Irish Genealogist*, Vol. 9 (1994–1995).

Finn's Leinster Journal (Kilkenny), 1767–1770

Biographical notices from the run held by the National Library, published in the *Irish Genealogist*, Vols 6–8 (1984–1991 & 1993).

Ramsey's Waterford Chronicle (Waterford), 1771, 1776, 1777, 1778 and 1786–1791

Biographical notices from surviving numbers, published in the *Irish Genealogist*, Vols 4–6 (1973, 1974 & 1976–1980).

Walker's Hibernian Magazine (Dublin), 1772–1812

Marriage notices published in abbreviated form in Henry Farrar's *Index to Irish Marriages in Walker's Hibernian Magazine* (London 1897).

Waterford Journal (Waterford), 1791–1796

Biographical notices from surviving numbers, in the *Irish Genealogist*, Vol. 6 (1980–1982).

Northern Star (Belfast), 1792–1797

Selective index by name, subject and place, published by the South Eastern Education & Library Board (SEELB), Library Headquarters, Windmill Hill, Ballynahinch, Co Down.

Anthologia Hibernica (Dublin), 1793–1794

Birth, marriage and death notices, published as an appendix to Farrar's *Index to Irish Marriages*.

Kerry Evening Post (Tralee), 1828–1864

All biographical notices, published in Vol. 6 (pp 2067–2371) of

O'Kief, Coshe Mang (see Glossary) and covered by the full name index at the end of the volume.

The Search for Missing Friends: Irish Immigrant Advertisements Placed in the Boston Pilot, 1831–1856

Three volumes, published by the New England Historic Genealogical Society, Boston.

Northern Herald (Belfast), September 1833–January 1836

Selective index published by SEELB.

Downpatrick Recorder (Downpatrick), 1836–1886

Selective index published by SEELB.

Newtownards Independent (Newtownards), July 1871–January 1873

Selective index published by SEELB.

Newtownards Chronicle (Newtownards), 1873–1900, 1901–1939

Selective indexes published by SEELB.

County Down Spectator (Bangor), 1904–1964

Selective index published by SEELB.

Mourne Observer (Newcastle, Co Down), 1949–1980

Selective index published by SEELB.

TRADE DIRECTORIES

Trade directories can be used to locate an ancestor who ran a business, or to supplement information already obtained from other records. Generally speaking, they are more than directories of trades, as they may include names of nobility, gentry, clergy, professionals and various officials. Their coverage can be erratic. The early editions of publications tend to be narrower in scope than those of later years.

The earliest trade directory for any part of Ireland is *Wilson's* for Dublin in 1751, and from 1761 there are annual editions for the city. In relation to provincial cities and towns, occasional directories for certain areas appeared in the late 18th century, but it was not until 1820 that a nation-wide book was attempted. Their use in relation to business people is broadly outlined in the City and Town Merchants and Traders section in Chapter 8.

Dublin

While all directories for the city are generally referred to as the *Dublin Directory*, there were in fact a number of distinct publications, which overlapped in the 1830s or 1840s. *Wilson's* continued to appear (as one third of the *Treble Almanack*) until 1837, but it was joined in 1832 by the *Post Office Directory* and in 1834 by Pettigrew and Oulton's *Dublin Almanac and General Register of Ireland*. Pettigrew and Oulton continued publication until 1849, and was joined in 1844 by Thom's *Irish Almanac and Official Directory*, which continued into the 20th century. The *Post Office Directory* also continued annual publication into the 20th century, but it was very much overshadowed by its rival.

The first editions by Wilson (1751–1753) were simply alphabetical lists of Merchants and Traders, stating the occupations and addresses. From 1761, the next edition in existence after 1753, similar listings of attorneys, barristers, physicians and surgeons were included (see Chapter 8, Legal Profession and Medical Profession). A separate section of Nobility and Gentry was added in 1815. Pettigrew and Oulton introduced the first street by street list in 1834, along with the names of the magistrates for each county in Ireland. By degrees the separate lists of Merchants and Traders, and Nobility and Gentry were merged into one alphabet.

By the 1850s Thom had incorporated all the elements of the earlier directories and these were to continue for the next hundred years. In relation to Dublin, the principal features are the alphabetical list of residents and the street-by-street section, which eventually covered all suburbs and outlying towns. Those living in flats or in smaller houses are not named in either of these, but the coverage certainly widens as the 19th century progresses. Not everyone named in the street by street section is recorded in the alphabetical list, so it is often difficult to trace someone who moved home. There is also a section of traders arranged by occupation, but it is far from complete. The separate lists concerning the various professions are for the most part complete. Thom broadened the scope of the directory to include certain national information. As well as the magistrates for the various counties, lists of clergy for the various denominations were added, along with a biographical section on such people as peers, bishops, Privy Councillors, Members of Parliament and senior officials. In the 20th century a commercial directory covering principal towns was added.

Provincial and National

The earliest existing directory for anywhere outside Dublin is Ferrar's *Limerick Directory* of 1769. In 1787 and 1788 Richard Lucas produced two volumes. The first was his *Directory of Cork*, which covered Cork city and the towns of Bandon, Cove (now Cobh), Innishannon, Kinsale, Passage (West) and Youghal. The second was his *General Directory of Ireland*, which covered a further 27 places, Kilkenny, Limerick and Waterford cities and various towns in Cos Carlow, Clare, Kildare, Kilkenny, Queen's (now Laois), Tipperary, Waterford, Wexford and Wicklow. The section for Cork city was republished in the *Journal of the Cork Historical and Archaeological Society* in 1967, while all the other lists from both volumes were reproduced in the *Irish Genealogist* in 1965–1968. The only other 18th century directory in existence is Nixon's *Cork Almanack* of 1797 which contains a list of merchants and traders.

Cork is well covered by various directories throughout the early and mid-19th century, as is Belfast. From 1852 the *Belfast and Province of Ulster Directory* appeared intermittently, covering the larger towns throughout the province. Guy's *Directory of the County and City of Cork*, 1875, *Postal Directory of Munster*, 1886 & 1893, and *City and County Cork Almanac and Directory*, from 1889 onwards, do the same for their area. From the 1860s to the 1880s George Henry Bassett produced once-off directories for various counties. However, the only publications covering the entire country, including Dublin, which appeared in the 19th century are *Pigot's Directory of Ireland*, 1820 and 1824, and *Slater's Directory of Ireland*, 1846, 1856, 1870, 1881 and 1894. While the 1820 book only includes large towns, the scope had widened so much by 1894 that practically every village is listed. Of course, you can only be sure of the more prosperous shopkeepers being recorded in the early years. Tradesmen such as blacksmiths were usually ignored until later in the century. As well as merchants and traders, the local gentry, clergy, professionals and officials were named. The 1894 edition also included farmers. *Kelly's Directory of Ireland*, 1905, continued the tradition of Pigot and Slater into the 20th century.

A detailed list of directories covering the various towns within each county is given in Rosemary ffolliott and Donal F. Begley's 'Guide to Irish Directories' in *Irish Genealogy: A Record Finder*.

VOTERS' LISTS

Lists of voters are useful when you are trying to trace a family forward. Unfortunately, no one Dublin repository has a comprehensive set relating to counties within the Republic. Generally speaking, those for the early 20th century (and in some cases the 19th century) can be found in the National Archives. For the reference, check the volume of the 'Records of Circuit Court' (formerly Crown & Peace) calendar for the relevant county, located on the open shelves. As the lists are in off-site storage you will not be given them until the day after you place the order. The National Library's holdings are mainly for the late 20th century and they are quite patchy. You simply need to quote the year and the county. PRONI has voters' lists for counties in Northern Ireland. The references for these are found in the Crown & Peace calendars on the open shelves, which are similar to those at the Archives.

10 Record Repositories

This chapter gives you basic information on the main offices you may need to visit or contact while tracing your Irish ancestors. First we deal with the national record repositories and LDS Family History Centres in Dublin and Belfast. We then give a brief guide to the main holdings of Irish material in London, Sydney, Boston and Salt Lake City. However, you should remember that many local libraries and family history societies throughout the world have basic sources for Irish research, so enquire at home before going further afield.

DUBLIN REPOSITORIES

The telephone area code for Dublin from overseas (and Northern Ireland) is 353-1 and from within the Republic of Ireland is 01.

Genealogical Office (GO)

2 Kildare Street, Dublin 2
Telephone: 6030200
Fax: 6621062
Website: None
Opening hours: M–F 10.00 a.m.–12.30 p.m.; 2.00 p.m.– 4.30 p.m.

The GO manuscripts are made available for consultation through the National Library (see p. 234), either in its Microfilm Room or (in the case of those not yet microfilmed) in its Manuscript Reading Room. There is no fee for consulting them but you will need a National Library Manuscript Reader's Ticket. The GO's in-house researcher will conduct searches in the manuscripts for a fee. Enquiries for this service should be made in writing.

Main holdings: The manuscripts held by the GO mainly record the heraldic achievements and pedigrees of the aristocracy and gentry and of the senior branches of Gaelic families. There are also transcripts of parts of 18th-century census-type material (see Chapter 3) and collections of will abstracts and transcripts as well as other assorted material (see Chapter 7). Because of their contents these records would not be relevant to the initial stages of your research and you would very likely have no occasion to use them at any point.

Further reading: McAnlis, Virginia W.: *The Consolidated Index of the Records of the Genealogical Office* (Issaquah, WA: by author 1994–1997).

General Register Office (GRO)

Joyce House, Lombard Street East, Dublin 2
Telephone: 6711000; 24-hour recorded information 6711863
Fax: 6711243
Website: None
Opening hours: M–F 9.30 a.m.–12.30 p.m.; 2.15 p.m.–4.30 p.m.
Conditions: Fee payable

Procedure: The Search Room is upstairs on the first floor. There you must pay to conduct a general or a specific search (five years) in the indexes. For a further fee you can obtain on-the-spot photocopies from the registers, rather than purchasing certificates.

Main holdings: Civil records of non-Catholic marriages 1845–1863; births, deaths and marriages for all Ireland 1864–1921; for the Republic of Ireland 1922 to date (see Chapter 2).

LDS Family History Centre

The Willows, Finglas Road, Glasnevin, Dublin 11 (opposite Glasnevin Cemetery, on Number 40 bus route)
Telephone: 8309960
Fax: None
Website: None
Opening hours: vary – best to enquire
Conditions: By appointment

Procedure: Space is limited and it is often necessary to book a place weeks in advance. It is of use primarily to residents of the Dublin area. Visitors from overseas would be advised to check the holdings of the LDS Centre nearest them before travelling to Ireland.

Main holdings: Microfilm copies of GRO indexes up to 1958; GRO registers: Births 1864–March 1881 and 1900–1913, Marriages 1864–1870 and some earlier years, Deaths 1864–1870 (see Chapter 2); microfilm copy of Mount Jerome cemetery records (see Chapter 9); *International Genealogical Index* (see Glossary).

National Archives

Bishop Street, Dublin 8
Telephone: 4783711
Fax: 4072333
Website: http://www.kst.dit.ie/nat-arch
Opening hours: M–F 10.00 a.m.–5.00 p.m.
Conditions: Ticket required; pencils only allowed

Procedure: In the foyer you will be given an application form for a reader's ticket. You will be asked to sign in and to deposit anything other than your research material in the lockers (pencils are provided if you don't have any). Then take the lift or the stairs to the fifth floor and report to the counter in the Reading Room where your completed form will be processed and a ticket valid for the current year will be issued. If you are unsure of sources the counter staff will assist you or introduce you to the archivist on duty. You may use any of the finding aids or reference books on the open shelves. When requesting any other material, use the Order Docket. Up to three separate items may be requested at a time and remember that last orders are at 4.30 p.m. In the case of original wills, Voters' Lists and teachers' salary books, which are held off-site, the order must be placed a day in advance. Cards for self-service print-outs from the microform printer/readers may be purchased at the counter.

Main holdings: 1901 and 1911 Census returns, *Largy Books Full Names Index to the 1901 Census for Cos. Fermanagh & Tyrone*, surviving parts of 19th-century census material, Census Search Forms and original or transcript copies of parts of 18th-century census-type material (see Chapter 3); microfilm copies of various Church of Ireland parish registers and *Parish Register Society of Dublin* publications (see Chapter 4); Index of Surnames, Griffith's *Primary Valuation*, Valuation Office surveyors' notebooks and Tithe Applotment Books (see Chapter 5); Landed Estates Court rentals and various estate papers (see Chapter 6); indexes to wills, administrations and marriage licence bonds, as well as surviving original testamentary records and various transcripts and abstracts (see Chapter 7); police career records, National School teachers' salary books and *Dublin Directories* (see Chapter 8); Catholic Qualification Rolls, convict transportation records, Cantwell's Memorials of the Dead for Cos. Wicklow & Wexford, Egan's Dublin City and County Gravestone Inscriptions and some voters' lists (see Chapter 9).

National Library of Ireland

Kildare Street, Dublin 2
Telephone: 6030200
Fax: 6766690
Website: http://www.hea.ie/natib/homepage.html
Opening hours: M–W 10.00 a.m.–9.00 p.m.; Th & F 10.00 a.m.–5.00 p.m.; Sa 10.00 a.m.–1.00 p.m.
Conditions: Ticket required; pencils only allowed for manuscript reading

Procedure: You will need to present two passport-size photographs. In the foyer you will be given an application form for a reader's ticket. You will then be interviewed by a library assistant and issued with a ticket bearing your photograph, which will allow you access for a period ranging from a few months to five years. If you feel you may need to use manuscripts you should apply for an additional ticket.

Reading Room and Microfilm Room: To gain access to the main Reading Room and the Microfilm Room you must show your ticket and deposit anything other than your research material in the lockers. Pens are allowed in this area. The Reading Room is at the top of the stairs. Sign the register and make any enquiries at the counter. You may use any of the books on the open shelves. Others must be ordered up (three items at a time). For these the catalogues are the key. The computer catalogue may be searched by author or subject but it only relates to acquisitions since 1990. For earlier printed books the 'Author Catalogue' is the key. It is divided into two sections. The first concerns books acquired before 1969 and is in 446 large volumes. The second is a card catalogue of books acquired between 1969 and 1989. Both may be checked by author or title. They are located in an adjoining room. There is also a 'Subject Catalogue' which runs to 62 volumes. It is a less efficient source for locating a call number and it has not been updated since the 1970s. The finding aids for Roman Catholic parish registers and other microform sources, as well as all newspapers, are available on the open shelves. For users of the National Library's Genealogical Service, a same-day, non-renewable ticket is available, allowing access to some of the facilites of the Reading Room and Microfilm Room.

Manuscript Reading Room: To gain access to the Manuscript Reading Room you must go to a separate building a few doors down Kildare Street. It is the building which also houses the Genealogical Office. You must deposit anything other than your research material in the lockers (pens are not allowed here) and show your manuscript reading ticket before taking the lift to the Reading Room on the first floor. Sign the register and make any enquiries at the counter. The National Library Reports on Private Collections, the *Hayes Catalogue* and some reference books are on the open shelves. Manuscripts must be ordered at the counter.

Main holdings: Transcripts of parts of 18th-century census-type material (see Chapter 3); microfilm copies of most Roman Catholic parish registers and of birth, marriage and death records housed in the Dublin Friends (Quaker) Historical Library, and *Parish Register Society of Dublin* publications (see Chapter 4); Index of Surnames, Griffith's *Primary Valuation*, *All-Ireland Heritage Indexes* and Tithe Applotment Books (see Chapter 5); Landed Estates Court rentals, various estate papers and indexes/catalogues to Land Commission estate records (see Chapter 6); various transcripts and abstracts from testamentary records (see Chapter 7); trade and professional directories, newspapers, ffolliott's newspaper indexes, periodicals, published gravestone inscriptions, Cantwell's Memorials of the Dead for Cos. Wicklow & Wexford and Egan's Dublin City and County Gravestone Inscriptions, as well as most printed sources and some voters' lists (see Chapters 8 and 9).

Registry of Deeds

King's Inns, Henrietta Street, Dublin 1
Telephone: 6707500
Fax: 8048406
Website: None
Opening hours: M–F 10.00 a.m.–4.30 p.m.
Conditions: Fee payable

Procedure: The first step is to pay a search fee (£2 for the day) in the ground floor office and sign the register. Take the lift or stairs to the second floor, where all the relevant records are located. The Index of Grantors is in the room closest to the lift. The Lands Index is on the mezzanine off the corridor which is to the right of the top of the stairs. The volumes containing the memorial transcripts are in both these locations and in a third room to the left of the top of the stairs.

Holdings: Deeds registered since 1708 (see Chapter 6).
Further reading: Rosemary ffolliott, 'The Registry of Deeds for Genealogical Purposes', *Irish Genealogy: A Record Finder*, ed. Donal F. Begley (Dublin 1981)

Representative Church Body Library (RCB)

Address: Braemor Park, Rathgar, Dublin 14 (near Mount Carmel Hospital; on 14 bus route)
Telephone: 4923979
Fax: None
Website: None
Opening hours: M–F 9.00 a.m.–1.00 p.m.; 1.45 p.m.–5.00 p.m. – best to make appointment
Conditions: Pencils only allowed

Procedure: The RCB is not near any of the other Dublin repositories. It may be best to travel by taxi if you are unfamiliar with the city, but do telephone first to make sure the records you require are there. It has a small staff who are generally busy and cannot deal with general genealogical enquiries. However, they will guide you on how to call up specific records. Some general genealogical reference books and the published clerical succession lists are on the open shelves in the reading rooms. Manuscripts (including original parish registers) must be called up.

Main holdings: Transcripts from 1740 Protestant Householders' Lists for some parishes (see Chapter 3); various original Church of Ireland parish registers and microfilm copies of most from Cos. Cavan, Donegal, Louth and Monaghan (see Chapter 4); some transcripts and abstracts from testamentary records (see Chapter 7); career records of Church of Ireland ministers (see Chapter 8); various original Church of Ireland vestry minute books.

Valuation Office (Land Valuation Office, LVO or VO)

Irish Life Complex
Middle Abbey Street
Dublin 1
Telephone: 8171000
Website: None
Opening hours: M–F 9.30 a.m.–12.30 p.m.; 2.00 p.m.–4.30 p.m.
Conditions: Fee payable

There is a fee of £2 per volume or £12 per hour.

Main holdings: Manuscript revisions of valuation since Griffith's

Primary Valuation; accompanying revision maps; a portion of the perambulation books in preparation for Griffith's *Valuation* (see Chapter 5).

BELFAST REPOSITORIES

The telephone area code for Belfast from within the United Kingdom is 01232, from the Republic of Ireland it is 08-01232 and from elsewhere it is 44-1232.

General Register Office of Northern Ireland

Oxford House, 49–55 Chichester Street, Belfast BT1 4HL
Telephone: 252000
Fax: 252044
Website: None
Opening hours: M–F 9.30 a.m.–4.00 p.m.
Conditions: By appointment; fee payable

Procedure: Because of limited space it is necessary to make an appointment up to six months in advance of a visit. A staff member will assist you in your search, providing the indexes and checking the registers.

Main holdings: Civil records of births, deaths and marriages for Northern Ireland 1922 to date; original civil registers of births and deaths for same area 1864–1921 (see Chapter 2).

LDS Family History Centre

401 Holywood Road, Belfast BT4
Telephone: 768250
Fax: None
Website: None
Opening hours: W, Th 10.00 a.m.–4.00 p.m.; Sa 9.00 a.m.–1.30 p.m.
Conditions: None

Procedure: It is of use primarily to residents of the Belfast area. Visitors from overseas would be advised to check the holdings of the LDS Centre nearest them before travelling to Ireland.

Main holdings: Microfilm copies of GRO indexes up to 1958, GRO registers: Births 1864–March 1881 and 1900–1913, Marriages 1845–1870, Deaths 1864–1870 (see Chapter 2); *International Genealogical Index* (see Glossary).

Linen Hall Library

17 Donegall Square North, Belfast BT1 5GD
Telephone: 321707
Fax: 438586
Website: None
Opening hours: M, Tu, W, F 9.30 a.m.–5.30 p.m.; Th 9.30 a.m.–8.30 p.m.; Sa 9.30 a.m.–4.00 p.m.
Conditions: None

Procedure: The Linen Hall is a public reference library. It has a genealogy section with a good selection of general reference books on open shelves. The rarer publications and manuscripts must be called up.

Main holdings: Files of the *Belfast Newsletter* with index; *Belfast Directories* and many printed sources (see Chapters 8 and 9).

Public Record Office of Northern Ireland (PRONI)

66 Balmoral Avenue, Belfast, BT9 6NY (near the King's Hall; Balmoral train station)
Telephone: 251318
Fax: 255999
Website: http://proni.nics.gov.uk/index.htm
Opening hours: M,Tu,W,F 9.15 a.m.-4.45 p.m.; Th 9.15 a.m.-8.45 p.m. (annual closure of two weeks in November/December)

Conditions: Ticket required; pencils only allowed for Reading Room; fee payable by professional researchers

Procedure: In the foyer you will be given an application form for a reader's ticket, allocated a number (valid for the current year) and asked to sign the register. You must deposit anything other than your research material in the lockers. A video explaining PRONI's services is worth viewing on a first visit. A staff member will deal with your application form in the Search Room. This room contains the finding aids for all of PRONI's holdings as well as a selection of reference books. The Search Room connects to the Reading Room. Manuscripts may be ordered up on computer in the Search Room or at the counter in the Reading Room. Three individual documents may be ordered at a time and orders may be placed up to half an hour before closing. Microfilm copies of church registers are made available on a self-service basis in a separate building in the complex. As PRONI is some distance from cafes and pubs, readers may use the staff canteen.

Main holdings: Copies of the 1901 Census returns, of surviving parts of 19th-century census material and of parts of 18th-century census-type material relating to Ulster, as well as a set of Census Search Forms (Form 37s) relating to counties now in Northern Ireland (see Chapter 3); transcript or microfilm copies of most surviving church registers throughout Ulster and of some from other parts of Ireland (see Chapter 4); 'Householders' Index' (Index of Surnames), Griffith's *Primary Valuation* (all Ireland), Valuation Office surveyors' notebooks, revisions of valuation and revision maps (Northern Ireland) and Tithe Applotment Books (Ulster) (see Chapter 5); various estate papers (see Chapter 6); various transcripts and abstracts from testamentary records (see Chapter 7); *Belfast Directories* and some voters' lists (see Chapter 9).

Further reading: *An Irish Genealogical Source – Guide to Church Records* (Belfast: PRONI, 1994).

LONDON REPOSITORIES

British Library Newspaper Library

Colindale Avenue, London NW9 5HE

Main Irish holdings: Microfilm and hardcopy collections of most surviving Irish national and provincial newspapers (see Chapter 9).

Further reading: James O'Toole, *Newsplan: Report on the Newsplan Project in Ireland* (published by the British Library and National Library of Ireland, 1992)

Irish Genealogical Research Society (IGRS)

c/o The Irish Club, 82 Eaton Square, London SW1W 9AJ
Opening hours: Sa 2.00 p.m.–6.00 p.m.
Conditions: Fees payable by non-members

Procedure: The library, in the basement of the building, holds an impressive collection of Irish material, but space is limited. It is run by a team of volunteers who will give guidance on the use of the records. The fee for non-members is £5 for the afternoon.

Main holdings: *Largy Books Full Names Index to the 1901 Census for Cos. Fermanagh and Tyrone* and Manning's index to surnames in the Elphin Census (see Chapter 3); *Parish Register Society of Dublin* publications (see Chapter 4); Index of Surnames and Griffith's *Primary Valuation* (see Chapter 5); published will abstracts and indexes to wills, and some transcripts and abstracts from testamentary records (see Chapter 7); various printed sources relating to occupations (see Chapter 8); most published gravestone inscriptions, Cantwell's Memorials of the Dead for Cos. Wicklow and Wexford, Egan's Dublin City and County Gravestone Inscriptions and many other printed sources (see Chapter 9).

Public Record Office

Address: Ruskin Avenue, Kew, Richmond, Surrey TW9 4DU
Main Irish holdings: British Army, Militia, Yeomanry, Coastguard, Navy and Royal Irish Constabulary records (see Chapter 8); some convict transportation records (see Chapter 9).

Further reading: PRO's *Records Information* sheets (also available on the Internet: http://www.open.gov.uk/pro/genealog.htm)
Stella Colwell, *Dictionary of Genealogical Sources in the Public Record Office* (London 1992)
Alice Prochaska, *Irish History from 1700: A Guide to Sources in the Public Record Office* (British Records Association 1986)

Society of Genealogists

14 Charterhouse Buildings, Goswell Road, London EC1M 7BA

Main Irish holdings: copies of *Largy Books Full Names Index to the 1901 Census for Cos. Fermanagh and Tyrone* (see Chapter 3); *Parish Register Society of Dublin* publications (see Chapter 4); Index of Surnames; sections of Griffith's *Primary Valuation* and most *All-Ireland Heritage Indexes* (See Chapter 5); some published will abstracts and indexes to wills and some abstracts (principally by Rosbottom) from testamentary records (see Chapter 7); various printed sources relating to occupations and Civil Service Commission: Evidences of Birth (currently being sorted) (see Chapter 8); some published gravestone inscriptions and various other printed sources (see Chapter 9); Cary collection of miscellaneous genealogical abstracts.

Further reading: Anthony J. Camp, *Sources for Irish Genealogy in the Library of the Society of Genealogists* (London 1990)
Anthony J. Camp: 'Sources for Irish Genealogy at the Society of Genealogists', *Aspects of Irish Genealogy* eds M.D. Evans and E. Ó Dúill (Dublin 1993)

SYDNEY REPOSITORIES

Society of Australian Genealogists

120 Kent Street, Sydney, New South Wales 2000

Main Irish holdings: *Largy Books Full Names Index to the 1901 Census for Cos. Fermanagh and Tyrone* and Manning's index to surnames in the Elphin Census (see Chapter 3); *Parish Register Society of Dublin* publications (see Chapter 4); Index of Surnames, Griffith's *Primary Valuation* and most *All-Ireland Heritage Indexes* (see Chapter 5); most published will abstracts and indexes to wills and a copy of the Rosbottom will abstracts from the Society of Genealogists, London (see Chapter 7); various printed sources relating to occupations (see Chapter 8); many convict transportation records, most published gravestone inscriptions, ffolliott's newspaper indexes and many trade directories (see Chapter 9); *International Genealogical Index* (see Glossary).

Further reading: Heather Garnsey, Perry McIntyre and Angela Phippen, *Irish Holdings of the Society of Australian Genealogists* (Sydney 1996)

BOSTON REPOSITORIES

New England Historic Genealogical Society

101 Newbury Street, Boston, Massachusetts 02116

Main Irish holdings: Index of Surnames, *Griffith's Primary Valuation* and Tithe Applotment Books (see Chapter 5); various journals and printed sources.

Further reading: Marie E. Daly, 'The Irish Collection at the New England Historic Genealogical Society', *Aspects of Irish Genealogy* eds M.D. Evans and E. Ó Dúill (Dublin 1993)

SALT LAKE CITY

LDS Family History Library

35 N. West Temple Street, Salt Lake City, Utah 84150

Main Irish holdings: Microfilm copies of GRO indexes to 1958, GRO registers: Births 1864–March 1881 and 1900–1913, Marriages 1845–1870, Deaths 1864–1870 (see Chapter 2); microfilm copies of 1901 Census returns, surviving parts of 19th-century census material and PRONI's set of Census Search Forms relating to counties now in Northern Ireland (see Chapter 3); microfilm copies of most Roman Catholic parish registers and of birth, marriage and death records housed in the Dublin Friends (Quaker) Historical Library (see Chapter 4); Index of Surnames, Griffith's *Primary Valuation*, Valuation Office revisions to 1900 and Tithe Applotment Books (see Chapter 5); Registry of Deeds indexes and records to 1929 and various estate papers (see Chapter 6); microfilm copies of indexes to testamentary records at the National Archives and PRONI (see Chapter 7); microfilm copies of miscellaneous records from various Irish repositories.

Further reading: Dean J. Hunter, 'The Church of the Latter-day Saints and Irish Records', *Aspects of Irish Genealogy* eds M.D. Evans and E. Ó Dúill (Dublin 1993).

Glossary

Barony

For administrative purposes a group of civil parishes formed a barony (see **Parish** entry). However, a parish might extend over the boundary of the barony into another one. Certain records are arranged by barony so it is important to establish the name of the one you are dealing with. It was not a land division most people on the ground would have been conscious of, so your ancestor would not have spoken of coming from this or that barony.

Civil Registration District

The administrative structure for civil registration of births, marriages and deaths (see Chapter 2) is based on the Poor Law (Ireland) Act, 1838 and Amendment Acts (see **Poor Law Union** entry). Each union has a superintendent registrar; and within each Superintendent Registrar's District are several Registrars' Districts, usually co-extensive with the dispensary district. The Poor Law Union, or PLU, and the Superintendent Registrar's District are co-extensive. You can identify the appropriate PLU of a townland with the help of the *Townlands' Index*; the County District replaced the PLU in the 1901 edition of the *Townlands Index* (see **Townland** entry).

County

A group of baronies (see **Barony** entry) formed a county. The county was and still is an administrative division of great significance. If you are lucky enough to find a record overseas of a place of origin for an emigrant ancestor other than simply 'Ireland', it will usually be the county. There are 32 counties in Ireland, six of them being now in Northern Ireland (see **Ireland** entry). Though they have all been in existence since the early 17th century, it is worth remembering that some boundary alterations took place as late as the

1830s. For example, three detached parts of Co. Dublin, lying on the border between Cos. Kildare and Wicklow were transferred to those counties at that time. King's and Queen's Cos. became Cos. Offaly and Laois (also called Laoghis and Leix) after 1922. The only other county with an alternative name is Londonderry, which many people call Derry.

County Districts

County Districts were formed under the Local Government (Ireland) Act, 1898. County Districts consist of groups of District Electoral Divisions (see **Registrar's District** entry), and the two classes of County Districts are Urban and Rural County Districts. (see **Civil Registration District** entry).

Diocese

For ecclesiastical administrative purposes in both the Roman Catholic and Church of Ireland churches, parishes were grouped together to form dioceses. With the exception of the RC diocese of Galway (which covers part of Tuam diocese) and some other minor differences, both denominations have the same basic framework. Their dioceses, however, have been differently amalgamated over the years.

District Electoral Division (DEDs)

These consist of groups of townlands (see **Townland** entry) and were formally called Poor Law Electoral Divisions. In 1901 there were 3751 DEDs.

Hayes Manuscripts

Manuscript Sources for the History of Irish Civilisation consists of an

11-volume published catalogue (ed. R.J. Hayes, USA 1965). National Library manuscripts, deeds and manuscript maps processed up to 1965 are listed. Manuscript material of Irish interest in other repositories and in private custody in Ireland and overseas are also included (much of this material is available on microfilm at the National Library). Entries are arranged by person, subject, place (arranged by county), dates and with regard to material not held in the National Library, by institutions.

Manuscript Sources for the History of Irish Civilisation: Supplement, a three-volume published supplement covering the years 1965–1975, is also available.

Hayes Periodicals

Periodical Sources for the History of Irish Civilisation consists of a nine-volume published index (ed. R.J. Hayes, USA 1970). Articles, reviews, obituaries and other substantial items, which appeared in a wide section of Irish periodicals prior to 1970, are indexed, arranged by person, subject, place (arranged by county) and date.

International Reply Coupon (IRC)

International Reply Coupons can be purchased worldwide through any post office. They enable you to advance, in an internationally accepted method, the cost of postage to your respondent. Some people include a stamped, self-addressed envelope with their letter of enquiry when writing to an individual or repository in Ireland but an envelope with a non-Irish stamp cannot be sent from Ireland. However, one IRC represents the minimum charge of sending a letter by airmail. You are advised to send two IRCs if the occasion arises.

International Genealogical Index (IGI)

Refer to Chapters 1 and 3. The *International Geneological Index* is a very useful research aid. It is available on microfiche (and in many cases on CD-Rom) in Mormon libraries across the world and the microfiche can even be purchased at a very reasonable price. It consists of a listing of birth/baptismal and marriage records for people in various countries all over the globe and can be of enormous assistance in pinpointing places of origin. The 1992 edition is the most up-to-date microfiche edition. However, in relation to Ireland it is most certainly *not* anywhere near a comprehensive listing.

Among the Irish records indexed are virtually all births registered during the first three years of civil registration – 1864, 1865 and 1866 – together with a substantial number registered during the later 1860s (see Chapter 2). Many of the baptismal and marriage parish registers published by the Parish Register Society of Dublin in the early 1900s are also included in the *IGI*, as are many of those registers published in *O'Kief, Coshe Mang* (see **O'Kief ...** entry and Chapter 4). Entries are indexed alphabetically by surname (distinct surnames sometimes are lumped together under a common surname heading), under (a) all counties; (b) specific individual counties; and (c) county unknown. You need to check the entries you have noted against what is recorded in the original registers, for possible errors and of course for extra information.

Index of Surnames

Refer to the Index of Surnames section in Chapter 5, page 133.

Ireland

The island of Ireland consists of four provinces, within which are 32 counties (see the **County** and **Province** entries).

The Government of Ireland Act, 1920, passed by the Parliament of the United Kingdom on 23 December 1920, provided for the establishment of two subordinate Irish parliaments and administrative structures: one in the north of the country and the other in the south. General elections followed; the Northern Ireland general election was held 24 May 1921 and parliament was opened at Belfast City Hall on 22 June. The 128 candidates nominated for election to the Southern Ireland parliament were returned unopposed. The Southern Ireland parliament met on 28 June, with some four elected members of the possible 128 in attendance. On 16 August 1921 the elected Sinn Féin M.P.s met in the Mansion House, Dublin, as the second Dáil Éireann (the first Dáil Éireann – Irish Parliament – was held on 21 January 1919 at which Sinn Féin M.P.s had adopted a provisional constitution and made a declaration of independence. The third week of January 1919 saw the beginning of what became known as the War of Independence).

On 14 September 1921 delegates were appointed by Dáil Éireann to negotiate with the British Government. The Anglo-Irish Treaty, which brought the War of Independence to an end, was signed in London on 6 December 1921 and was approved by Dáil Éireann on 7 January 1922. The Irish Free State (Agreement) Act, 1922, which came into effect 31 March 1922, provided for the transfer of power to the provisional government and for the dissolution of the parliament of Southern Ireland.

Civil war between the Irish Free State Provisional Government and the anti-Treaty forces began on 28 June 1922, with the Provisional Government's attack on the Four Courts, within which were barricaded members of the anti-Treaty forces; the destruction of the Four Courts, including the treasury of the Public Record Office, ensued on 30 June – the often-mentioned disaster recounted throughout the various chapters of this book. (The Civil War ended in May 1923.)

The Irish Free State Constitution Act, 1922 (of the United Kingdom), enacted on 5 December 1922, ratified the Constitution of the Irish Free State (Saorstát Éireann) Bill, which had been approved by the Dáil, and the Anglo-Irish Treaty articles. On 7 December the Northern Ireland parliament opted out of the Irish Free State.

A referendum on a new constitution was held on 1 July 1937 and came into effect on 29 December 1937. Éire (Ireland) supeseded the title Saorstát Éireann (Irish Free State). Ireland became a republic on 18 April 1949 following from the Republic of Ireland Act, 1948.

The Republic of Ireland is a sovereign state, consisting of 26 of the 32 counties of the island.

Northern Ireland is politically a part of the United Kingdom of Great Britain and Northern Ireland. The territory consists of six of the nine counties of Ulster: Cos. Antrim, Armagh, Down, Fermanagh, Londonderry and Tyrone.

Lewis' Topographical Dictionary:

A Topographical Dictionary of Ireland, two volumes, and one volume of maps of the counties, showing barony and parish details, edited by Samuel Lewis, was first published in 1837.

Lewis' and the *Townlands Index* (see **Townland** entry) are essential tools for family and local-history research. *Lewis'* contains historical, statistical and contemporary information (1837) on the counties, dioceses, baronies, cities, boroughs, market towns, post towns, parishes (civil) and villages in Ireland. Similar to a dictionary, the entries are presented in alphabetical order. Information on individual (civil) parishes includes the name(s) of the corresponding Roman Catholic parish(es) and usually the location(s) of the church(es) (see p. 82, Roman Catholic Records). The spelling of placenames followed in *Lewis'* can be inconsistent or archaic. *Lewis'* has been reprinted and is available. A substantial alphabetical list of the names and addresses of the subscribers (1837) is published at the beginning of volume 1.

O'Kief, Coshe Mang, Slieve Lougher, and Upper Blackwater in Ireland: Historical and Genealogical Items relating to North Cork and East Kerry
(Edited by Albert E. Casey and published at Birmingham, Alabama USA, 1952–1971.)

This 15-volume work is a compilation of assorted genealogical sources relating to an area covering most of east Kerry and north west Cork. Each volume has a full name index. An index to the series, compiled by Albert E. Casey, Eleanor L. Downey-Price and Ursula Dietrich, was published in 1979. It is a catalogue or guide rather than an alphabetical index.

If your ancestor was associated with a townland, parish or less

NORTH CORK & EAST KERRY PARISH REGISTERS

When consulting Roman Catholic parish registers from this area, remember that permission is needed beforehand from the relevant bishop's office if you wish to examine a microfilm copy of a parish register (see Chapter 4). However, it is quite possible that the particular register of a parish in North Cork and East Kerry was published in *O'Kief, Coshe Mang* ... For example, the registers of the Catholic parish of Killarney, Co. Kerry up to 1900 were published.

With Church of Ireland registers also, you could be greatly facilitated by *O'Kief, Coshe Mang* .... For example, the National Archives holds the baptismal, marriage and burial registers for Macroom parish from 1727 to 1837; not only are these registers published in *O'Kief*, but, so are the continuation registers up to the year 1913.

specific area within the boundaries of North West Cork and East Kerry, this series should be consulted. Among the North Cork and East Kerry sources published are: Roman Catholic and Church of Ireland parish registers (see Chapter 4); civil registration records; gravestone inscriptions (see Chapter 9); Consistorial or Diocesan testamentary records and indexes (see Chapter 7); Will Books 1858–1900 for the District Registries of Cork and Limerick; Biographical notices from Cork and Kerry newspapers (see Chapter 9); Summaries of memorial transcripts at the Registry of Deeds (see Chapter 6); Summaries from historical publications, and printed family and parish histories.

The print quality of much of *O'Kief, Coshe Mang* is not easy to read; you are strongly advised to use a magnifying glass.

Parish

Civil Parish: For administrative purposes a group of townlands formed a civil parish. It is important to establish the name of the civil parish you are dealing with, especially in relation to land valuation records (see Chapter 5).

Ecclesiastical Parish: The Church of Ireland (C. of I.) or Anglican parish was basically the same unit as the civil parish, but it sometimes went by a different name. For example, Rathbran (civil) parish in Co. Wicklow was called Stratford in the Church of Ireland administration. Quite often a number of parishes were amalgamated to form a C. of I. 'union' of parishes and occasionally a large parish was subdivided. The Tithe Applotment Books are based on Church of Ireland parish divisions (see Chapter 5). The Roman Catholic (RC) parish was very different. Sometimes it equated to the civil parish, but generally it covered a larger area, taking in various civil parishes and frequently covering only parts of a number of them. It is, therefore, often hard to define the exact dimensions of RC parishes. The other big problem with them is that they may be known by various names. For example: Killann or Bailieboro, Co. Cavan (Diocese of Kilmore); Ballinahowen, Boher and Pollough or Lemanaghan, Cos. Offaly and Westmeath, (Diocese of Ardagh and Clonmacnois; Annagh or Ballyhaunis, Co. Mayo (Archdiocese of Tuam). However, except in towns or cities with more than one parish, they are never known by the name of their church. Other religious denominations did not use a strict parish structure.

Poor Law Union

In 1838 the Poor Relief (Ireland) Act, and subsequent amending Acts, made provision for the maintenance of 130 Poor Law Unions (PLUs) throughout Ireland, and within the 130 Unions were 2049 electoral divisions. The townland was the basic unit (not the county); groups of townlands were formed into District Electoral Divisions and several electoral divisions formed a Union. In 1857 the number of Unions was increased to 163; by 1901 the number of PLUs was fixed at 159. From the mid-19th century the PLUs and DEDs more or less replaced the baronies for administrative purposes. Of the 159 PLUs in 1901, 113 were totally contained within specific counties, 38 straddled two counties and 8 extended into three counties.

A standard reference book relating to the Irish Poor Law is *History of The Irish Poor Law* by Sir George Nicholls (London 1856). If you have difficulty identifying a townland (see **townland** entry) but you know the PLU/Superintendant Registrar's District, a very useful publication is George B. Handran's *Townlands in Poor Law Unions: A Reprint of Poor Law Union Pamphlets of the General Registrar's Office* (Massechusetts, USA, 1997).

Province

Ireland has four provinces but they have no administrative function. Ulster (in the north) contains nine counties, six of which now form the territory known as Northern Ireland. Munster (in the south) has six counties, Leinster (in the east) has 12 and Connaught (in the west) has five.

Registrar's District
Registrar's Districts and Dispensary Districts, which are usually co-extensive, consist of groups of District Electoral Divisions (see **District Electoral Division** entry). There were some 829 Registrars' Districts throughout Ireland in 1901. See **Civil Registration District.**

Soundex
The soundex system of indexing groups together different surnames of a similar sound, making it largely unnecessary to check for variant spellings. The soundex code consists of the initial letter of the surname, followed by a series of three numbers representing the subsequent consonant sounds (other than 'h', 'w' and 'y', which are disregarded). In the absence of such consonant sounds, zero (0) is inserted. For example, Forbes would be found under F612, while Kehilly would be under K400, along with Kelly and Kiely. Carney would appear under C650, but Kearney would also have to be checked under K650.

Within the soundex group the entries are arranged alphabetically by forename. Therefore, all the Kehillys, Kellys and Kielys called John would be found together.

Superintendent Registrar's District
See **Civil Registration District** entry.

Town
Most villages in Ireland are colloquially referred to as towns. Within large villages and small towns the most precise address you can hope to find is a street. It is only in larger towns and cities that houses within streets were numbered. You will find in such sources as Griffith's *Primary Valuation* (see Chapter 5) that for administrative

purposes towns are subdivided by the townlands over which they extend. Towns are also included in the *Townlands Index*, identifiable by the letter 'T' following their name. You might also find that a cluster of houses whose status as a 'town' was dubious might appear in one edition of the *Index* and not in the others.

Townland

In rural Ireland the most precise address you can hope to find is a townland. Townlands are not towns but are instead basically collections of farms. They are irregularly shaped and generally consist of a few hundred acres, though the largest townland contains over 7000 acres. Occasionally you will find that there are local names for parts of a townland or for a cluster of houses (see **Town** entry), but townlands are the smallest official division of land in Ireland. Most have existed for hundreds of years. Their boundaries were formalised by the Ordnance Survey in the 1830s, when some were subdivided, with designations such as 'North' , 'South', 'Upper' and 'Lower', and others were newly invented.

If you have a placename, the *General Alphabetical Index to the Townlands and Towns, Parishes and Baronies of Ireland*, which is more usually called the Townlands Index or Index to Townlands, is the place to check. There are three editions – 1851, 1871 and 1901. That for 1851 has been reprinted and may be purchased. They all give the Ordnance Survey map reference and the civil parish, county, barony and Poor Law Union (or county district) in which the townland is located. The 1901 edition also gives the district electoral division name and number, which are necessary if you are using the 1901 Census (see Chapter 3).or, working in the Valuation Office (see Chapter 5).

Ward

The act of 15 March 1839, amending sections of the Poor Relief (Ireland) Act, 1838, allowed for any city borough or town with a population in excess of 10,000, or any other place, within an area of three miles, with a similar population, to be divided into an electoral division. An electoral division could be divided further into wards for administrative purposes, which included the election of poor law guardians.

Select Bibliography

BOOKS

Donal F. Begley (ed) *Irish Genealogy; A Record Finder* (Dublin, 1981)

Mark Bence-Jones: *Burke's Guide to Country Houses, vol. 1 – Ireland* (London 1978)

Kyle J. Betit & Dwight A. Radford *Ireland A Genealogical Guide for North Americans* (Salt Lake City 1995)

M. D. Evans (ed.) *Aspects of Irish Genealogy II: Proceedings of the 2nd Irish Genealogical Congress* (Dublin 1996)

M. D. Evans & Eileen Ó Dúill (eds.) *Aspects of Irish Genealogy: Proceedings of the 1st Irish Genealogical Congress* (Dublin, n.d.[1993])

Margaret Dickson Falley *Irish and Scotch-Irish Ancestral Research*, 2 Vols. (USA 1962, reprinted 1988)

John Grenham *Tracing Your Irish Ancestors* (Dublin 1992)

Seamus Helferty & Raymond Refaussé *Directory of Irish Archives* (2nd Ed., Dublin, 1993)

Samuel Lewis *A Topographical Dictionary of Ireland*, 2 Vols (London 1837)

Tony McCarthy: *The Irish Roots Guide* (Dublin, 1991)

Edward MacLysaght *Irish Families* (Dublin 1972)

Edward MacLysaght *More Irish Families* (Dublin 1982)

Edward MacLysaght *The Surnames of Ireland* (Dublin 1978, 1991)

Robert E. Matheson	*Varieties and Synonymes of Surnames and Christian Names in Ireland* (Dublin 1901)
Robert E. Matheson	*Special Report on Surnames in Ireland, with notes as to numerical strength, derivation, ethnology and distribution* (Dublin 1909)
Brian Mitchell	*A Guide to Irish Churches and Graveyards* (Baltimore, USA 1990)
Brian Mitchell	*A New Genealogical Atlas of Ireland* (Baltimore, USA 1986; 3rd printing 1992)
William Nolan	*Tracing the Past: Sources for Local Studies in the Republic of Ireland* (Dublin 1982)
Alice Prochaska	*Irish History from 1700: A Guide to the Sources in the Public Record Office* (British Records Association 1986)
James G. Ryan	*Irish Records; Sources for Family Local History* (Dublin 1988)
James G. Ryan	*Irish Church Records* (Dublin 1992)
Rev. Patrick Woulfe	*Irish Names and Surnames* (Dublin 1923; reprint USA 1992)
No attributed author (*'presented to both Houses of Parliament'*)	*Return of Owners of Land of One Acre and Upwards in Ireland* (Dublin 1876; reprinted Baltimore, USA 1988)

MAPS

Derry Youth and Community Workshop, under the direction of Brian Mitchell: *Townland Maps of Ireland* (depicting all townlands within a civil parish: Cos. Armagh, Donegal, Londonderry and Tyrone) (Pennsylvania 1988)

Townland Maps (for the nine counties of Ulster; the six counties of

Munster; the five counties of Connacht; and Cos. Kildare, Louth, Meath and Wicklow of Leinster are available on microfiche)

JOURNALS AND MAGAZINES

The Irish Genealogist Journal of The Irish Genealogical Research Society, London (1937 forward)

The Irish Ancestor (ed. R. ffolliott) vols. I–XVIII (1969-1986)

Irish Roots (ed. Tony McCarthy) Quarterly magazine, Cork (1992 forward).

The Irish At Home and Abroad (eds. Kyle J. Betit & Dwight A. Radford). Quarterly magazine, Salt Lake City (1993 forward)

Nimmo, The five centuries of Simpsons ... [illegible]

[illegible]

Family Record Summaries

Because ancestor-hunting can, by the very nature of the source materials, be a complex process, our hope is that you will take this book with you on your research outings in order to have an easy reference guide to hand as you work through the various types of record that you will encounter.

To assist you in this process, we include here tables that can be used as a working record of the key genealogical details of your ancestors which can be used not only as an *aide memoire* but also as a notepad to record your findings *in situ.*

Generation bands

Each table has a space to record the generation band of the particular ancestor, that is, the generation they are removed from your generation. For example,

Generation 0: your generation (i.e you and any brothers, sisters or cousins)
Generation 1: your parents' generation (i.e parents, aunts and uncles)
Generation 2: your grandparents' generation, etc.

For generations younger than you, these can be assigned negative band numbers, for example, your children would be -1, your grand-children -2, and so on. Marking which band a particular ancestor falls in will assist you in keeping track of particular individuals as the number of identified forebears mounts.

GENERATION BAND

HUSBAND:

Birth/baptism: **Place:**

Parents:

Marriage: **Place:**

Other marriages:

Occupation:

Death: **Place:**

Burial place:

Children's names	Birth date/place
1.	
2.	
3.	
4.	
5.	
6.	

Wife:

Birth/baptism: **Place:**

Parents:

Marriage witnesses:

Other marriages:

Occupation:

Death: **Place:**

Burial place:

Death date/place **Marriages/Spouse(s)**

GENERATION BAND

HUSBAND:

Birth/baptism: **Place:**

Parents:

Marriage: **Place:**

Other marriages:

Occupation:

Death: **Place:**

Burial place:

Children's names	Birth date/place
1.	
2.	
3.	
4.	
5.	
6.	

WIFE:

Birth/baptism: **Place:**

Parents:

Marriage witnesses:

Other marriages:

Occupation:

Death: **Place:**

Burial place:

Death date/place **Marriages/Spouse(s)**

Generation Band

Husband:

Birth/baptism: **Place:**

Parents:

Marriage: **Place:**

Other marriages:

Occupation:

Death: **Place:**

Burial place:

Children's names	Birth date/place
1.	
2.	
3.	
4.	
5.	
6.	

Wife:

Birth/baptism: **Place:**

Parents:

Marriage witnesses:

Other marriages:

Occupation:

Death: **Place:**

Burial place:

Death date/place | Marriages/Spouse(s)

Generation Band

Husband:

Birth/baptism: **Place:**

Parents:

Marriage: **Place:**

Other marriages:

Occupation:

Death: **Place:**

Burial place:

Children's names	Birth date/place
1.	
2.	
3.	
4.	
5.	
6.	

WIFE:

Birth/baptism: **Place:**

Parents:

Marriage witnesses:

Other marriages:

Occupation:

Death: **Place:**

Burial place:

Death date/place **Marriages/Spouse(s)**

☐ **GENERATION BAND**

HUSBAND:

Birth/baptism: **Place:**

Parents:

Marriage: **Place:**

Other marriages:

Occupation:

Death: **Place:**

Burial place:

Children's names	Birth date/place
1.	
2.	
3.	
4.	
5.	
6.	

WIFE:

Birth/baptism: **Place:**

Parents:

Marriage witnesses:

Other marriages:

Occupation:

Death: **Place:**

Burial place:

Death date/place **Marriages/Spouse(s)**

☐ **GENERATION BAND**

HUSBAND:

Birth/baptism: **Place:**

Parents:

Marriage: **Place:**

Other marriages:

Occupation:

Death: **Place:**

Burial place:

Children's names	Birth date/place
1.	
2.	
3.	
4.	
5.	
6.	

WIFE:

Birth/baptism: **Place:**

Parents:

Marriage witnesses:

Other marriages:

Occupation:

Death: **Place:**

Burial place:

Death date/place **Marriages/Spouse(s)**

☐ Generation Band

Husband:

Birth/baptism: **Place:**

Parents:

Marriage: **Place:**

Other marriages:

Occupation:

Death: **Place:**

Burial place:

Children's names	Birth date/place
1.	
2.	
3.	
4.	
5.	
6.	

WIFE:

Birth/baptism: **Place:**

Parents:

Marriage witnesses:

Other marriages:

Occupation:

Death: **Place:**

Burial place:

Death date/place **Marriages/Spouse(s)**

☐ GENERATION BAND

HUSBAND:

Birth/baptism: **Place:**

Parents:

Marriage: **Place:**

Other marriages:

Occupation:

Death: **Place:**

Burial place:

Children's names	Birth date/place
1.	
2.	
3.	
4.	
5.	
6.	

WIFE:

Birth/baptism: **Place:**

Parents:

Marriage witnesses:

Other marriages:

Occupation:

Death: **Place:**

Burial place:

Death date/place **Marriages/Spouse(s)**

GENERATION BAND

HUSBAND:

Birth/baptism: **Place:**

Parents:

Marriage: **Place:**

Other marriages:

Occupation:

Death: **Place:**

Burial place:

Children's names	Birth date/place
1.	
2.	
3.	
4.	
5.	
6.	

WIFE:

Birth/baptism: **Place:**

Parents:

Marriage witnesses:

Other marriages:

Occupation:

Death: **Place:**

Burial place:

Death date/place **Marriages/Spouse(s)**

Generation Band

Husband:

Birth/baptism: **Place:**

Parents:

Marriage: **Place:**

Other marriages:

Occupation:

Death: **Place:**

Burial place:

Children's names	Birth date/place
1.	
2.	
3.	
4.	
5.	
6.	

Wife:

Birth/baptism: **Place:**

Parents:

Marriage witnesses:

Other marriages:

Occupation:

Death: **Place:**

Burial place:

Death date/place **Marriages/Spouse(s)**

Generation Band

Husband:

Birth/baptism: **Place:**

Parents:

Marriage: **Place:**

Other marriages:

Occupation:

Death: **Place:**

Burial place:

Children's names	Birth date/place
1.	
2.	
3.	
4.	
5.	
6.	

WIFE:

Birth/baptism: **Place:**

Parents:

Marriage witnesses:

Other marriages:

Occupation:

Death: **Place:**

Burial place:

Death date/place **Marriages/Spouse(s)**

Generation Band

Husband:

Birth/baptism: **Place:**

Parents:

Marriage: **Place:**

Other marriages:

Occupation:

Death: **Place:**

Burial place:

Children's names	Birth date/place
1.	
2.	
3.	
4.	
5.	
6.	

WIFE:

Birth/baptism: **Place:**

Parents:

Marriage witnesses:

Other marriages:

Occupation:

Death: **Place:**

Burial place:

Death date/place **Marriages/Spouse(s)**

GENERATION BAND

HUSBAND:

Birth/baptism: **Place:**

Parents:

Marriage: **Place:**

Other marriages:

Occupation:

Death: **Place:**

Burial place:

Children's names	Birth date/place
1.	
2.	
3.	
4.	
5.	
6.	

Wife:

Birth/baptism: **Place:**

Parents:

Marriage witnesses:

Other marriages:

Occupation:

Death: **Place:**

Burial place:

Death date/place	Marriages/Spouse(s)

The Catholic Family History Socy